D1234743

# Managing
# New Product
# Innovations

# Managing New Product Innovations

William E. Souder
School of Engineering
University of Pittsburgh

**Lexington Books**
*D.C. Heath and Company/Lexington, Massachusetts/Toronto*

*Library of Congress Cataloging-in-Publication Data*

Souder, William E.
  Managing new product innovations.

  Includes index.
  1. New products—Management.  I. Title.
HD69.N4S634   1987      658.5'75       85-40104
ISBN 0-669-10809-X (alk. paper)

Published simultaneously in Canada
Printed in the United States of America
International Standard Book Number: 0-669-10809-X
Library of Congress Catalog Card Number: 85-40104

The paper used in this publication meets the minimum requirements of American National Standard for Information Sciences—Permanence of Paper for Printed Library Materials, ANSI Z39.48-1984. ∞™

90  8  7  6  5

*This book is dedicated to the new product innovators of yesterday, today, and tomorrow. May your spirit endure forever.*

# Contents

# Figures

# Tables

# Preface

I believe this is a unique book. It is based on life cycle data from 289 new product development innovations. These projects were studied over a 10-year period using numerous telephone interviews, 584 depth interviews and 27 data collection instruments at 53 firms. This author has firsthand knowledge of all these projects, except for a few occasions when he was absent from the field interviews.

I believe this book is also a unique handbook. It shows the best ways to manage new product innovations. These prescriptions are not based on ivory-tower theories. Everything in this book is based on what was seen, described, and verified with actual project events. Some of the data, information, concepts, and conclusions are familiar. Some of it provokes skepticism. And some of it provokes disbelief. Remember, it is all empirically based; it describes what was found in the real world of new product innovations.

This book is unique in other ways. It is a blend of theory, wisdom, and practice. The field sites and subjects contributed theories, stimulated ideas, and provided a wealth of advice that is synthesized here. This book contains advice for managers that will help them increase the outputs from their new product development processes. It contains advice for innovators that will help them implement their ideas. And it contains many suggestions for additional study by other researchers and students of innovation processes. I hope these qualities will afford this book a prominent place on student's, innovator's, and manager's book shelves.

This book takes the reader through the inside workings of corporate America. Chapter 1 defines the concepts and chapter 2 describes the methodology of the research which led to this book. Chapter 3 presents three truly exciting and rich cases of innovations that typified the 289 new products studied here. Chapter 4 deals with answers to the important questions of how long it takes and how much it costs to innovate. There are numerous surprises among the data in this chapter. Chapter 5 looks at various conditions that were found to relate to project success and failure. Several important factors were found that encourage success when they are in constellation and retard it when they are not. Chapter 6 discusses how to organize for successful new product innovation. No universally best way was found. Rather, several good ways were found, depending on the circumstances. Chapter 7 examines the influence of organization climates on new product success rates. The results show that climates do, indeed, make a real difference. Chapter 8 describes the decision processes and methods used by the 53 firms in the data base to determine which projects they should pursue. Those firms that used the most systematic approaches were the most successful. Chapter 9 examines 10 commonly used approaches for managing new product development projects. Several very specific "how to do it" lessons are clearly prescribed by the results here. Chapter 10 explores the fascinating behavioral dynamics of the interface between R&D and marketing. Many crystal clear lessons are contained in the data in this chapter. Chapter 11 discusses the various roles that R&D and marketing must play in order to achieve successful innovations. Several prescriptions for effective behaviors are presented. Chapter 12 investigates the surprising influence of the nature of technology on the outcome of new product development efforts. Some ways to successfully manage difficult technologies are presented. Chapter 13 discusses several pertinent lessons for managers on how to transfer their technologies. Finally, chapter 14 summarizes the findings in this book in a set of ten principles for managing new product innovations.

These ten years of field research have taught this author a great deal. Many things have been learned beyond how to improve new product development processes. Above all, this author has acquired a deep regard for the power and yet the delicacy of innovation processes. The objective of this book is to share some of that appreciation with you.

# Acknowledgments

It is literally impossible to acknowledge all of the many persons who have contributed to this research. But some stand out. First and foremost are the legions of anonymous individuals who opened their files, thoughts, feelings, and experiences for this project. They spent countless hours patiently detailing events and experiences, willingly ferreting out various small details, and responding to endless questions. To all the field site personnel: a very big thank you. It is only through your trust and openness that innovation processes can be studied, and that this book becomes possible.

Research funds and support from the National Science Foundation under grants 79-12927 and 75-17195, from the Carl Foundation in Pittsburgh, from the U.S. Departments of Energy and Interior, and from the Faculty Development Fund at the University of Pittsburgh all made this research possible. However, as usual in projects of this nature, the research funds were used up before all the data collection and analyses were completed. Then that wondrous thing called serendipity occurred. A totally unexpected phone call came from Bob Spear, Technical Director at Alcoa. He had selected our research group, the Technology Management Studies Group, to receive a grant. That grant enabled this book to be completed.

Thanks to my graduate assistants Paul Shrivastava, Paul Slovik, Arlan Stehney, Abdul Quaddus, James Loscar, Bob Cicchinelli, and John Houston for a variety of backup assistance on this research, and to Penny Brown, who tirelessly typed most of the field notes. Thanks to my colleague research associates Bob Avery, Jay Bourgeois, Tom Bonoma, Alok Chakrabarti, Bob O'Keefe, and James Comer, who provided some thoughts, helpful comments, and various kinds of assistance with the field data. My colleagues at the Department of Industrial Engineering are acknowledged for tolerating my zealousness in demanding space for field notes and commandeering computer time, and for tolerating my constant grumbling about the heavy demands of field research while carrying a full teaching load.

A number of individuals contributed to this work in a variety of important ways. Gene Palowitch and Bob Evans at the U.S. Bureau of Mines started me thinking about the longwalls and water jet cutting cases. Clarence Schatz at Scott Paper Company started a thought process that led to chapter 12. Francis Brown, then at Gulf Oil Corporation, suggested some of the materials in chapter 13 in a discussion I had with him one day. My late father—a tinkerer, inventor, innovator and entrepreneur in every sense of these words—contributed many of the rich details on the hybrid corn case in chapter 3 from his experiences as a farmer-salesman. Chapter 3 is dedicated to him.

Very special thanks to Edie for her constant support, for tolerating such a single-minded husband, and for her efficient word processing and proof-reading of this manuscript. Thanks to C. Merle Crawford, Yorham Wind, and Robert Spear for their valuable comments on an earlier draft of this manuscript. Though I have not faithfully adopted all their recommendations, their ideas were very helpful. Thanks to E. William Rossi for drafting the figures and to Vivian Manfredi for typing several tables. I am sure to have missed a few persons who deserve some credit. Forgive my oversights.

# 1
# Concepts of Innovation

> A man may die, nations may rise and fall, but an idea lives on.
> —John F. Kennedy, 1963

This book is the result of over 10 years of field research on 289 new product development innovation projects at 53 firms. Detailed life cycle data were collected on each project, from its inception to its termination or completion. The data revealed many new insights about new product innovation processes, provided numerous prescriptions for managers that can help them increase project success rates, and suggested many opportunities for further research.

The subsequent chapters of this book share these details with the reader. However, before turning to these details, it is important to establish some definitions and basic concepts.

## Innovations

### Some General Observations

Innovation is a very old word. It appears to have its origins in the Latin "innovare," meaning to renew, to make new or to alter. The Romans, early French, and the old English all wrote about innovations. In his 1796 farewell address President George Washington counseled Americans on "preserving a spirit of innovativeness."

"Innovation" has become such a part of our everyday modern vocabulary that we seldom stop to define it. We are quick to speak of someone whose ideas we like as being innovative or some new gimmick or technique that impresses us as being an innovation. It has become stylish to innovate.

Innovation has a thousand faces. It has been variously defined as a process from idea generation to commercialization, the adoption of change, a radical change in traditional ways, a new device or something new to society. Accordingly, there are many examples of products, processes, services, organization structures, ideas, technologies, procedures, and behaviors that have been awarded the lofty title of "innovation." Some things are considered innovative because they improve our quality of life. Other things are innovative because they have a radical impact. Still other things are considered innovations simply because they are new. Sometimes innovations do not even have to be new: old things in new forms or combinations are often considered to be innovations. Some common definitions of innovation are presented in table 1-1.

### Types of Innovations

Innovations come in different degrees of radicalness. Some innovations are radical departures from traditional ways. Others are "incremental" innovations or small departures from traditional ways. Innovations also come in different degrees of familiarity. Some innovations arise in response to a documented need or demand. They are often referred to as "needs-generated" or "technology pull" innovations. This is in contrast to "means-generated" or "technology push" innovations, which arise from a technical capability. The firm that makes a new device without concern for the existence of a docu-

**Table 1–1**
**Some Common Definitions of Innovation**

A creative process in which two or more existing things are combined in some novel way to produce a unique new thing

A complex set of activities from the conceptualization of a new idea to its reduction to practice

The invention and implementation of a new device

The process of social change in response to a new technology

The sequence of events from the generation of an idea to its adoption

A novel new device, concept, or idea

The adoption of a change that is new to the organization, group, or society

A new modification or new combination of existing entities

Anything that is new because it is different from the existing forms

Any idea, practice, or thing perceived to be new by the adopting entity

Anything perceived by the individual or user as new

mented market or need is engaging in a means-generated innovation effort.

Though these distinctions seem reasonable, they are not easy to apply. For example, a laboratory curiosity is clearly a means-generated technology. But how about a unique new device that was developed in the hope that a market might then be created for it? This is not a clear case. If a user requests the device after seeing it, does it now become a needs-generated innovation? The answer is not obvious. And when is a technology radical? A radical innovation to you may fill an incremental need for me.

Perhaps this is enough to show that the terminology is not standardized. Innovations sometimes exist primarily in the eye of the beholder. In fact, this is often the ultimate test of an innovation. If you perceive that something is so significant that you feel it is an innovation, who is to say that it is not an innovation in terms of your well-being? Perhaps it is not an innovation in terms of my experience. But does that make it any less an innovation for you?

## Definition of Innovation

In view of the above discussion, it is important to set out some clear definitions. This book uses the term "innovation" to refer to a high-risk idea that is new to the sponsoring organization, and which the organization believes has high profit potential or other favorable commercial impacts for them. "New to the sponsoring organization" means they have not had one like it before. Commercial impact means that there exists someone who will pay money to get it. High impact means that this idea will significantly increase the organization's financial welfare. High-risk means that the sponsors perceive that this idea exposes them to higher than normal chances of severe personal, financial or other loss.

Note that the above definitions refer to a *sponsoring* organization rather than an *originating* organization. The innovating organization need not be the originator of the idea. Note also that there need not be an actual willing customer waiting for the innovation. The belief that there is a potential customer is sufficient. In fact, it is typical of innovations that customers must be convinced to buy them for their own benefit.

These definitions may seem obvious and trivial. Yet, as the above discussion noted, a lack of clear definitions has resulted in considerable arbitrariness in our concepts of innovation.

## Innovation Processes

### Nature of Innovation Processes

Reference is often made to *the* innovation process as if it were a single, unique process. Nothing could be further from the truth.

Processes for generating, developing, and implementing innovations usually involve complex combinations of other processes like those listed in table 1-2. Moreover, every innovation typically involves a different blend of the processes listed in table 1-2. The ways in which these processes are combined and blended is the art of managing innovations. To complicate matters further, there are perhaps as many different ways to manage innovations as there are different innovations. Some ways are better than others. Some ways are totally ineffective. Some ways are only effective under some specific circumstances.

This latter point is an important one. There is no one best way to innovate. Rather, there are several effective ways. The surrounding conditions and environments determine which way is the most effective in each case. The nature of the technology, the nature of the end markets, the capabilities of the organization, the prevailing economic climate, and the available managerial expertise are only some of the factors that determine the best choice of an innovation process. Several different innovation processes are described in this book. The relative effectiveness of each process is analyzed within various environments.

Thus, innovation processes are sequences of other multifaceted, multistage processes that are carried out by many different parties. Most innovation processes involve the dynamic interplay of several different individuals who supply thoughts, ideas, and resources at several different levels of abstraction and reality. The success of these processes usually involves hurdling many obstacles and overcoming many resistances. Because of this, innovations often involve large human, organizational, and social costs. Personnel,

**Table 1–2**
**Some Components of Innovation Processes**

Invention processes

Product development processes

Decision processes

Need recognition processes

Evaluation processes

Trial and adoption processes

Selling and persuasion processes

Attitude formation and change processes

Market analyses processes

Demand creation processes

ideas, wants, hopes, and desires are sometimes badly bent and bruised as a result. It has been said that organizations must have a few fanatics within them in order to innovate.

## Roles and Interpersonal Dynamics

To be successful, innovation processes require that a number of roles be played by several different persons. One important role is the creative inventor or idea generator. Someone must generate the idea or invent the device that is the basis for the new product. Then there are various idea carrier roles. Several persons must interact dynamically to carry the idea across fields of natural barriers. Some of these barriers can be anticipated. Others cannot.

The primary idea carrier is often referred to as the entrepreneur. Sometimes, the word "intrapreneur" is reserved for a particular kind of entrepreneur: the company employee or inside entrepreneur. The successful entrepreneur (or intrapreneur, as the case may be) will enlist a cadre of other role-persons to assist him. He will usually need a variety of blockers, receivers, and passers. But he will quarterback their efforts with the game plan, the risk-money, and other supporting personnel. The entrepreneur is usually motivated solely by the thrill of the game and the lure of success. Getting the ball across the goal line is his driving ambition. He may variously behave like a guerilla warfare agent, a negotiator, a beggar, a bargainer. He will do whatever it takes to get the job done.

Entrepreneurs (and intrapreneurs) usually need the support of many others from the sidelines. A variety of different coaching roles exist within most innovation processes. Like good coaches, these supporters give counsel and experience-based advice, but they stay off the playing field. Other persons may play information-provider roles. Still others play the roles of bankers and funding agents. There are also a variety of idea-selling roles that must be played. Some of the important roles played during one innovation process observed in this study are listed in table 1-3.

Innovation processes are sometimes described as if they were a set of prescriptions, linear procedures, or a recipe. In reality innovations seldom occur linearly, in a smooth flow of roles, behaviors and events. Rather, the movement is a series of jerky starts and stops that grope in the general direction of the end goal. The roads to successful innovations are littered with the trials and errors of past attempts. However, if we can improve our understanding of innovation processes, there is hope that we can increase their efficiency.

## Definition of Innovation Processes

In this book, an innovation process is any system of organized activities that

**Table 1–3**
**Some Important Innovation Roles**

| Role | Description of Role |
|------|---------------------|
| Leader | Coordinates the work of the technical specialists; coordinates tasks and activities |
| Capitalist | Finds various sources of funds within the organization to sustain the project during its periods of financial drought |
| Exciter | Stimulates and inspires colleagues; generates enthusiasm |
| Integrator | Oversees the whole project and coordinates its various components |
| Scout | Watches new developments outside the organization and channels pertinent external information into the organization |
| Linchpin | Provides liaison between departments and stimulates interdepartmental interactions |
| Champion | Promotes new ideas and advocates their support by the organization |
| Mentor | Coaches the junior staff and provides constructive feedback to them |
| Translator | Represents new technologies to potential users and communicates user needs to the technology developers |
| Spotter | Identifies technical problems and barriers that are not obvious |

transforms a technology from an idea to commercialization. This definition does not say anything like "to commercial success." The process may or may not lead to a commercially successful innovation.

Thus, innovation processes include invention, development or elaboration, engineering or performance optimization, market development or user awareness stimulation, reduction to practice, and sales or adoption by the user. Note that an invention is not necessarily an innovation. An invention is a unique idea. It may or may not have commercial relevance. Moreover, it is not sufficient just to have an idea with commercial relevance. An innovation process is needed in order to fully exploit the potentials of that idea and achieve user adoption.

## New Product Development Projects

A project is an organized effort consisting of human and nonhuman resources. It is dedicated to the accomplishment of a specific goal in a prescribed time, within some prescribed budget. This book focuses on a particular type of project: those where the goal is the successful development of some new product innovation. Thus, this book is only concerned with projects that are organized, managed, or otherwise follow an innovation process, as discussed above.

Although this definition of a project is perhaps the most unequivocal of all the definitions in this book, it too has it problems. The biggest dilemma is determining the boundaries of a project. A project is considered to begin at the point when someone within the sponsoring organization recognizes the need or opportunity for a new product. Thus, the very early beginnings of the idea for a new product are included here as part of the project. For example, a one-person effort consisting of browsing in the library or sitting and thinking is considered to be part of the project, assuming a formal project is subsequently assembled from these activities. If there is no subsequent effort, the solitary research is not counted as a project and is not studied here. Moreover, the project extends to the adoption of the product by the user, or the failure to adopt, whichever occurred. Of course, management may terminate the project before it reaches its completion. Projects with those outcomes are also studied here.

Thus, this book considers the new product development project to begin with the recognition of a need or opportunity. The life cycle of the project extends to the point where either a user adopts the newly developed product or management terminates the project. Table 1-4 illustrates the typical life cycle of a successful new product development project.

## Table 1–4
### Key Items in the Typical Life Cycle of a Successful New Product Development Project

Start of the project: recognition of a need or an opportunity

Idea definition and elaboration

Product research and development

Product engineering

Prototype pilot testing and product adjustment

Pilot production of the new product

Market stimulation

User adoption trials and product establishment

Completion of the project: adoption of the new product by the user or customer

## Problems in Managing Innovations

Innovative new products are essential to the progress of any society. The processes of developing new products provide employment and economic well-being for those directly associated with them, as well as for persons employed in supporting industries. The new products respond to the wants of the populace and stimulate higher standards of living. Thus, when innovation processes are properly managed, an expanding variety of new products stream forth. These products respond to the changing needs of a fully employed workforce whose economic welfare is constantly increasing. However, managing innovation processes to achieve this happy state is difficult.

Nine common problems in managing innovation were encountered in this study. They are:

1. Avoiding technologies that fail.
2. Designing the best organization for innovation.
3. Developing organization climates that stimulate innovation.
4. Picking projects that have the best chances of success.
5. Determining how much effort to spend on innovation projects, and when to terminate unsuccessful projects.
6. Managing innovation projects for timely completion.
7. Handling problems at the R&D and marketing interface.
8. Coping with uncertain technologies.
9. Transferring technologies and new products to other parties.

Based on the results from this study, several management principles were developed for overcoming these problems. The subsequent chapters of this book discuss these principles.

## Summary

New product innovations are responsible for employment, economic growth, technological progress, and high standards of living. Therefore, the study of new product innovations and the processes through which they emerge is important.[1,2,3]

This book reports the results from one such study. The study analyzed the ways in which new product innovations are born, developed, and taken to the marketplace by firms in the United States. Several common management problems were encountered in this survey. Principles for overcoming these problems were formulated.

This chapter has presented the definitions and concepts which guided the study. Three important points were made in this chapter. First, the focus of the study was projects: organized efforts to achieve established goals. Second, the study was limited to one particular type of project: those where the goal was the development of a new product innovation. Third, the entire project life cycle was studied, from the birth of the new product concept to its adoption (or rejection) by the customer.

## Notes

1. For a summary of definitions and concepts of innovation processes the reader should consult Gerald Zaltman, Robert Duncan, and Jonny Holbek. *Innovation and Organizations* (New York: Wiley, 1973). This book has become a classic work.

2. Two recent works on innovation processes are Victor Kiam's *Going For It! How To Succeed As An Entrepreneur* (New York: Morrow, 1986) and Peter Drucker's *Innovation and Entrepreneurship: Practices and Principles* (New York: Harper & Row, 1985). Kiam examines the roles of the entrepreneur. Drucker focuses more on corporate innovations and intrapreneurs.

3. A good summary of the problems of managing innovations can be found in Andrew H. Van De Ven, "Central Problems in the Management of Innovations", *Management Science,* 32, no. 5 (May 1986), 590-607. This paper is also a good entry into the vast literature on innovation.

# 2
# New Product Innovation Data Base

> Nothing in life is to be feared; it is only to be understood.
> —Marie Curie, 1928

T he central focus of this study was on projects for successfully developing new product innovations. The objective was to learn how to manage those projects better. The data base for this study consisted of life cycle data on 289 new product innovation projects. This data base was developed through an extensive field research methodology. A series of personal and telephone interviews, 584 in-depth interviews and 27 instruments were used to collect the data at 53 firms. This chapter discusses this methodology.

## Focus of This Study

New product innovation processes do not occur in isolation. As depicted in figure 2-1, it is necessary to be concerned with some events outside the project environment. Specifically, the effect of organization structures, strategies, climates, external environments, and technologies must be taken into account. The external environment for innovation includes various governmental actions, the behaviors of competitors, the influence of trade and professional organizations, the impact of standards set by regulatory agencies, the economic conditions, and legal constraints. The climate for innovation within particular organizations may be deeply influenced by these environmental conditions. This climate includes top management's attitudes, the risk-taking posture of the firm, the competitive position of the firm, the financial condition of the firm, the research and development (R&D) intensiveness of the firm, the autonomy and license given to innovators within the firm, and the discretionary funds available for innovative activities.

As figure 2-1 suggests, all these factors are considered in this book in an attempt to gain a complete picture of new product innovation processes. The aim is to develop some general rules about how to manage innovation projects under various technological, organizational, and environmental conditions in order to maximize the number of successful projects.

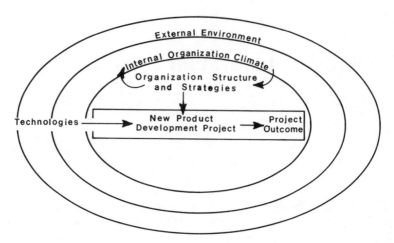

Figure 2–1. Focus of This Study

## Measurement of Innovations

In chapter 1, an innovation was defined as a high-risk idea that was new to the sponsoring organization, which that organization believed would significantly increase its financial welfare. In the research study reported here, each firm was free to dimension risk and financial welfare in any way it chose. The dimensions could be dollar profits, costs, sales, or other monetary measures. Or the dimensions could be nonmonetary: numbers of new customers, probabilities of various outcomes, degrees of market penetration, or other measures. If the firm's officers perceived that an idea was new, risky, and had high potential commercial impacts for them, then it was largely accepted here as an innovation. The qualifier "largely" is used here because personnel at each firm were thoroughly queried to ensure that their definitions did in fact conform to the definitions in chapter 1.

This approach embodies the viewpoint that an innovation is situationally determined. As a hypothetical illustration of this, suppose the Carbon Company has an idea for a new high-density semiconductor made from one of their by-products. The Carbon Company is a small, old-line mining firm, and its executives view this new product as highly risky since they have no background in chip manufacturing. But this venture has the potential to significantly increase their profits and eliminate the cyclical nature of their sales. By comparison, suppose a well-established chip producer, the Chip Company, is also developing the same product from raw materials they are purchasing. The product is very similar to their existing lines. The Carbon Company managers feel they are working on an innovation. The Chip Company managers do not, though they do count it as a new product. This is consistent with the above definitions.

But doesn't permitting each firm to have its own definitions raise havoc with firm-to-firm comparisons? Not if one takes the viewpoint that *perceptions* and associated behaviors are precisely what we want to measure. Perceptions may be the most realistic measure of innovations. Perceptions may be reality, in the case of innovations. The perception (or its absence) sets in motion various behaviors that result in successes or failures. In any event, this viewpoint served remarkably well in the research described in this book.

## Measurement of Newness

Since the research reported here focused on *new* product developments, it was important to have a good measure of newness. Unfortunately, the concept of newness in new products is a troubling matter. When is a product really new? For example, a chemical compound unlike any others is clearly a new one. But suppose this compound now has a methyl group added to its sixth carbon atom. Is this a new product or just a modification of an old product?

If the organization never had a product like this before, and if the organization felt it was new to them, then it was generally counted as a new product in this study. Indeed, to one firm the product may be so simple that they would call it a product modification. But to another firm, it may truly be a new product. This book focuses on things that are new to the sponsoring organization. The fact that it is not new to their competitor or to some other firm is of no relevance here.

A product can be new in many different ways. The newness may take the form of lower prices, greater convenience, improved performance, newer appearance, or new markets. To take an extreme example, suppose a firm advertises heavily and successfully convinces its customers that it has a new product. In fact, the product is only cosmetically changed. Is this a new product? In the scheme used in this book, it would be new if the sponsoring organization categorized it as *new to them*. That is the key: newness to the sponsoring organization.

Admittedly, this definition can be a tenuous one. For example, in spite of a firm's insistence that their new blue detergent is truly new, chemical analyses may show that the only thing new is the package. But, can anyone say for sure that the consumer has not derived some psychic value from the product anyway? Can the value of the increased employment from the production of the new blue detergent be denied? These are not easy questions to answer unequivocally. In the research described in this book, personnel at each firm were challenged to defend their definitions of newness. In some cases, their definitions failed the challenge and the product was not selected for study. However, in the end, it was the firm's own decisions that were accepted. It seemed preferable to error on the side of including a few new blue detergents than to impose another definition that might be even less realistic.

## Project Outcome Measurement

### Obstacles in Measuring Project Outcomes

The precise measurement of project outcomes is central to the research described in this book. However, this is a troubling aspect. Though intuitively appealing, the use of "success" versus "failure" as labels to assess project outcomes is too limiting for new product innovations. Most innovation projects experience varying degrees of success and failure. Moreover, it is unusual for a project to be a total failure, in the sense that none of its outputs are useful.

Sometimes a project that is perceived as a failure at one time may be rejuvenated as a success at a later time. A success does not always endure for very long: a competitor may issue a superior product or unexpected regulations may inhibit the sale of the product. Partial successes are common when a project meets some but not all of its original objectives.

Sometimes, the original objectives for a project turn out to be unattainable and management changes the goals, thus converting a potential failure into a success. How should this outcome be counted? External events can also alter the fate of a project, posing several measurement dilemmas. For example, suppose a competitor issues a superior product that captures the available market. Management therefore terminates the project. Should this project be counted as a failure? What about the fact that the termination decision saved the firm money? What would have happened if the effort had continued instead of being terminated prematurely? Was management right, or would an even more superior product have resulted if the project had been allowed to continue?

### Focus on Actual Outcomes

This book does not deal with the philosophical issue of what might have happened if this or that had occurred. It deals only with actual project outcomes. Moreover, temporal success/failure is dealt with only when it occurs within the time span of this study. For example, suppose the project that seemed so successful at first becomes a failure later. If the failure happened within the 10 year time period of this study, it is so recorded. Otherwise, it is counted here as a success. Therefore, it is possible that some of the successes recorded here eventually became failures, and vice versa. However, there is reason to believe that these cases are minimal in this data base.

The study reported in this book simply accepts the last outcome of the project as the correct one. That is, a project that looked like a failure but succeeded because its goals were changed is simply counted here as a success (though the events leading to that goal change are carefully noted).

*Project Outcome Scale*

Table 2-1 presents the scale that was used to assess the outcomes of the projects studied here. Respondents at each firm rated each project on this scale. Several other scales were tried, but they were less suitable. The scale shown in table 2-1 was partially suggested by one of the firms, and it served remarkably well for the entire study. Note that both technical outcomes (from the laboratory, engineering, or other technical department) and commercial outcomes (final adoption by the user) are measured by this scale.

Because various levels of any organization can have different perceptions, the outcome assessments were made by consensus among the commercial, technical, and top management respondents. Projects where consensus could not be achieved were not studied.

## Field Study Methods

*Sample of Firms*

Using data from *Business Week*, the U.S. Bureau of Commerce, and the Industrial Research Institute, an industry by industry compilation of firms with significant new product activities was generated. This population was further stratified by several characteristics, including whether the firm produced industrial or consumer products, whether the firm had centralized or decentralized R&D, the size of the firm in terms of sales dollars, and the size of the firm in terms of R&D expenditures.

Firms were then randomly selected from each strata to build a representative sample of significant new product sponsoring organizations. It should be noted that several firms were active in both consumer and industrial products and several firms had both central and divisional R&D departments. Because of the dual strata represented by these firms, the sample size could be reduced somewhat without compromise.

A total of 56 target firms were selected, based on a compromise design that considered the cost of traveling to distant firms, the need for some geographic dispersal of firms and the need to maintain a representative sample. The 10 United States industries having the highest preponderance of new

**Table 2–1**
**Project Outcome Measurement Scale**

| Degrees of Success or Failure | Success Outcome Descriptors | | Failure Outcome Descriptors | | |
|---|---|---|---|---|---|
| | Techical Outcomes | Commercial Outcomes | Technical Outcomes | Commercial Outcomes | Other Outcomes |
| High | Breakthrough | Blockbuster | Complete Dud | Took a Bath We Won't Forget | SE = Stopped the Effort Early Due to Poor Prognosis |
| Medium | Enhancement | Above Expectations | Gained Some Technology | Protected Our Position But Lost Money | |
| Low | Met the Specs | Met Expectations | Learned a Lot | Below Expectations | |

product activities were represented in the sample, which was checked to ensure that it contained a range of the strata characteristics.[1]

### Site Selection and Entry Procedures

Figure 2-2 presents the site selection algorithm used to identify the firms that were willing to cooperate in this study. In the contingent or dual-entry procedures, site entry letters were sent or telephone calls were made to acquaintances within the firm in parallel with the top-down entry. Of the original 56 target firms, 53 agreed to be studied.

Figure 2-3 presents the field site entry algorithm that was followed at each firm. The major activity of the site entry was the assembly of the population of development projects initiated at each firm during the previous 5 years. To assemble this population, the entire project portfolios were reviewed at each firm. Then, using the definitions in chapter 1, the relevant population of new product development *innovation* projects was assembled. It may be noted that numerous small obstacles were encountered in assem-

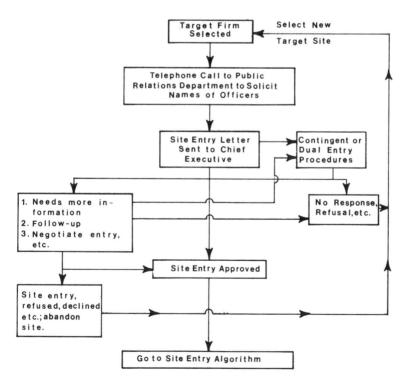

Figure 2–2. Site Selection Algorithm

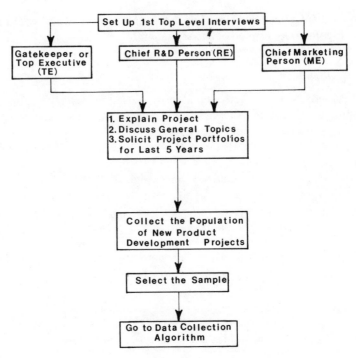

**Figure 2–3. Site Entry Algorithm**

bling this population. These problems included coping with the enormous numbers of projects at the larger firms and dealing with scanty records at other firms.

## Empirical Data Base

### Sample of Projects

As discussed above, the site entry procedures involved the collection of the population of new product development innovation projects initiated during the previous 5 years at each of the 53 firms. A random sampling of equal numbers of success and failure projects (using the scale in table 2-1) was then taken from this population at each firm. Several ongoing projects whose success or failure was not yet fully known were intentionally included in this sampling. A 10 percent project sample (5 percent success and 5 percent failure projects) was the goal at each firm. However, it soon became obvious that this provided too many projects at the larger firms and too few at the smaller firms, and the rule was modified accordingly.

A very large sample resulted from these procedures. Each project in the sample was then examined to see if it contained all the data sought in this study. Many projects were eliminated from the sample because they did not meet this requirement. The remaining sample was then checked to ensure that it contained a balance of success and failure outcome projects, projects with various degrees of difficulty, a diversity of technologies, both consumer and industrial products, both central and divisional R&D efforts, both means-generated and needs-generated innovations (see chapter 1) and a variety of sizes of projects. Repeated sampling was carried out to achieve this desired balance.

A final sample of projects was thus defined and data collection was initiated on them. But as in most field studies, organization changes, personnel changes, and other factors arose that caused twelve of the originally selected projects to be abandoned during the 10-year study period. However, during this time, many interesting new projects were initiated at several of the firms. These projects were sampled in a way that maintained the balance established in the original sample. Thus, complete life cycle data were collected on a total of 289 new product innovation projects.

*Data Collection Process*

Following the data collection algorithm outlined in figure 2-4, a total of 27 instruments, numerous telephone and personal interviews, and 584 in-depth cascading interviews were administered. Various subjects who worked on the 289 projects participated in these procedures to provide the life cycle data.[2,3]

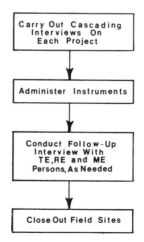

Figure 2–4. Data Collection Algorithm

The cascading interview procedure developed for this study is illustrated in table 2-2. This procedure was essential to ensure the validity of the data and information. Cascading interview procedures were used with four types of personnel on each project: primary subjects, key project personnel, key departmental personnel, and informants. The primary subjects were the firm's top managers. The key project personnel included all the personnel who had worked on the project. The key departmental personnel included management representatives from R&D, marketing, production and other departments who had dealt with the project. The informants were various persons who had little formal connection with the project, but who could confirm or otherwise add details to the project histories. The exact numbers of these persons varied with the project, the firm, and the availability of information.

## Some Caveats and Cautions

The reader should bear in mind that this study is based on a relatively broad sample. Though such a sample affords the ability to generalize conclusions, it may not always provide the desired depth in specific areas. This is the necessary compromise that must often be made in choosing a sample.

The analyses presented in the following chapters were not all made on the entire 289 project sample. In spite of rather thorough data collection, some gaps always remain in any study. Thus, the statistical significance of some of the analyses may vary from one chapter to another because of vary-

**Table 2–2**
**Cascading Interview Process**

| This Subject | Identifies |
|---|---|
| Top Manager | |
|    Mr. A | Critical events $e_1$, $e_2$, $\boxed{e_3}$ |
|    Mr. B | Critical events $\boxed{e_3,}$ $e_4$ |
| Middle Manager | |
|    Mr. C | Critical events $\boxed{e_3,}$ $e_6$ under conditions $c_1$, $\boxed{c_2,}$ $c_3$ |
|    Mr. D | Relations $\boxed{e_3}$ to $c_1$, $\boxed{e_3}$ *to* $\boxed{c_2}$ |
| Project Manager | |
|    Mr. E | Conditions $c_1$, $\boxed{c_2}$ |
| | Relation $\boxed{e_3}$ to $\boxed{c_2}$ |

The conclusion is: There is considerable support for the relatedness of $e_3$ and $c_2$.

ing sample sizes. This is pointed out where it is pertinent in the various chapters.

Age is the inherent enemy of all data. Field research on completed projects takes time to collect, time to analyze, and time to disseminate. During this elapsed time, people learn and practices change. The very fact that a project has been completed means that the participants learned some things. They may consequently change their behaviors the next time they have a similar situation. Attempts were made to minimize such time lapse effects by selecting the most recently completed and ongoing projects for study here.

## Notes

1. The 10 industries were metals, glass, transportation, plastics, machinery, electronics, chemicals, food, aerospace, and pharmaceuticals. Both automotive and mass transit products are included in the transportation industry classification. Computer products and instruments are included in the electronics classification.

2. The instrument package is available from the author.

3. The methodologies used here were developed and established in two other studies. They are discussed in detail in William E. Souder, et al., *An Exploratory Study of the Coordinating Mechanisms between R&D and Marketing as an Influence on the Innovation Process*, National Science Foundation Final Report, August 26, 1977 and in William E. Souder, et al., *A Comparative Analysis of Phase Transfer Methods for Managing New Product Developments*, National Science Foundation Final Report, August 15, 1983. Copies are available from the author.

# 3
# Benchmark Cases of New Product Innovations

E very successful innovation has its ups and downs. Few innovations have a smooth ride to stardom. Most evolve through painful cycles of growth and decline. Eventually, they become strong enough to break through their performance thresholds and win a place in society. Institutionalized walls of resistance fall only after repeated battering by increasingly powerful versions of the innovation.

## Growth-Decline Patterns

Figure 3-1 shows the growth-decline cycles that characterized one of the innovations observed in this study. As the first version of the innovation, version A, took shape, it acquired believers and users. But flaws were soon discovered and version A fell from favor. A new, improved version B was developed from these experiences. Though stronger than its predecessor, it too soon succumbed to the more powerful forces in its environment and died out. Phoenix-like, a subsequent version C was borne from the ashes of its predecessor. But it was even less potent. However, learning from these failures, a superior version D was developed that overcame the performance and societal barriers. It was adopted by so many users that it became the standard practice for the industry.

## Benchmark Cases

In this chapter, the life cycles of three new product innovations are described. They provide many rich insights into the fascinating system of technical, social, institutional, organizational, personal, and individual factors that must be in harmony for successful innovations.

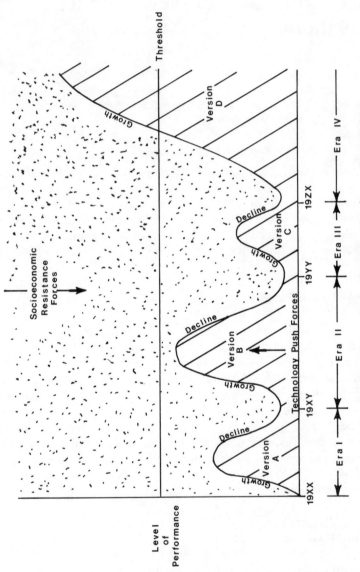

Figure 3–1. Typical Growth-Decline Patterns for an Innovation

The three cases detailed here are: hybrid seed corn, longwall coal mining, and water jet cutting. These technologies were originally researched because of the need to know more about the backgrounds of several projects in the data base. However, once their histories were written, it became apparent that these three cases embodied the types of information, events, variables, insights, understandings, and explanations that should be sought for all 289 projects in the data base. Thus, these three became "benchmark cases" or models that guided all the data collections and analyses throughout this research.

## Hybrid Seed Corn

Hybrid seed corn was a radical innovation that was fervently resisted by most farmers, who had become dependent on open-pollinated corn farming practices for their livelihoods.[1,2] But over a 50 year period, hybrid corn emerged and completely revolutionized farming practices. It ushered in farm mechanization, scientific soil management practices, several new industries, dramatic increases in farm productivity, improved nutritional sources for farm animals, and an array of new food products for the consumer.

The hybrid corn story shows how radical technological progress can occur in a relatively short period of time, even under depressed economic conditions, if there is a proper confluence of technical, economic, and social forces. The story contains many lessons for basic researchers, new product developers, product planners, policy planners, and commercializing agents.

### Origins of This Innovation

In March of 1896, animal nutritionists at the University of Illinois Agriculture Experiment Station initiated corn plant crossbreeding experiments. In 1896, farmers were planting the same type of open-pollinated corn that the Indians had shown them how to grow 400 years earlier. It is noteworthy that these first experiments were not conducted by plant scientists. Rather, this work was carried out by animal nutritionists who were concerned that open-pollinated corn would not produce sufficient animal food to sustain America's fledgling beef, poultry, and pork industries.

By 1899, news of these experiments began to arouse interest. A prominent grower of open-pollinated seed, Eugene Funk, gave a grant to the University of Illinois Station to further their hybrid research. Hybrid technologies were a potentially serious competitor to open-pollinated technologies. Funk was obviously a very forward thinking producer. However, by 1906 few advances had been made and the original research team had disbanded.

## The First Wave

One of the original team members, Murray East, continued his work at the University of Connecticut Agriculture Experiment Station. The Connecticut Station had a reputation for innovation and an interdisciplinary staff of prominent researchers.

In the winter of 1909, East presented a paper on his work at the American Corn Breeders Association. His paper did not arouse much interest among the corn breeders. But a prominent basic researcher, George Shaw, was impressed. East and Shaw subsequently joined forces and combined their respective empirical and theoretical backgrounds to develop a revolutionary inbreeding theory. Using this theory, the Nebraska State Agriculture Experiment Station successfully grew hybrid strains for the first time under field conditions in 1913. This was the first state experiment station to show any interest in hybrid seeds. All the previously interested stations had been at universities.

Though superior yields were obtained, the fragile hybrid plants did not survive the next two years of unusually harsh Nebraska winters. Shaw interpreted these results as a failure of his inbreeding theory and abandoned further studies. East felt that he had exhausted his limited knowledge of plant genetics and turned his attention to other issues. By 1916, interest in hybrid seed corn appeared to have died off.

## The Second Wave

In 1917, a young plant scientist named Donald Jones joined the University of Connecticut Station and re-interested East in hybrid seeds. Jones was the first formally trained applied plant geneticist to enter hybrid corn breeding. By 1918, Jones and East had created a double cross hybrid that yielded 20 percent more than all other corn under laboratory conditions. By 1919, a book by Jones and East had revolutionized corn breeding theories and unraveled many long-standing mysteries. But almost 20 years would pass before the principles in their book would be used to mass produce commercial scale hybrid seed stock.

From 1917 to 1919, Jones and East became prolific writers in various farm magazines. They predicted yields of 112 bushels per acre for hybrid corn, as opposed to the 40 to 60 bushels per acre common for open-pollinated corn. But most of the leading agronomists, state experiment stations, and agriculture specialists remained steadfastly opposed to the new hybrids. No one in authority wanted to risk blessing an untested product on the basis of a few laboratory results. It was essential to find convincing field-scale trials outside of the favorable New England climate. By the fall of 1918, Jones and East knew that time was of the essence: commercial growers of open-pollinated seed were fighting back with slick full color advertisements and convincing photographs of the earlier Nebraska failures. Interest in hybrid seed corn was again on the wane.

## The First Field Trials

A scientist named Jim Holbert at the Minnesota State Agriculture Experiment Station had followed the East-Shaw-Jones work with great fascination. Early in 1918, Holbert left the station and went to work for Eugene Funk at his commercial seed growing facilities in Iowa. This was the same Funk who had funded some of the original hybrid work nearly 20 years earlier. Funk was a very open-minded producer. He felt he owed it to his customers to try out the promising new hybrids, even though his whole business was founded on rival open-pollinated technologies.

Working with Jones and East, by late 1918 Holbert had perfected a new hybrid plant strain at Funk's growing facilities. In the spring of 1919, Funk convinced the local county agent to run a comparison test, as a county-sponsored project, in the corner of a corn field owned by one of the most influential local farmers. The superiority of the hybrid strains was overwhelmingly demonstrated in that unusually hot summer of 1919. The open-pollinated corn withered, became diseased, and died. The adjacent hybrid corn prospered.

## The Transition Period

The dramatic results of these first field trials were met with skepticism by many farmers. Their livelihoods depended on their corn crops. Most felt they could not risk their livelihoods for a chance at improvement on the basis of one field test. Sometimes, those who are the least well-off are also the least likely to take a chance to improve their lot!

However, these results were very convincing to the U.S. Department of Agriculture. In October 1919, the first federal Agriculture Experiment Station was established on Eugene Funk's commercial seed growing farm with Holbert as the director. The goal of the station was to find an effective way of controlling corn disease, which the U.S. Department of Agriculture had declared to be the number one menace to corn farming. As a result, later in 1919, special appropriations were secured from Congress which established six more federal field stations within the corn belt. These stations provided a critical mass of scientific talents, focused on a national problem. The stations were linked with both the universities and the commercial seed growers, and they were devoted to field-scale research.

Henry C. Wallace, the editor and publisher of a highly respected Iowa farm magazine, accepted the post of Secretary of Agriculture in 1921. Because Wallace favored hybrid corn, the interest of the U.S. Department of Agriculture in hybrids became more intense. Wallace used Funk's commercial farm and its experiment station as a showcase for numerous visitors and dignitaries. Subsequently, the first successful hybrid corns were grown on a large-scale basis at Funk Farms. By 1924, Holbert's hybrids were being successfully grown in several farmer's test plots throughout Illinois and Iowa from seed supplied by the Funk Seed Company.

Lester Pfister, a prominent Midwestern farmer and personal friend of Holbert, was a commercial seed grower with an extensive marketing organization. Working with Holbert and Funk Farms, Pfister developed a new hybrid strain which he began to market in Indiana, Illinois, and Iowa in 1929. Though Pfister had made his fortune selling open-pollinated corn, he was quick to recognize the superiority of hybrid strains. Most of the new hybrids developed at the Funk Farms station were mass marketed through Lester Pfister's organization.

Thus, from 1896 to 1917, a number of influences propelled the development of hybrid corn out of its early beginnings at university experiment stations. From 1917 to 1929, these foundations were built on through the entry of the federal government and the commercial seed growers. The federal government supplied research funds and the commercial seed growers supplied the production and mass-distribution resources. A decisive factor in the story of hybrid seed corn was the resulting network of relationships that formed among the federal field stations, the commercial seed growers, and the local farmers. This network was the basis for the eventual widespread adoption and diffusion of hybrid corn.

## The Diffusion Period

During the early 1930s, the federal field stations and the hybrid seed corn marketers worked together to recruit the most influential farmers to sell hybrid corn to their neighbors. By the mid-1930s, a small army of these "farmer-salesmen" were merchandising hybrid corn through a variety of clever methods. In one scheme, the farmer-salesmen offered to pay for half the seed if his neighbor would give him one-quarter of his increased yields from using it. Every farmer-salesman made a profit from this deal. Another tactic was to give the local farmer just enough seed to plant a few rows of the hybrid corn, if he agreed to plant it near the road or in some conspicuous place adjacent to his other corn. Neighboring farmers passing by his field would immediately see the comparative superiority of the hybrid corn and tell other farmers about it. This "neighborhood effect" was one of the major factors in the rapid spread of the awareness of hybrid seed corn.

It is important to note that these farmer-salesmen were not directed by high-powered sales executives who were imported into the industry. Each farmer-salesman was trained by a more experienced farmer-salesman, thus generating a sales chain. These depression era farmers were motivated in part by the extra income from selling seed corn. But they were also motivated by the learning experience. A springboard for exchange of opinions and findings developed among the farmers and the farmer-salesmen, and the hybrid seed corn experience fostered a receptive frame of mind to other new ideas.

*Significant Factors in the Hybrid Corn Case*

The story of the development, introduction, and adoption of hybrid seed corn demonstrates how innovation depends on many different parties and roles. It shows the power of ideas. It shows how partnerships between government agencies and others can promote the diffusion of a radical innovation. And it shows how innovative selling methods can overcome seemingly insurmountable odds. This story is all the more impressive because it occurred with a class of adopters who were generally resistant to change, during the worst economic crisis the United States has ever faced. In a relatively short period of time, hybrid seed corn completely displaced open-pollinated corn, revolutionized traditional farming practices, ushered in radical changes in mechanized farming, and changed the culture of the farm belt. The traditional value, "It was good enough for my father, so it's good enough for me," was replaced by cosmopolitan values, an openness to change, and a receptivity to new practices.

Several factors can be cited that fostered the success of this innovation. Hybrid seed corn was born from basic research in several disciplines. A spirit of fierce dedication and zeal was present among the early laboratory researchers (like East), the established producers (like Funk), and the existing commercial agents (like Pfister). They were variously motivated by the chances for scientific fame, public recognition, and economic gain. The availability of basic research funds and the promotive organizational climates at the early development stage of this technology, such as at the Connecticut Experiment Station, fostered sound research. There was a network of scientists and scientific societies that encouraged open scientific exchange and debate. There was an emerging mass media that quickly picked up the news of the new hybrids, translated it into laymen's terms and carried it to every farmer. There was a distribution network of commercial seedsmen who were dedicated to supplying the best possible seeds to their customers. They owned and operated the major seed producing facilities of the nation, which they were willing to donate for the trial of the new hybrid seed. The network of established federal experiment stations became dedicated to improving the nutritional value of corn. As a result, close personal rapport developed between many government experiment station employees and several prominent commercial seedsmen. Experiment station researchers often took jobs with the seedsmen's organizations, then subsequently rejoined the experiment station. This provided enormous scientific cross-fertilization and intellectual growth.

There was a high-level champion, Henry Wallace, who became secretary of agriculture at the time when the hybrid corn movement was snowballing. As a result of his efforts, Congress provided funds for seven breeding stations at the commercial growers' facilities, where many farmers could see the new corn as it was being grown. The federal government and the commercial seedsmen, literally, formed an economic partnership to further the development and distribution of hybrid seeds. Several county agents, experiment station personnel, and government researchers formed their own production and distribution companies. These individuals had either a captive audience of loyal potential customers, or a wealth of know-how about hybrid breeding, or both. In some cases, scientists and county agents jointly formed commercial enterprises.

There was a serious economic need and an established market demand for improved corn. There was a heritage of seed-producing institutions and the association of "good" products with them. The names Funk, Pfister, and Wallace inspired confidence. It was fortuitous that hybrid corn was a highly "divisible" innovation. It could be sold (or given away) and planted in amounts ranging from a single kernel to several bushels. Thus, it was "trialable" at different levels of commitment, from low risk to high risk.

An army of farmer-salesmen was recruited, in chain letter fashion, to sell hybrid corn. Free samples, promotions, cost-sharing methods, neighborhood farmer comparisons, and other clever merchandising methods were employed. The most highly regarded neighborhood farmers were chosen as the targets for conversion to hybrid corn. Once these influential adopters were convinced, the rest of the community usually followed, in a neighborhood effect. Farm youths were encouraged to adopt hybrid corn through Future Farmers of America organizations and college programs, in an attempt to change farming practices by changing the behavior of future farmers.

## Longwall Coal Mining

In the longwall method of mining underground coal, the roof above the coal bed is supported only while the coal is extracted. After extraction, the equipment is removed and the roof is purposely collapsed.

This method has the advantage of providing a higher percentage of the available coal from the mine. Unlike conventional methods, virtually all the coal in the mine can be recovered.[3] Moreover, since the roof is collapsed after mining, there is no subsequent danger of further subsidence or uncontrolled disturbance to the countryside around the mine. Cave-ins, sudden faults, and surface subsidence are a constant danger around conventional mines. People often build houses above old, abandoned conventional mines that sometimes suddenly collapse, severely damaging or even swallowing up the houses.

## Overview of This Technology

Since its beginnings in the United States during the 1800s, seven varieties of longwall technologies have evolved. They differ with regard to the nature of the roof supports and the methods used to cut and haul the coal from the mine. The evolutionary history of the technology is cyclical, with the birth of a new method overlapping the death of a prior one. Typically, a new variety of longwall mining would appear in response to some need. It would be adopted first by a few venturesome innovators, and later by many imitators who joined the bandwagon. But costs and other imperfections in the technology would cause most of the adopters to discontinue their use. Because the original need remained, another variety of longwall would emerge from the ashes of the old one, and the cycle would be repeated.

Figure 3-2 depicts the life cycle diffusion pattern which characterized each variety of longwall.[4,5] The cycles varied in their duration and maximum net percentage diffusion. However, the seventh and latest longwall does not exhibit the discontinuances shown by the others. And it appears from all other indications that this version will have a very long life.

Figure 3-3 summarizes the census of longwalls in operation from 1875 to 1985. Cycles like the one shown in figure 3-2 are embedded in these statistics. They can be discerned by disaggregating these data.[4,5,6]

## The 1875–1945 Period

Early style longwall mining (with wooden roof supports and hand cutting of the coal) and old style longwall mining (with mechanical steel jack roof supports and machine cutting of the coal) were used to some extent in the United States from 1875 to 1945. These methods were introduced by immigrant Welsh mining engineers during the westward expansion of the United States. These technologies were quite crude, inexact, and unreliable. Unexpected roof collapses and severe injuries were frequent. The spread of unionization and the introduction of improved coal cutting and haulage methods made these costly labor-intensive longwalls obsolete.

In 1945, the U.S. Bureau of Mines dedicated itself to promoting improved mine productivity to assist the postwar expansion. When the Bureau learned of successful coal plow longwall trials in Germany, an observational team of coal mining executives, engineers, and government employees was assembled. This team became a significant factor in the subsequent history of longwalls.

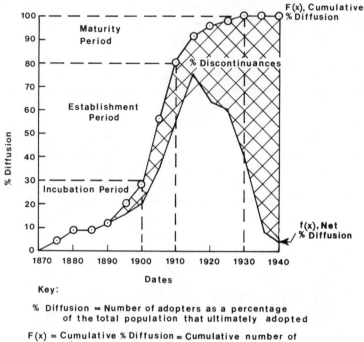

Figure 3–2. Typical Longwall Life Cycle Diffusion Pattern

*Source:* Adapted from William E. Souder and E. R. Palowitch, "Growth of Longwall Technologies in the U.S.," chapter 1 of *Longwall-Shortwall Mining State of Art*, R. V. Ramani, ed. (New York: American Institute of Mining Engineering, 1981), pp. 3–9 by permission.

*Coal Plow Longwalls*

The observational team recommended the trial of coal plow longwalls in the United States. In the coal plow longwall, a unit resembling a farm plow is pulled across the coal face, slicing the coal off. Several American mining firms were willing to try the units, but none had the financial strength to fund those trials. The U.S. Bureau of Mines responded with a series of government funded demonstrations of coal plow longwalls. The government bought the equipment; the mining companies supplied the labor and kept the coal produced by the demonstration.

Though much was learned from each demonstration, the experiences

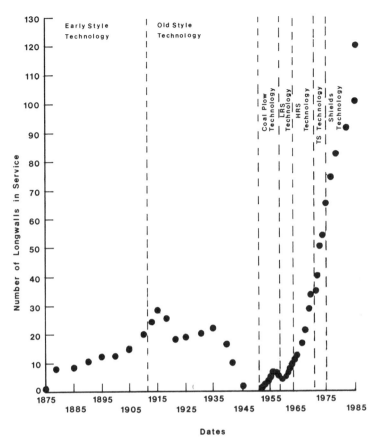

*Source:* Adapted from William E. Souder and E. R. Palowitch, "Growth of Longwall Technologies in the U.S.," chapter 1 of *Longwall-Shortwall Mining State of Art*, R. V. Ramani, ed. (New York: American Institute of Mining Engineering, 1981), pp. 3–9 by permission.

**Figure 3–3. Census of Longwalls, 1875 to 1985**

were generally plagued by roof and water problems, a lack of spare parts, and equipment unreliabilities. By the late 1950s, this surge of renewed interest in longwalls was dying out. Theories of roof fall were not well developed, so the only prudent course was the costly over-design of the mechanical roof supports. Even these over-designed supports did not substantially reduce the high frequency of often violent, unexpected, and deadly roof collapses. The inherent unreliability and hazards of the method, the large numbers of men required to set and retrieve the mechanical roof supports, the influence of rising wage rates and the invention of continuous miner machines combined to doom the coal plow longwall.

But the potentials of this new technology had been demonstrated. The experience gained led to the advent of self-advancing hydraulic roof supports and shields, improved conveyors, and high-velocity coal cutting devices in a subsequent era. These components eventually evolved into an articulated, engineered longwall system with enormous potential.

## LRS And HRS Longwalls

The European longwall equipment manufacturers began to take more notice of the U.S. market during the late 1950s, when their domestic markets began to saturate. Thus, when British and European hydraulic self-advancing roof supports were displayed at the Cleveland coal show in 1959, latent interest in longwalls was rekindled in American mining companies.

In 1960, Eastern Gas and Fuel Associates, one of the firms that had participated in the Bureau's earlier coal plow demonstrations, purchased and installed one of the European units. Their experiences in the earlier demonstrations allowed them to select the optimum conditions for this low resistance support (LRS) unit. It operated nearly trouble-free and set a world production record. This experience finally convinced the skeptics. From 1960 to 1965, many imitators adopted LRS longwalls. However, most of these LRS units eventually proved too fragile for the demanding conditions of many mines in the United States. They, too, were discontinued. Like its predecessors, the LRS longwalls soon died off.

Several prominent mining engineers felt that U.S. longwall failures could be prevented by higher resistance roof supports. The LRS experiences convinced the European manufacturers of the need for high resistance support (HRS) longwalls in the United States, and they were introduced in 1964. This event opened the floodgates. Those who had adopted LRS longwalls immediately upgraded to the HRS technologies. Many other imitators followed.

## Total Systems (TS) and Shield Longwalls

In spite of successes with the HRS longwalls, few manufacturers produced a total system (TS) longwall. This is an articulated system of roof supports, coal cutting devices, and coal conveying technologies. The typical HRS longwall was an ad hoc combination of equipment from various manufacturers, assembled by the mining firms to meet their individual conditions. This created many problems, and the interest in HRS longwalls soon began to dwindle. It was not until 1975 that the state of the art had advanced to the point where, given the wide variety of equipment, TS longwalls could be scientifically engineered to fit specific individualized U.S. mine conditions.

By 1978, TS longwalls were being replaced with shield longwalls. A shield is a massive steel canopy that effectively protects the workers and the coal cutting equipment from roof falls under even the most adverse conditions. It may be the ultimate in roof support and worker protection. It is interesting that shields nearly double the basic cost of a longwall, yet the mining companies are now adopting them at unprecedented rates.

### Analysis of the Longwalls Case

As the data in table 3-1 show, the elapsed time for longwall technologies to reach their maximum diffusion among the user population has steadily decreased. For example, the early style longwalls required 30 years to reach the end of their incubation period and 10 more years to become established. By comparison, the TS longwalls were snatched up much more quickly.

As indicated by the data in table 3-2, the users' degree of success with longwall technologies increased with the more recent types of longwalls. Discontinuances occurred later in the lives of the more recent technologies (larger percentage of era elapsed). Moreover, the percentage of adopters who discontinued (percentage discontinuances) declined with the more recent types of longwalls.

Table 3-3 presents some interesting comparisons. The elapsed times from the awareness to the adoption stages has shortened considerably in recent years. Longwall adopters have begun to behave more like the adopters of other innovations. However, note that the longwall imitators remain slow to

**Table 3–1**
**Comparative Diffusion Patterns**
*(years)*

| | Period | | | |
|---|---|---|---|---|
| *Types of Longwalls* | *Incubation* | *Establishment* | *Maturity* | *Total Life* |
| Early Style | 30 | 10 | 20 | 60 |
| Old Style | 12 | 8 | 10 | 30 |
| Coal Plow | 2 | 3 | 2 | 7 |
| LRS | 2 | 3 | 1 | 6 |
| HRS | 2 | 2 | 1 | 6 |
| TS | 2 | 2 | 1 | 5 |
| Shields | 1 | 1 | [a] | [a] |

Source: Adapted from William E. Souder and E. R. Palowitch, "Growth of Longwall Technologies in the U.S.," Chapter 1 of *Longwall-Shortwall Mining State of Art,* R. V. Ramani, ed. (New York: American Institute of Mining Engineering, 1981), pp. 3–9, by permission.

[a]This period has not yet ended.

**Table 3–2**
**Comparison of Diffusion Statistics**

| Types of Longwalls | Percentage of Era Elapsed when Discontinuances Began | Percentage Discontinuances at the End of the Era |
|---|---|---|
| Early Style | 30 | 98 |
| Old Style | 25 | 90 |
| Coal Plow | 28 | 82 |
| LRS | 30 | 91 |
| HRS | 40 | 25 |
| TS | 60 | 13 |
| Shields | 60 | a |

Source: Adapted from William E. Souder and E. R. Palowitch, "Growth of Longwall Technologies in the U.S.," Chapter 1 of *Longwall-Shortwall Mining State of Art*, R. V. Ramani, ed. (New York: American Institute of Mining Engineering, 1981), pp. 3–9, by permission.
aThis period has not yet ended.

**Table 3–3**
**Average Years of Elapsed Time**

| Stages | Longwalls 1945–65 | Longwalls 1968–78 | Longwalls 1978–80 | Other Comparable Innovations |
|---|---|---|---|---|
| Awareness-to-Trial | | | | |
| Innovators | 5.5 | 1 | 1 | 1.5 |
| Imitators | 5 | 5 | 4.5 | 3.5 |
| Trial-to-Adoption | | | | |
| Innovators | 2.5 | 2 | 2 | 1 |
| Imitators | 2.5 | 2 | 2 | 1 |
| Awareness-to-Adoption | | | | |
| Innovators | 8 | 3 | 3 | 2.5 |
| Imitators | 7.5 | 7 | 6.5 | 4.5 |

Source: Adapted from William E. Souder and E. R. Palowitch, "Growth ot Longwall Technologies in the U.S.," Chapter 1 of *Longwall-Shortwall Mining State of Art*, R. V. Ramani, ed. (New York: American Institute of Mining Engineering, 1981), pp. 3–9, by permission.

adopt, relative to the innovators. The imitators continue to be especially slow to trial longwalls once they become aware of them. Why? The search for an answer leads to some interesting observations.

Innovators and imitators play reciprocal roles. The innovator effectively debugs the technology for the imitator, reducing the technological risks and economic uncertainties. But the subsequent diffusion of this technology through an imitator population erodes the innovator's captive markets and monopoly profits as other producers and users join the bandwagon. A rapidly diffusing innovation therefore motivates an innovator to further improve his product or adopt a new innovation so that the cycle repeats. Thus, the increased speed of diffusion shown in tables 3-1 to 3-3 for recent longwalls must be viewed as a beneficial trend.

However, one factor was found in the longwalls case that distinguished the innovators from the imitators and explained why the imitators were so slow to adopt. This factor was the extent to which the firm's managers were active in their environment. In the most innovative firms, the decision makers attended more conventions and trade shows, visited more competitors' mines, read more journals, and generally had more diverse contacts outside their firms. These firms were more outward-looking. They were always seeking new things that they could bring into their firms. It should be noted that the financial health of the firms was not correlated with their willingness to adopt longwalls. The firms that could least afford it were the first to adopt. In effect, their backs were to the wall. They had to adopt or go out of business.

It is interesting to note how this differs from the hybrid corn case, where willingness to adopt was directly correlated with the wealth of the farmer. The poorest farmers were the most reluctant adopters. Why? The explanation is socioeconomic in nature. The farmer was putting his personal economic livelihood on the line. Mining company executives were putting the stockholder's capital at risk, not their own.

Thus, we have a rather pessimistic picture of innovation and adoption in the case of longwall technologies. Adoptions appear to occur only as a last resort, when the firm has no other alternative for survival. Other firms that are less destitute and more financially robust continue to resist new technologies. They remain inward-thinking, unconcerned and unaffected by events outside their own firms until some cataclysmic economic or technical event puts their backs to the wall. Clearly, longwalls are not unique in this regard; the iron, steel, automotive and railroad industries in the United States provide some analogous pictures. Also, it is clear that encouraging potential users to adopt the longwall technology is a different matter than encouraging potential hybrid corn users. Different strategies are required.

*Barriers to Adoption*

Throughout the long history of longwalls, adoption was encouraged by the ever present promises of lower cost, higher productivity, greater recovery of coal from the mine, and improved safety. But, as table 3-4 shows, there were seven major barriers that slowed the spread of longwalls. The lack of appreciation for longwalls as an engineered system has been a serious barrier. The industry has for so long dealt with handicraft methods and incremental innovations that it was hard for the users to grasp the concept of a total mining system. The size of the investment, the long payback period, and the high-output breakeven point dissuaded all but the most venturesome. The lack of reliable theories of ground movement and long-term comparative data under real conditions were other serious barriers.

The culture of the coal mining industry is itself a barrier. The industry consists of a heterogeneous collection of entrepreneurs, each of whom faces a slightly different set of mining and economic conditions, technical problems, and markets. Though there is open communication with regard to technical information, the perceived uniqueness of conditions at each mine limits real technology transfer and useful information exchange. There is an apparent pride of ownership in being the first user. But this motive seldom extends to any technology that is not well proven, low risk, and highly incremental. Mine operators are quick to listen to new ideas but equally quick to state how "that wouldn't work at our mine because. . . ." This cultural openness and willingness to communicate new technical ideas may in fact discourage the entry of outside-the-industry innovations. Why? Because it undermines any long-term technical advantage or monopoly profits for an innovator.

## Table 3–4
## Barriers to the Adoption of Longwalls

1. Lack of appreciation and comprehension

2. Perceived risk and uncertainty

3. Disbelief by equipment manufacturers that a U.S. market existed

4. Lack of comprehensive information

5. Culture of the coal mining industry

6. The all-or-nothing characteristics of longwalls

7. General supply and demand uncertainties

Source: Adapted from William E. Souder and E. R. Palowitch, "Growth of Longwall Technologies in the U.S.," Chapter 1 of *Longwall-Shortwall Mining State of Art*, R. V. Ramani, ed. (New York: American Institute of Mining Engineering, 1981), pp. 3–9, by permission.

This may also explain why there is little R&D within the industry. Thus, there are serious barriers to innovation from both inside and outside the industry.

It must be noted that longwalls are not easily tried in piecemeal fashion. The longwall mining technology is a large, high-investment item that must either be used in its entirety or not at all. Thus, the very nature of the innovation discourages its adoption. It is much easier to adopt things on the installment plan than all at once, especially in an industry that resists even incremental innovations. Finally, it must be noted that the history of roller coaster prices and the short economic boom-or-bust cycles of the coal industry discourage the adoption of any long payback innovations.

## Water Jet Cutting

Cutting operations are an integral part of many industrial processes. There is hardly any manufacturing operation that does not involve some kind of cutting or sizing. It is therefore surprising that it has taken over 2,000 years for water jet technologies to reach widespread application.[7]

### Low-Pressure Technologies

The use of water pressure from naturally occurring lakes, streams, and water reservoirs to cut stones and to mine minerals is a very old idea. The ancient Romans used inclined sluices and reservoirs to mine gold. This old art found its way to California during the gold rush of the 1800s, where it was known as "booming." It was soon upgraded into a pump and hose affair called a "giant" or "monitor," with a nozzle velocity of up to 8 feet per second. By 1867 this technology had found its way back to Europe, where it was used to mine peat and cut soft minerals.

This low-pressure period was characterized by a crisscross evolutionary pattern as the technology crossed back and forth between various users. With each new application, the user made changes to adapt the technology to a particular use. This further encouraged other new applications. However, substantial technological progress was not made until the basic idea of water jet cutting was augmented with the invention of manual pumps. They became an important facilitating technology for water jet cutting at that time.[7]

### Medium-Pressure Technologies

However, as time passed, manual pumps added only marginally to the basic water jet technology. It was the invention of the steam engine that really facilitated the advancement of water jet cutting. Steam engines provided the first possibility for efficient pump power capable of creating serious water pressures. In 1905, Russia's Leningrad Institute developed the first 700 pounds per square inch (psi), steam-powered water cannon. It had the capability to cut light industrial materials.

Further efforts seemed simply to fade away for lack of any real need. Then, in 1946, a special hydraulic institute was constructed at Stalinsk and a resurgence of Soviet interest occurred with the U.S.S.R.'s postwar industrialization efforts. From 1946 to 1950, Western European nations also rediscovered water jet cutting as a means for simultaneously cutting, cleaning, and cooling some hot-formed industrial materials. A variety of swiveling and pulsating jet pumps were devised for cutting and cleaning, as part of the European postwar rebuilding effort.

Soviet and European publications detailed numerous applications that the American Gilsonite Company attempted to duplicate. However, it was not until 1954, when higher pressure pumps became available, that the company was able to assemble a 2,300 psi system. This system proved highly effective for cutting gilsonite, a natural ore that could not be safely mined by any other known method. Thus, the technology came back to the United States.

The medium-pressure era was characterized by two distinct pathways of effort. In one path, the Soviets emphasized theoretical work and applications that supported their industrialization needs. In the other path, Western Europe and the United States extended these results by making mechanical augmentations that facilitated the advance of the basic technology.

*High-Pressure Technologies*

The 1946 to 1954 experiences demonstrated the potentials of water jets. But higher pressures were needed if this technology was ever to achieve widespread use. The development of higher pressure pumps during the late 1950s and early 1960s made this a real possibility.

During the ensuing years, the United States devoted considerable research activity to the development of 15,000 to 20,000 psi cavitation and percussion jet nozzles. Seeded by monies from the National Science Foundation, the National Aeronautics and Space Administration, and private industry, by the end of the 1960s new equipment and practices in water jet cutting and cleaning had been spawned. Today, water jet technologies are widely used throughout the world to economically cut a variety of materials. Simple techniques have been devised to contain the excess water, protect the machine operators, and recycle the water for repeated use in the same operation.

Thus, the 1945-70 period was marked by an emphasis on basic research to develop two key components of the system: pumps and nozzles. Higher pressure pumps quickly eroded the nozzles. Once better nozzles were designed, pumps again became the limiting factor. Eventually, the state of the art in both of these technologies came together to facilitate significant advances in water jet technologies.

Figure 3-4 traces the impacts of various facilitating technologies and inventions on water jet cutting. As time passed, each technology (booming, giants, water cannons) was gradually improved, thereby increasing its capability to produce higher pressures. These patterns are indicated by the family of curved lines in figure 3-4. But each technology eventually reached its maximum performance threshold ($T_1$, $T_2$, and so on), at which time it was replaced by a superior technology. However, the advent of each superior technology had to await the introduction of some facilitating technology like better pumps and nozzles.

*Observations about the Water Jet Cutting Case*

Figure 3-5 summarizes the key events in the history of cutting by water jets. The technology evolved through five stages: adaptation from nature; research and extrapolation; development and improvement; modification and reduction to practice; and adoption and implementation. The initial adaptation of water cutting from natural streams and the embodiment of water jet concepts in mechanical cannons was "pulled" by the need for greater productivity in mining precious metals. The desire for more fundamental knowledge led to basic research and extrapolations of the concept. The industrialization movements of the 1800s and 1900s further "pushed" the technology to greater heights. The invention of facilitating technologies like the steam engine, the hydraulic pump, and the jet nozzle fostered new users and new applications. The desire for greater capabilities then pulled the technology into new uses and applications. Imitators began to take up the technology, modifying it for their applications and encouraging its spread.

The water jet cutting case suggests several factors that are a key to the successful development and diffusion of any technology. First, a body of basic knowledge must exist. The water jet practices of the sixteenth and seventeenth centuries were such a base, as crude as they were. Second, a technology "pull" or real need must exist. It must be a need that can be filled by the technology, or at least some extension of it. Third, there must be a human desire to improve the status quo. If people do not care about improving their lot, nothing will happen. People must have sufficient motivation to seek new knowledge that will solve problems. Fourth, facilitating technologies must be available. Without the invention of jet nozzles, powerful pumps, and sources of power to run them, it is hard to see how water jet cutting could have advanced to its current state. Fifth, basic research monies must be available at the times when they are needed. Finally, many users must be willing to take the risk of trying and adopting the new technology. A few innovators are required who will take the first venturesome steps. But it is not enough that

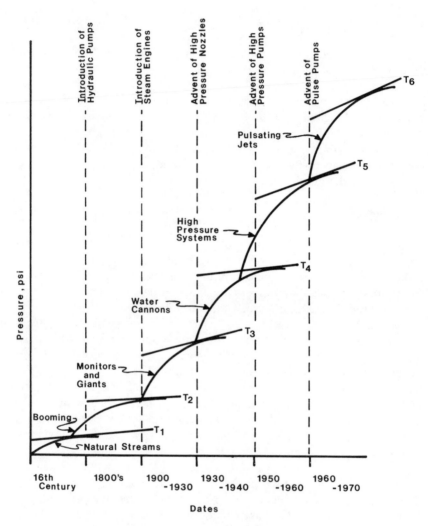

*Source:* William E. Souder and R. J. Evans, "Water Jet Cutting: The Resurgence of an Old Technology," chapter 22, *RETC Proceedings*, vol. 2 (1983), pp. 712–740, by permission.

**Figure 3–4. Impacts of Facilitating Technologies**

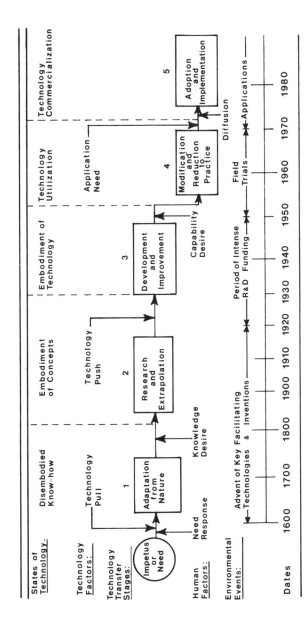

**Figure 3–5. Technology Evolution Model**

*Source:* William E. Souder and R. J. Evans, "Water Jet Cutting: The Resurgence of an Old Technology," chapter 22, *RETC Proceedings*, vol. 2 (1983), pp. 712–740, by permission.

**Table 3–5**
**Summary of the Three Cases**

| Factors Important to Innovation Success | Hybrid Corn | Longwall Coal Mining | Water Jet Cutting |
|---|---|---|---|
| Basic research | X | O | X |
| Pioneering spirit | X | X | X |
| Profit motive | X | X | X |
| Desire for fame | X | O | O |
| Opportunity for recognition | X | X | X |
| Communication networks | X | X | X |
| Favorable organization climates | X | O | O |
| Mass media | X | X | O |
| Government agencies | X | X | X |
| Research institutes | X | X | X |
| Distribution networks | X | O | X |
| Commercial agents | X | O | X |
| Production facilities | X | X | X |
| Entrepreneurs | X | X | X |
| Intrapreneurs | X | X | O |
| Product champions | X | O | O |
| Government-industry partnerships | X | X | X |
| User need | X | X | X |
| Promotional techniques | X | X | O |
| Neighborhood effects | X | X | X |
| Working prototypes | X | X | X |
| Successful demonstrations | X | X | O |
| Comparison tests | X | O | X |
| Field trials | X | X | X |
| Funding agents | X | X | X |
| Linchpins[a] | X | X | O |
| Translators[a] | X | X | O |
| Spotters[a] | X | O | X |
| Capitalists[a] | X | X | X |
| Exciters[a] | X | X | O |
| Integrators[a] | X | X | X |
| Scouts[a] | X | O | X |
| Time to mature | X | X | X |
| Facilitating technologies | X | X | X |
| Adaptation in each use | X | X | X |

*Table 3–5 continued*

| Factors Important to Innovation Success | Hybrid Corn | Longwall Coal Mining | Water Jet Cutting |
|---|---|---|---|
| Desire to improve | X | X | X |
| Technology push and pull | X | X | X |
| Willingness to take risks | X | X | X |
| Leaders and followers | X | X | X |
| Confluence of above factors | X | X | X |

*Key:* X = important factor
O = unimportant factor
ªSee table 1-3 for definitions of these factors.

a few innovators accept the technology. They must also be sufficiently influential within their user community that others will emulate their behaviors, and the innovation will spread widely. These factors are all embedded within or implied by the model shown in figure 3-5.

Thus, we see why water jet cutting technologies took over 2,000 years to develop. The reason was a combination of the lack of technology pull, the lack of human desire for betterment, the absence of facilitating technologies, the lack of basic research monies, and the lack of influential innovators at the most opportune times throughout the long history of this technology.

## Summary

The hybrid seed corn, longwall coal mining, and water jet cutting stories are rich with lessons for managers of new product innovations. Though fundamentally very different, these three cases demonstrate the principles of sound management of successful innovations. They yield many insights into the workings of innovation processes, as summarized in table 3-5. One lesson is echoed by these three cases: Perseverance is the lifeblood of an innovation.

The three cases vividly testify to the importance of multiple persons playing many roles throughout the processes of innovation. Successful innovations are not achieved by one person acting alone. Innovations do not normally arise from a single source or from a solitary theory or practice. Rather, innovations usually involve several theories and a combination of technologies and practices. Innovation processes do not follow a straight line from start to finish. Rather, the process is an evolutionary one of many fits and starts, jerkily groping its way to success. The cases demonstrate how innovations must frequently overcome substantial barriers that threaten their longevity at every turn. These barriers fall very grudgingly, only after repeated battering.

Managers and students of innovation processes are well-advised to read these three cases carefully. They are rich in lessons that dispel many myths.

## Notes

1. Prior to the advent of genetically controlled seed corn, farmers simply saved a portion of their crop to be used as next year's seed. This "open-pollinated" seed corn contained the uncontrolled weak strains and diseases of whatever species happened to pollinate the parent plant during the previous growing season. One poor corn year could lock the farmer into several future bad years as the weak seeds begot still other weak seeds. By contrast, hybrid seeds are bred to retain only the strong traits of several species of corn plants. However, the idea of buying new seed each year was not intuitively appealing to many farmers, who naturally thought their low yields from open-pollinated corn were the best they could get.

2. One of the most comprehensive references on the hybrid seed corn story is Richard Crabb's *The Hybrid Corn Makers* (New Brunswick, N.J.: Rutgers University Press, 1947). It is a scholarly and thorough treatment of the entire history of the hybrid seed corn movement, chronicled by a professional journalist.

3. In conventional mining methods, the roof of the mine is supported by leaving pillars of coal and by constructing wooden and steel supports that are left in the mine. The disadvantage of this approach is that considerable amounts of coal are left behind in the pillars, and the supports are expensive. Moreover, the pillars and the supports may decay over time, so that roof collapses (subsidence) can occur several years after a mine has been worked out. It is not uncommon for homes and factories constructed above old mine sites to suffer severe structural damage from subsidence. In the longwall method, the roof is supported only long enough for the coal in one section to be removed, then it is purposely collapsed in a controlled fashion. The advantages of this method are that all the coal can be removed, and once a roof has been collapsed it will not subside any further. Today's longwalls are so precise and safe that they have been successfully used to mine under rivers, lakes, and whole towns without any disturbance to the surface.

4. The detailed history and the complete census of U.S. longwalls is contained in William E. Souder and E. R. Palowitch, "Growth of Longwall Technologies in the U.S.," Chapter 1 in *Longwall-Shortwall Mining, State of Art,* R. V. Ramani, ed. (New York: The American Institute of Mining Engineering, 1981), pp. 3-9. As of this writing, this is the only published census of U.S. longwalls that chronicles their history from their first appearance in the United States.

5. Longwalls follow a typical diffusion pattern for a new technology. For more about technology diffusions, see the classic landmark analytical work on the adoption and diffusion of innovations: Everett Roger's *The Diffusion of Innovations* (New York: Free Press, 1983).

6. For more details on this process see William E. Souder and Abdul Quaddus,

"A Decision Modeling Approach to Forecasting the Diffusion of Longwall Mining Technologies," *Technological Forecasting and Social Change*, 21, no. 1 (1982) 1-14.

7. The evolution of water jet cutting technologies is chronicled in William E. Souder and R. J. Evans, "Water Jet Cutting: The Resurgence of an Old Technology," Chapter 22 in *RETC Proceedings, Vol. 2* (New York: The American Institute of Mining Engineering, 1983), pp. 719–739.

# 4
# Cost and Duration of New Product Innovations

> Money is the Lorelei of innovation; there is never enough of it, except when there is too much.
> —William E. Souder, 1980

W hat does it cost and how long does it take to convert a laboratory idea to a commercial success? To answer this question, 80 new product innovation projects were examined from the data base. The analyses revealed that there is no simple answer to the above question.

## Methodology

To obtain the 80 projects analyzed here, all the means-generated projects (see chapter 1 for a definition) were retrieved from the 289 project data base. Each project was then scrutinized for its completeness of information. Some candidates were rejected as a result of this operation.[1] The remainder were classified into "success" and "failure" categories based on the outcome assessments provided by the respondents at each firm (see table 2-1). This summary dichotomization into success and failure was used in lieu of the expanded categories in table 2-1, in order to avoid small sample sizes. Projects were then randomly sampled from each success and failure category until 40 commercial success and 40 commercial failure projects were obtained for analysis. This design resulted in approximately 10 projects within each of the 8 industries analyzed in this chapter, with each industry having about 5 success and 5 failure projects.[1]

It is important to note that the innovations discussed here are means-generated innovations. As explained in chapter 1, this is quite different from needs-generated innovations that originate in response to a documented customer need or an explicit customer request. On the other hand, these technologies were not laboratory curiosities with no apparent uses. In all the projects studied here, there was good reason to believe there might be many users. But there was no substantiation of this belief. The rationale for limiting the analyses to means-generated projects here was to ensure that these were truly first-time efforts by the firms. Otherwise, it was feared that learning effects from repeating similar experiences might distort the cost and time data.

## Life Cycle Costs

### Eight Stages

The collected data revealed the presence of eight identifiable stages of innovative activities, as shown in table 4-1. It must be noted that these stages are not mutually exclusive. Some overlaps were found. For example, stages 1 and 2 (exploratory and concept development) were inseparable for some projects. Moreover, some projects did not appear to have a distinct stage 1 (exploratory). Others did not have a stage 3 (prototype development) that was different from their stage 4 (prototype testing). Thus, though the eight-stage model in table 4-1 is not necessarily universal, it is the model that was most often observed among the 80 projects studied here.[2]

**Table 4–1**
**Life Cycle Stages**

| Stage Number | Stage Label | Stage Description |
|---|---|---|
| 1 | Exploratory | Search and inquiry activities, often funded by corporate monies, usually phenomenon oriented |
| 2 | Concept Development | Concept elaboration, extension, and substantiation activities aimed at the clarification or elaboration of previously generated ideas or concepts |
| 3 | Prototype Development | Differs from stage 2 in that a commercially relevant prototype, first model, or product has been identified and is targeted |
| 4 | Prototype Testing | Laboratory, field, or production-scale evaluations |
| 5 | Market Development | Market generation, demand stimulation, and market analyses activities |
| 6 | Manufacturing Start-up | Initial production runs, scale-up, and preparation for full-scale activities |
| 7 | Marketing Start-up | Preparation for full-scale market entry |
| 8 | Technical Service | Follow-on market and technical activities that accompany the introduction of the new product |

## Costs by Stages

Variations in accounting for indirect costs and other methodological vagaries made it impossible to collect comparable interfirm raw cost data. However, by reconstructing the manpower buildup and phase-down patterns on each project and appropriately monetizing that data, remarkably consistent stage-wise cost patterns emerged within each industry.

Table 4-2 presents a summary of the life cycle cost data by industry classification. Because total project costs varied considerably from one industry to another, the data are shown here as percentages. This effectively normalizes for the different industry cost structures and aids the focus here, which is on the stage patterns.

The metals industry data in table 4-2 includes both ferrous and nonferrous R&D projects, for both industrial and consumer applications. The glass industry classification includes projects relating to bulk glass and fabricated glass products. The transportation industry includes new products for mass transit and personal transportation applications. The machinery industry is restricted to new products for industrial uses. The other industries follow the familiar Standard Industrial Classification (SIC) codes.

The percentage cost allocations for stage 1 (exploratory) activities shown in table 4-2 are generally smaller than the conventional wisdom leads us to expect. Doesn't exploratory R&D cost a great deal? Perhaps not. Bear in mind that exploratory research is often relatively inexpensive per unit of time: one or two persons running relatively inexpensive conceptualization tests and exercises. The means-generated innovations studied here were often born in the mind of an inventor, who then confirmed his idea with a few simple experiments. The project then often officially began on the firm's record books as a stage 2 development effort. Moreover, exploratory work on means-generated innovations is sometimes funded "under-the-table." That is, the researcher pays for his experiments from some discretionary fund or charges his time to some other company approved project. Thus, accurate cost data for stage 1 activities may not be available from the firm's official cost records. For this reason, the interview and manpower record reconstruction procedures used here may lead to more accurate data, especially for stage 1 activities.

The data in table 4-2 contain a few surprises, but they also support certain conventional wisdom. As expected, the food industry shows rather high percentage costs in stages 4 and 5 (prototype testing and market development). But, the chemicals, machinery, and transportation industries also show surprisingly high stage 4 percentages. The stage 6 data (manufacturing start-up) also seem high for several industries. The electronics industry shows an extremely high percentage here: 51 percent. Yet the metals industry shows only 11 percent, the machinery industry shows 5 percent, and the food industry shows only 11 percent costs in stage 6. The stage 8 data (technical

Table 4–2
Average Percentage of Total Project Life Cycle Cost Allocated to Each Stage[a]
(*in percents*)

| Industry | Stage 1 Exploratory | Stage 2 Concept Development | Stage 3 Prototype Development | Stage 4 Prototype Testing | Stage 5 Market Development | Stage 6 Manufacturing Development | Stage 7 Marketing Start-up | Stage 8 Technical Service | Totals |
|---|---|---|---|---|---|---|---|---|---|
| Metals | 2 | 7 | 18 | 12 | 33 | 11 | 9 | 8 | 100 |
| Glass | 1 | 25 | 20 | 14 | 5 | 19 | 10 | 6 | 100 |
| Transportation | 1 | 15 | 25 | 20 | 10 | 20 | 8 | 1 | 100 |
| Plastics | 5 | 21 | 30 | 5 | 14 | 10 | 8 | 7 | 100 |
| Machinery | 2 | 25 | 20 | 28 | 10 | 5 | 7 | 3 | 100 |
| Electronics | 1 | 5 | 12 | 5 | 13 | 51 | 7 | 6 | 100 |
| Chemicals | 1 | 7 | 9 | 24 | 25 | 20 | 9 | 5 | 100 |
| Food | 2 | 19 | 12 | 14 | 32 | 11 | 7 | 3 | 100 |

[a]Data are rounded to the nearest whole percent.

**Table 4–3**
**Combined Percentage Stage Costs**
*(in percents)*

| Industry | Development Costs (Stages 2 and 3) | Marketing Costs (Stages 5 and 7) |
|---|---|---|
| Metals. | 25 | 42 |
| Glass | 45 | 15 |
| Transportation | 40 | 18 |
| Plastics | 51 | 22 |
| Machinery | 45 | 17 |
| Electronics | 17 | 20 |
| Chemicals | 16 | 34 |
| Food | 31 | 39 |

service) also contain some expected results, a few surprises and some mysteries. In the transportation industry, stage 8 is virtually nonexistent. On the other hand, the metals figure for stage 8 (8 percent) seems high. The food statistic for stage 8 is also a mystery: it is only 3 percent.

## Aggregation of Stage Costs

It is reasonable to aggregate the stage 2 (concept development) and stage 3 (prototype development) costs to obtain the total development costs for the project. This aggregation is shown in table 4-3. Now some of the anomalies are eliminated. But still other surprises occur. The electronics and chemicals industries are at the low end of the spectrum of percentage costs devoted to development. The glass, transportation, plastics, and machinery industries are at the high end of the spectrum. This is generally consistent with conventional wisdom, except for the glass industry results. One would not expect the glass industry to spend so much on product development.

It is also reasonable to aggregate the stage 5 and stage 7 data to get a picture of the emphasis on total marketing costs. These data are also presented in table 4-3. The glass and machinery industries allocate the lowest percentage of project costs to marketing activities. Food, chemicals, and metals spend the most. These high percentages in marketing for chemicals and metals is puzzling, especially since these are industrial markets.

## Discussion of Cost Data

The seeming anomalies found in the data in tables 4-2 and 4-3 were quickly resolved by the interviews. Consider that not only are these innovation projects, they are also means-generated innovations. Thus, industries that traditionally spend little on development, marketing, and other activities may find it necessary to increase their allocations in the case of means-generated innovations. Means-generated innovations must be viewed as rather radical departures from these firm's usual operations.

The news that unconventional cost allocations were needed surprised many of these firms. Many of the respondents described scenes of severe interpersonal conflict and consternations that were raised about escalating costs on these projects. Examples were often cited of projects that were tenuously kept alive in spite of severe pressures to terminate them simply because their stage costs were high. Budget overruns are, unfortunately, one of the key items that attract managerial attention. Anyone who is not fully prepared for the cost patterns of innovations may be much too quick to terminate what appears to be a poor fiscal performance. It must be noted that many of the projects that barely survived being terminated due to "unusual" cost allocations went on to become successes. There is thus a lesson in these experiences: Being aware of how innovations differ from more traditional projects can help prevent great organizational tension and poor decisions.

## Controlling Project Costs

Table 4-4 shows the cumulative percentage life cycle costs for the eight industries studied here. These data were obtained by cumulating the costs in table 4-2 at each stage.

### Analysis of Cost Build-Ups

Table 4-4 shows that the glass, transportation, plastics, and machinery industries have relatively high cumulative percentage costs through stage 4. The metals, electronics, chemicals, and food industries have relatively low cumulative costs through stage 4. Or, to put it another way, the former show a pattern of rapid buildup while the latter show a pattern of slow buildup.

Table 4-5 shows the results from casting the eight industries into two categories, fore-load and aft-load, based on the data in table 4-4. The fore-load industries have the bulk of their life cycle costs in stages 1 through 4. The aft-load industries have the bulk of their life cycle costs in stages 5 through 8. It may be noted here that several other three- and four-category schemes were tried, but they were not as robust as this two-category scheme for distinguishing industries.

The results thus show that the glass, transportation, plastics, and machinery industries are characteristically fore-loaded in the case of means-generated innovations. That is, research, development, and testing activities

**Table 4–4**
**Cumulative Average Percentage of Total Project Life Cycle Cost Allocated to Each Stage**
*(in percents)*

| Industry | Stage 1 Exploratory | Stage 2 Concept Development | Stage 3 Prototype Development | Stage 4 Prototype Testing | Stage 5 Market Development | Stage 6 Manufacturing Development | Stage 7 Marketing Start-up | Stage 8 Technical Service |
|---|---|---|---|---|---|---|---|---|
| Metals | 2 | 9 | 27 | 39 | 72 | 83 | 92 | 100 |
| Glass | 1 | 26 | 46 | 60 | 65 | 84 | 94 | 100 |
| Transportation | 1 | 16 | 41 | 61 | 71 | 91 | 99 | 100 |
| Plastics | 5 | 26 | 56 | 61 | 75 | 85 | 93 | 100 |
| Machinery | 2 | 27 | 47 | 75 | 85 | 90 | 97 | 100 |
| Electronics | 1 | 6 | 18 | 23 | 36 | 87 | 94 | 100 |
| Chemicals | 1 | 8 | 17 | 41 | 66 | 86 | 95 | 100 |
| Food | 2 | 21 | 33 | 47 | 79 | 90 | 97 | 100 |

### Table 4–5
### Two-Category Load Analysis

| Fore-Load Industries | Aft-Load Industries |
|---|---|
| Glass | Metals |
| Transportation | Electronics |
| Plastics | Chemicals |
| Machinery | Food |

make up the largest percentage of their project life cycle costs. This is in contrast to the aft-load metals, electronics, chemicals, and food industries, where marketing and production activities make up the bulk of the life cycle costs of means-generated innovations. Fore-load industries spend the bulk of their new product monies researching and developing their innovation. Aft-load industries spend most of their monies producing and selling their innovations.

### Terminating Failing Projects: Some Theoretical Considerations

In theory, this fore-load/aft-load buildup phenomenon has significant consequences for managing new product innovations. In the case of the rapid-buildup fore-load industries, early warnings of impending failures are important for saving money. If the project is not going to succeed in the marketplace, it becomes vital to know this early in the life of rapid-buildup projects, before the end of stage 2. Otherwise, funds will be needlessly spent on failing projects.

In theory, a great deal of money could be saved if failing fore-load projects are terminated before they reach the end of stage 2. In contrast, for the slow-buildup aft-load projects, where most of the funds are not spent until the late-life stages, it may not be vital to stop imminent failure projects as early. This is because large expenditures do not occur until stages 5 and 6 in the aft-load projects. Thus, the early termination of failing aft-load projects may not be as important. Moreover, at these late life stages, better information on the success likelihood of the project is usually available. Thus, a more reliable decision about whether to continue or terminate the project can be made. Fore-load projects are the ones where early indicators of success or failure are the most essential.

Accordingly, the theory says that the slow-buildup, aft-load metals, electronics, chemicals, and food industry projects are the fortunate ones. They are the industries that are theoretically the most able to economize on the cost of innovations. They are in the most favorable position to back away from potential failure outcome efforts before they must commit the bulk of their project expenditures.

This is a commonly held theory with many disciples.[3] Does it work? Let us use the data base to test the theory that imminent failure projects can be terminated early.

*Cost of Successes and Failures: Testing the Theory*

As summarized in table 4-6, an analysis of the project cost data indicated that the fore-load glass and transportation industries and the aft-load electronics industry spent more money on projects that ended in failure than on successes. Why? The interviews revealed that there was a very strong proclivity to tenaciously hang onto imminent failure projects in these three industries. This resulted in project cost overruns and stretch-outs. Thus, both fore-load and aft-load industries here evidenced severe cost overruns for their failure projects.

The interviews revealed a major reason why funding was not curtailed on failing projects in these industries: top management over interest. As shown in more detail in chapter 5, top management interest can create a kind of double bind. If top management wants it, how can lower level manage-

**Table 4–6**
**Comparative Costs of Successes and Failures**

| Industry | *Is the Average Cost of Successes and Failures More or Less Than the Average Cost for All Projects?[a]* | |
| | *Successes* | *Failures* |
| --- | --- | --- |
| Metals | More | Less |
| Food | Same | Same |
| Machinery | Same | Same |
| Electronics | Less | More |
| Transportation | Less | More |
| Glass | Less | More |
| Chemicals | Same | Same |
| Plastics | More | Less |

[a]If the difference is not statistically significant at the 95 percent confidence level, then "Same" is recorded here. Successes = all projects with success commercial outcomes. Failure = all projects with failure commercial outcomes. See table 2-1 for more information.

ment terminate it? Of course they can: by revealing all the project's weaknesses to the top management champion and by convincing him that his impressions are in fact wrong. But who put those impressions in top management's mind in the first place? Moreover, top management's interest usually results in preferential funding for projects. Now the difficulties of telling management that the project is a loser become even more complicated! How do you explain to your anxious boss that you are sorry you spent so much money and now you think the entire effort should be abandoned? Imagine his reaction: "What! But I presented this to the board just last month as one of our most promising projects!" Of course, this dilemma is easily resolved in an atmosphere of openness, trust, and honest communication. But real world organizational politics often get in the way of obvious solutions. Thus, the theory of terminating potentially failing fore-load projects can be rather impractical in the face of top management over interest.

There is another reason this theory does not work. Many projects were found in this study that suffered from the myth that success was just around the corner. This may, in fact, not be a myth. It may be true. Just a few more dollars may indeed permit the project to achieve a breakthrough.[3] The problem is that no one knows the truth. Nor is there any way to find the truth, except by continuing the funding until the project succeeds! Given enough time and money, nearly any project can succeed.

There is yet another common myth that disrupts the above theory. It is the myth that says, "If we quit now we won't get anything back." This myth is really a variation of the "Success is just around the corner" myth. It is also a variant of the sunk cost myth, "We must continue in order to recoup our costs." In fact, this is poor logic.[4] The past is past, and it should not bear on decisions about the future. Such logic will eventually lead the firm into bankruptcy if it continues to pursue the same bad idea to the exclusion of other opportunities. Many of the high-cost failure projects studied here experienced this myth. It was a powerful myth that sustained the project momentum, blotting out any consideration of terminating it to save money.

It must be noted that several of the high-cost failures had a truly enviable commitment. In these cases, management was unwilling to abandon anything that appeared to have a chance. They were willing to take high risks and sink funds into marginal projects. In these climates, the theory of early termination of potential failures to save money was not even considered. Here is another reason the theory is impractical: no one is willing to entertain any thoughts of termination.

Thus, the results here indicate that the effective management of aft-load and fore-load projects to conserve funds while maximizing success is a very complex matter. The theory of terminating potential failure projects early in their lives is appealing. But the lack of reliable advance indicators has traditionally kept this theory from being extensively applied. The preceding analysis and discussion adds still more reasons why the theory is impractical. Even if reliable indicators existed, there are powerful myths, organizational politics, risky commitments, and dogged tenacity that leave no room for the theory of early termination in the consciousness of the involved personnel.

## Life Cycle Project Durations

*Time Data Analyses*

Table 4-7 presents the averages of the percentage life cycle stage data which were collected. Let us subtract the percentage cost data in table 4-2 from the respective time data in table 4-7. The results of this subtraction exercise are presented in table 4-8. If the resulting number is positive, it indicates that the percentage duration of this stage was relatively greater than the percent cost of this stage. Analogously, a negative number shows that the cost was greater.

The data in table 4-8 indicate that time is approximately proportionate to dollars for the glass, transportation, and plastics industries. Time is money in these industries. On the other hand, for the metals, machinery, electronics, chemicals, and food industries, time and cost are disproportionate for several stages. For example, for the machinery industry, there are both large positive and large negative numbers in the early stages. Thus, depending on the stage, either cost or time is the dominant factor. The chemicals industry shows a similar pattern of alternating cost and time dominance. The food industry patterns resemble those in the chemicals industry. The electronics industry also has a mixed cost and time dominance phenomenon. The metals industry has one stage (stage 5) where costs dominate; time is more dominant in all the other stages. Thus, a very mixed situation exists with regard to which stages take relatively more time or more money.

An industry-by-industry examination of table 4-8 shows that stages 1, 3, and 4 are more often positive than negative. Thus, time is more often the dominant factor in exploratory research, prototype development, and prototype testing. Concept development (stage 2) and market development (stage 5) are more often cost-intensive. Manufacturing start-up (stage 6), marketing start-up (stage 7), and technical service (stage 8) are more often time-intensive. What are the implications of all this?

*Discussion of Cost-Time Data*

Table 4-8 contains information of considerable interest to technical managers, project managers, and project planners. It presents information about cost-time relationships that must be understood in order to effectively manage innovations. For example, the metals industry exhibits stage 5 (market

**Table 4–7**
**Average Percentage of Total Life Cycle Durations in Each Stage[a]**
(*in percents*)

| Industry | Stage 1 Exploratory | Stage 2 Concept Development | Stage 3 Prototype Development | Stage 4 Prototype Testing | Stage 5 Market Development | Stage 6 Manufacturing Development | Stage 7 Marketing Start-up | Stage 8 Technical Service | Totals |
|---|---|---|---|---|---|---|---|---|---|
| Metals | 3 | 9 | 21 | 12 | 16 | 15 | 13 | 11 | 100 |
| Glass | 5 | 25 | 20 | 10 | 5 | 20 | 10 | 5 | 100 |
| Transportation | 1 | 14 | 25 | 20 | 10 | 20 | 8 | 2 | 100 |
| Plastics | 5 | 19 | 29 | 5 | 15 | 11 | 9 | 7 | 100 |
| Machinery | 15 | 15 | 30 | 9 | 10 | 7 | 7 | 7 | 100 |
| Electronics | 1 | 9 | 20 | 15 | 11 | 18 | 25 | 1 | 100 |
| Chemicals | 1 | 5 | 14 | 36 | 14 | 25 | 3 | 2 | 100 |
| Food | 1 | 18 | 9 | 24 | 16 | 15 | 12 | 5 | 100 |

[a]All data are rounded to the nearest whole number.

**Table 4–8**
Time-Cost Data; Net Percentage Values

| Industry | Stage 1 Exploratory | Stage 2 Concept Development | Stage 3 Prototype Development | Stage 4 Prototype Testing | Stage 5 Market Development | Stage 6 Manufacturing Development | Stage 7 Marketing Start-up | Stage 8 Technical Service |
|---|---|---|---|---|---|---|---|---|
| Metals | +1 | +2 | +3 | 0 | −17 | +4 | +4 | +3 |
| Glass | +4 | 0 | 0 | −4 | 0 | +1 | 0 | −1 |
| Transportation | 0 | −1 | 0 | 0 | 0 | 0 | 0 | +1 |
| Plastics | 0 | −2 | −1 | 0 | +1 | +1 | +1 | 0 |
| Machinery | +13 | −10 | +10 | −19 | 0 | +2 | 0 | +4 |
| Electronics | 0 | +4 | +8 | +10 | −2 | −33 | +18 | −5 |
| Chemicals | 0 | −2 | +5 | +12 | −11 | +5 | −6 | −3 |
| Food | −1 | −1 | −3 | +10 | −16 | +4 | +5 | +2 |
| Totals | +17 | −10 | +22 | +9 | −45 | −16 | +22 | +1 |

development) cost allocations far in excess of the proportionate amounts one might expect. This is apparent from the minus 17 datum for the metals industry shown in stage 5 in table 4-8. This means that an unwary metals innovation project manager who estimates his budget on the basis of typical project allocations will surely be surprised. He will have to spend far more than he expected during this stage. The reason is that, in the metals industry, marketing costs for innovations involve huge outlays for demonstrations. These demonstrations are required to convince the customers of the value of a means-generated new product innovation.

On the other hand, the manufacturing and marketing start-up stages 6 and 7 for the metals industry are time-intensive. This is shown by the positive values in table 4-8 for these stages. Here, it is not so much a matter of having enough money as it is having sufficient time. Once the customer is convinced, huge expenditures are unnecessary. Note how these observations and conclusions run counter to the conventional wisdom for the metals industry. But, remember, conventional wisdom is based on conventional projects. Here, we are dealing with means-generated innovations. These are radical new product ideas, not the typical new metals product.

The glass industry shows two surprises in table 4-8. Stage 1, (exploratory activities) are time-intensive. This is indicated by the plus 4 datum in table 4-8 for stage 1 in the glass industry. Here, time is more important than cost. However, stage 4 (prototype testing) is just the opposite. Here, large costs are incurred relative to the time spent in this state. This is indicated by the minus 4 datum in table 4-8. Why is this? The reason is that, in this industry, exploratory innovation research is carried out by a few persons running relatively inexpensive tests that take a long time to analyze. But in the prototype testing of glass innovations, considerable funds must be spent on tests that do not take very long to run.

The machinery industry holds many pitfalls for the unwary innovation manager or budgeter. The exploratory stage (stage 1) is very time-intensive, as shown by the plus 13 datum in table 4-8. It requires a very long time to find a good innovative idea in this industry. Then stage 2 abruptly becomes very cost-intensive, as indicated by the minus 10 datum in table 4-8. In this industry, the elaboration of the innovative concepts found in stage 1 requires expensive testing. But, then stage 3 is time-intensive, followed by the cost-intensive stage 4. The poor unsuspecting innovation manager who does not properly budget for these phenomena will surely have some explaining to do to his bosses. His project will oscillate between seriously over-budget to seriously under-budget status! A more aware manager will properly budget and prepare for these swings.

The chemicals and food industries also exhibit oscillations from time-intensity to cost-intensity as one moves through the stages. Note the relatively high cost-intensity for food projects in stage 5, as indicated by the minus 16 datum in table 4-8. It costs a great deal to develop markets for innovative food products. By contrast, the electronics industry exhibits less oscillation. But it causes other problems for the budgeter. As shown in table 4-8, stage 2, stage 3, and stage 4 are time-intensive. But, just when this time-intensive pattern becomes well established, the electronics innovation project swings into extreme cost-intensity in stage 6. And then it abruptly swings back into extreme time-intensity in stage 7.

In summary, the data in table 4-8 are important guides for proper innovation project budgeting. Knowing which types of projects will require the most time or the most costs in which stages is important for accurate project planning and budgeting. Accurate planning and budgeting are essential to proper project control and monitoring. And such monitoring is vital to the smooth functioning of innovation projects. Without knowledge of the stage data shown in table 4-8, no intelligent decisions can be made about resource allocations or the significance of an over- or under-budget project. For example, suppose a machinery project in stage 4 is severely over its budget. Should it be terminated? Without knowledge of the data and the underlying phenomena shown in table 4-8 no intelligent decision would be possible. We would not have any idea how such a project should appear in the budget reports. When the knowledge contained in table 4-8 is not available, a gap is created that the myths discussed above will quickly fill. Thus, collecting, maintaining, and using data like that in table 4-8 eliminates myths, makes good management decisions possible, and fosters the spirit of innovation.

### Cost-Time Tradeoff: A Lesson

The minus 33 datum in table 4-8 for stage 6 of the electronics industry is a most interesting datum. It reflects an ineffective attempt to correct earlier errors in managing several electronics projects.

The interviews revealed that an attempt was made to accelerate several behind-schedule projects by flooding them with funds. This "flood money" was applied very late in the new product development process, at the manufacturing start-up stage (stage 6). These attempts to fix the deficient products at this late stage did not meet with success. Most of these projects were severe failures. That is, they were scored "Complete Dud" and "Took a Bath We Won't Forget" (see table 2-1).

Thus, the general belief that projects can be accelerated by time-versus-cost trade-offs may not apply in the case of innovations. At least, it did not apply here in the case of these means-generated innovations. Attempts to accelerate achievements and correct earlier errors and omissions created considerable frustrations for the project personnel. And such efforts did not appreciably increase the success of the projects. Thus, the lesson seems obvious:

Don't let project errors ride. Don't wait to fix them in the plant or in the field.[3]

## Summary

Conceptual and practical difficulties abound in obtaining valid historical life cycle cost and time data for innovation projects. The development of a general life cycle model is hindered by variations among industries and individual firms. Problems of confidentiality and variations in the detail of record keeping further compound the data collection problem.

In this chapter, data on the costs and durations of means-generated new product innovation projects in several industries were studied. Several general concepts and ideas were expressed for future testing and application. An eight-stage project life cycle model was presented and used to assess the cost and time patterns.

The records of innovation project cost buildups were analyzed and classified into two patterns. In the fore-load pattern, the bulk of the project's expenditures were in research, development, and engineering activities. In the aft-load pattern, the bulk of the project's expenditures were in marketing and production activities. The glass, transportation, plastics, and machinery industries projects were found to be primarily of the fore-load type. The metals, electronics, chemicals, and food industry projects were found to be primarily of the aft-load type. Several implications for effective project management and project control were deduced from these findings.

The cost patterns of success and failure outcome projects were examined for several industries. Some industries were found in which failure outcome projects cost significantly more than their successes. Unsuccessful attempts to accelerate some projects, unsuccessful attempts to correct research insufficiencies at the production stage, and a too intense devotion to pursue the projects explained why failures cost more than successes in some industries.

The common theory that imminent failures should and can be terminated early, thus saving considerable funds for better uses, was not found to be workable. First, top management over-interest and over-involvement typically occur when projects begin to overspend or run behind schedule. This often sets in motion political forces that make it even more difficult to terminate the project. Second, strong organizational myths normally arise that insulate and protect any overbudget project from termination.

The analyses suggested the following rules for fostering successful new product developments:

1. Make sure the product is perfected before it gets to the plant; after that it's too late. Bring the relevant production personnel on board well in advance of the product's transfer to the plant.

2. Carefully collect, model, and study the stage wise cost allocation patterns of innovation projects in your industry. Without an appreciation of these patterns, it becomes impossible to make judicious plans and budget decisions about innovation projects.

3. The effective financial control of innovation projects is a complex matter. The principles that are effective for non-innovation projects do not appear to work well for innovative efforts. In particular, innovation projects typically exhibit periods of oscillating high costs and low costs during their life cycles. Thus, the common practice of controlling projects on the basis of smooth cost-time functions is not feasible for innovation projects.

4. Because of the uncertain nature of innovation projects, myths, organizational politics and emotional commitments will naturally surround the project, obscuring the real facts and data on its status. Thus, managers must be especially carefully to distinguish fact from fiction.

## Notes

1. Two of the 10 industries in the data base (see Sample of Firms, chapter 2) did not have sufficient data for the analyses here. Thus, only eight industries are examined in this chapter.

2. Few cost studies of innovations exist, and fewer still that are comparable to the model and the details collected here. Thus, it is difficult to compare the results here with any other independent data base. Comparisons can be made with more general data bases, such as the McGraw-Hill surveys of U.S. industries. But these comparisons only reconfirm the observation that means-generated innovation projects have a different allocation pattern than other projects. The reader may want to consult two classic works here: Edwin Mansfield et al., *Research and Innovation in the Modern Corporation* (New York: W. W. Norton, 1971), pp. 110-35 and R. E. Roberts and C. E. Romine, "Investment in Innovation," in *Progress in Assessing Technological Innovation*, H. R. Clauser, ed. (Westport: Technomic, 1976).

3. See, for example, R. Balachandra and Joseph Raelin, "When to Kill that R&D Project," *Research Management*, 27, no. 4 (July-August 1984), 30-33.

4. See, for example, William E. Souder, *Project Selection and Economic Appraisal* (New York: Van Nostrand Reinhold, 1984), pp. 137-41 and William E. Souder, *Management Decision Methods* (New York: Van Nostrand Reinhold, 1980), pp. 299-315.

# 5
# Causes of Project Success and Failure

> Success has a thousand fathers; failure is an orphan.
> —Old saying, author unknown
> (sometimes included in Murphy's Laws)

W hat causes new product development project failures? This question does not have a simple answer.[1,2] Projects fail and succeed for numerous, complex reasons. A constellation of factors can usually be cited that "cause" a project to fail or succeed. Still, things are even more complex than this. The absence of only one important factor from this constellation can mean the difference between success and failure. Moreover, the presence of some factors may compensate for the absence of others. To complicate matters further, today's success may become tomorrow's failure. New laws, changes in consumer tastes, shifts in demands, and changes in needs can alter the status of a project overnight.

## Individual Factors and Combinations

Looking for the one universal factor that accounts for the difference between project success and failure is thus rather naive. But this does not mean that individual factors are unimportant. To obtain a complete understanding of how to increase the number of project successes, both the individual factors and their various combinations must be examined.

This is the perspective taken in this chapter, where the characteristics and outcomes of 235 projects from the data base are carefully scrutinized through various analyses. Because 54 other projects in the total 289 project data base did not have all the information on all the aspects analyzed here, they were excluded from these analyses.

## Conditions Influencing Project Outcomes

### Correlates of Success and Failure

Using a five-point scale instrument,[3] the respondents at each firm rated (5 equals high) several conditions surrounding each project. Correlational anal-

Table 5–1

**Conditions That Were Statistically Significantly Correlated with Project Success[a]**

| Conditions for Technical Success | Conditions for Commercial Success |
|---|---|
| Clarity of problem definition | Clarity of problem definition |
| Perceived level of fit between the company and the technology | Clarity of understanding of user requirements |
| Perceived technical expertise in the project area | Perceived technical expertise in the project area |
| Quality of available resources | Degree of detailed planning and control applied |

[a]High degrees of project success (see table 2-1) occurred when these conditions were high; high degrees of project failure occurred when these conditions were low; 95 percent confidence levels were used in the statistical tests.

yses were then run between these ratings and the six-point project outcome assessments (see table 2-1 of chapter 2) provided by the respondents. The conditions shown in table 5-1 were found to be statistically significantly correlated with the project outcomes.

A detailed examination of the data added some insights to the results in table 5-1. The number of projects achieving a technical "Breakthrough" or a technical "Enhancement" beyond those expected (table 2-1) was three times as great when the clarity of the problem definition was high. The number of projects that became a commercial "Blockbuster" (table 2-1) was three times as great when the clarity of the problem definition was high. Twice as many projects "Met The Specs" (table 2-1) when the perceived level of fit between the company and the technology was high. Three times as many projects achieved a technical "Breakthrough" when the perceived technical expertise in the project area was high. Four times as many projects "Met the Specs" when this factor was high. Three times as many projects became a commercial "Blockbuster" when both the clarity of understanding of user requirements and the degree of detailed planning and control applied was high. Thus, it seems clear that the conditions in table 5-1 are rather important for project success.

*Perceived Technical Expertise in the Project Area*

It is easy to understand why clarity of the problem definition and clarity of understanding of user requirements (table 5-1) are highly correlated with project outcomes. But why is perceived technical expertise in the project area significant for both technical *and commercial* success?

The interviews revealed that having the required technical expertise made two important commercial contributions. First, it permitted the organization to design a more perfect solution to the market needs. Second, high technical expertise in the area tended to occur along with well-developed R&D and marketing department interfaces. Well-developed interfaces were found to be vital to the success of most of the projects studied here (see chapter 10 for more details).

## Degree of Detailed Planning and Control Applied

The degree of detailed planning and control applied was not found to be significant for technical success. But it was significant *for commercial success.* This seems inconsistent. How should this result be interpreted?

Reference to the interviews and project histories indicated that detailed planning and control was often not feasible for the early life phases of projects. There simply was not enough information to develop a detailed project plan. Moreover, when close financial or activity control was applied, it tended to deflate the entrepreneurial euphoria that often seemed essential to the success of innovative efforts. However, once the project had advanced into its later stages, planning and control became more feasible and even essential to keeping the project on target. This result is thus quite consistent with the conventional wisdom that detailed planning and control are only appropriate for projects in the late life or commercialization stages of their life cycles.

## Quality of Available Resources

This condition refers to the existence of a diversity of qualified experts who can help overcome a variety of unexpected technical barriers that may arise. Throughout the data base, the most successful firms were those that maintained a diversity of up-to-date technical experts who could quickly be called upon. In most cases, the firms with the greatest diversity and most up-to-date personnel were the larger firms. Thus, these results run counter to the conventional wisdom that large firms are not innovative. In this regard, at least, the larger firms produce more successes because of their higher quality resources.

## Effects of Combinations of Conditions

Combinations of the conditions shown in table 5-1 were found to be especially potent. In general, the degree of success (table 2-1) of the projects appeared to increase exponentially as the conditions were added together. For example, having all the conditions together was significantly correlated with

**Table 5–2**
**Other Conditions That Were Important for**
**Project Commercial Success[a]**

Familiarity of the technology

Familiarity of the markets

Fit to the company philosophy

Own best customer

Lean-money funding

[a]High degrees of project success (see table 2-1) occurred when these conditions were high; high degrees of project failure occurred when these conditions were low.

a technical "Breakthrough" and a commercial "Blockbuster". This, of course, is precisely what one would expect.

### Other Important Conditions

The five conditions listed in table 5-2 were not statistically significantly correlated with project success. Nevertheless, they occurred with sufficient frequency to warrant their inclusion here.

Familiarity of the technology, familiarity of the markets and fit to the company philosophy were especially interesting conditions. Projects involving unfamiliar markets and technologies, or projects that did not fit the company philosophy often turned in low degrees of commercial success. In some of these projects, the firm "Took a Bath We Won't Forget" (see table 2-1). The following vivid illustration of this was provided by one of the firms in the data base.

### Effect of Unfamiliarity and a Poor Fit: An Illustration

Successful as a bulk producer of commodity goods, firm AK maintained a major market share with their entire commodity product line. Diversification into a specialty line was attractive for several reasons, since some of the same raw materials and production facilities could be used for both the commodity and specialty products. However, the commodity and specialty product users were reached through different distribution channels and sales strategies, and each had very different needs and wants. The firm's success in the commodity business afforded it no experience with the specialty market. Moreover, when field technical problems arose in the specialty area, the firm was unable to respond with the same depth of technical expertise that characterized the other specialty producers, who had built long-term reputations in the specialty area.

Firm AK soon found that the specialty product did not fit into their established philosophy of producing large volumes of standard products at low costs for mass markets. Procedures that the firm had used successfully in the commodity business failed in the specialty business. For example, when their specialty competitors offered increased services, the firm countered with their customary behavior of cutting prices. The result was a loss of the firm's sales volume and revenues in specialty products. Specialty customers were not price-sensitive. They identified high prices and increased services with a superior quality product.

Still more errors were made. When modified specialty products were introduced by competitors, the firm reacted in its customary fashion: it increased the promotion of its standard line of specialties. As a result, the firm's market share of specialties shrank even more. Specialty customers were eager for new models. They expected new models every few months, and they identified newness with increased capabilities.

Eventually, the firm withdrew completely from specialty products. The executives at the firm remember this experience as one of their worst failures. The firm had a history of success and market dominance in their familiar commodities markets. Their specialties failure cast a pallor on the entire firm, causing the executives to become increasingly cautious and risk-averse. This risk-aversion subsequently hindered the firm in maintaining its dominance in its familiar commodity markets!

Do these results imply that new product innovations involving radically different technologies, markets and management practices are infeasible? Is it implied that firms who want to succeed should stay close to familiar grounds?

Not at all. On the contrary, these results simply emphasize some of the basic characteristics of an innovation. In order to innovate, a firm has to be capable of changing its philosophies and behaviors (see chapters 6 and 7 for more details and discussion on this aspect). As the example emphasizes, long-term success in familiar areas can become a formidable barrier to future innovation, especially if the firm is unprepared for failure. Continued insistence on high success rates sometimes dooms an organization to perpetuating itself in its own image, while its competitors move on.

## Own Best Customer

One way firms can promote the success of their innovation is to be their own best customer for it, as noted in table 5-2. If the firm is able to use the innovation internally, or has a need for the product within its own operations, this promotes success.

Over 50 percent of those projects where the organization was its own best customer either met or exceeded their commercial expectations. Thus, being one's own best customer can substantially reduce the risk of failure and make the innovation more acceptable for funding by top management.

### Lean-Money Funding

The lean-money condition (table 5-2) is a most interesting one. More than one-fourth of the projects examined here were rated by the respondents as having excessive budgets or excess monies allocated to them, as a result of top management attention.

In a typical sequence of events, the project attracts the attention of top management and project personnel are flattered by the high-level visibility. Because of it, they tend toward over-optimism about the fate of the project. They also tend to protect top management from any bad news that might reflect badly on them or the project. Meaning only to help the project, top management authorizes additional funds. Project personnel are decidedly reluctant to refuse the additional funds. Thus, valuable project time is devoted to figuring out how to judiciously manage and spend the excess funds. Some of these expenditures detract from the major theme of the project. The amount of progress reporting, financial reporting, and top management presentations naturally escalates in this environment.

All these activities detract from the real purpose of the project, often delaying it and sometimes completely disrupting it. Fifty-six percent of the projects having excess monies allocated to them as a result of top management attention failed to meet their technical expectations. *That* is an important statistic. Thus, the lesson seems clear: do not overfund projects. Lean-money funding may be the best policy.

## Success Rates and Project Types

### Defensive versus Offensive Projects

Offensive projects aimed at capturing new customers or penetrating new markets often carry a sense of urgency. But a defensive project aimed at protecting current products from competitive threats would seem to carry an even stronger sense of urgency. Moreover, defensive projects involve familiar technologies. Wouldn't these two aspects create a strong impetus for success with defensive projects?

Table 5-3 answers this question. Threat-type projects were undertaken in response to immediate challenges to the firm's current market position. They arose from shifts in user demands, the appearance of a new technology or

Table 5–3
Project Success Rates by Project Impetus

| Type of Impetus for the Project | Category of Effort | Percentage of Projects within Each Type That Met or Exceeded Their Commercial Expectations[a] |
|---|---|---|
| Threat | Defensive | 61 |
| Line Protection | Defensive | 43 |
| Tactical Opportunity | Offensive | 39 |
| Strategic Expansion | Offensive | 49 |

[a]Includes all projects with commercial outcomes of "Met Expectations" and all other higher degrees of success; see table 2-1.

competitor, or the emergence of new laws and regulations. Line Protection projects arose in response to anticipated changes in user needs and practices. Tactical Opportunity projects were aimed at taking advantage of some favorable junction of products, markets or needs that strengthened the firm's current market position. Strategic Expansion projects differed from Tactical Opportunity efforts in that they represented planned ventures into new markets or product lines.

The results in table 5-3 support the idea that defensive efforts have a higher success rate than offensive efforts. Indeed, success appears to be more likely when the firm "has to succeed." However, the situation is more complex than this. A subsidiary analysis of the interview data revealed the absence of an important factor in those Threat projects that did not meet their commercial expectations. This factor is: the sense of urgency communicated to the project-level personnel. In over 50 percent of the Threat project failures, the personnel indicated that top management did not fully communicate the true sense of urgency to them. Statements like the following were expressed: "We had no idea of the urgency"; "We really weren't told the seriousness of the situation"; "No one told us how important it was for us to get this done on time." Thus, the sense of urgency communicated by management is clearly an important ingredient. It may be a more important factor than whether or not the project is defensive or offensive in nature.

In the case of the defensive Line Protection projects, marketing personnel often lamented that the anticipated markets turned out to be smaller and less cost effective than they originally expected. In fact, 40 percent of the Line Protection projects that did not meet their expectations fell into the failure category "Protected Our Position but Lost Money" (see table 2-1). Thus, the ability to accurately predict market consequences was surprisingly low for these defensive projects. This result provides more evidence that defensive projects do not necessarily have the high rates of success that conventional wisdom has accorded them.

It is interesting that table 5-3 shows a higher percentage success rate for the Strategic Expansion projects than for the Tactical Opportunity projects. Why? The interview data indicated that the Strategic Expansion projects generally had a greater degree of total organizational commitment. The Tactical Opportunity projects often involved relatively smaller rewards, uncertain targets, and a lack of consensus by marketing and research personnel.

Thus, it is apparent that the seemingly simple dichotomy between offensive and defensive projects involves many other complex dimensions. Because of this, it cannot be said that defensive innovations necessarily have higher success rates.

### Source and Sponsorship

Do project success rates relate to the source of the project idea? Are innovations suggested by customers highly likely to succeed? Are innovations likely to succeed if they originate in the firm's marketing department?

As the data in table 5-4 show, internally generated ideas had higher success rates than externally generated ideas. Perhaps the situation is much like one respondent stated: "We get a few good leads from our customers, but there are times when we can see the future better than they can. We're in a better position to see the whole picture. We know the technology better than

**Table 5–4**
**Project Success Rates by Source and Sponsorship of the Project Idea**

| Source or Sponsor of the Idea | Percentage of Projects from Each Source or Sponsor That Met or Exceeded Their Commercial Expectations[a] |
|---|---|
| Internal | |
|   R & D | 39 |
|   Marketing | 64 |
|   Management | 51 |
| External | |
|   Suppliers | 31 |
|   Customers | 36 |
|   Other[b] | 40 |

[a]Includes all projects with commercial outcomes of "Met Expectations" and all other higher degrees of success; see table 2-1.
[b]Independent inventors, agents, other firms, acquisitions, and technology purchases.

they do and we know what kinds of things can be made and what can't." As another respondent noted: "Every now and then one of our customers has a good technical idea. But he usually doesn't know any more than we do about whether or not that idea really has a market."

Note the relatively high rates of success for project ideas that originated from marketing and from management. Most of these projects were the relatively highly successful Threat and Strategic Expansion types in table 5-3.

*Technology and Success*

Do project success rates vary with the nature of the technology? As table 5-5 shows, this is indeed the case, based on information supplied by the respondents at each firm.[3]

In projects where the technology was a Well-Developed Science, the personnel maintained an attitude of confidence in their ability to overcome any challenges that might arise. Nevertheless, unexpected surprises and insolvable problems did arise, and many projects failed to meet their specifications. In several cases it was clear that the project personnel were over-optimistic and failed to appreciate the real obstacles that confronted them. Some of the failures were classified as a "Complete Dud" (see table 2-1). By comparison, personnel on Undeveloped Science projects were much less optimistic. Though they were confident of their own abilities, they were generally aware of the serious challenges that confronted them.

The Art-type projects were unique in several respects. Project personnel expected relatively low success rates and were not confident of their abilities to overcome emergent hurdles. However, most of the personnel working in the Art areas had spent their careers there. As one respondent noted: "I solve

**Table 5–5**
**Project Success Rates by Type of Technology**

| Type of Technology | Percentage of Projects within Each Type of Technology That Met or Exceeded Their Specifications |
|---|---|
| Well-Developed Science | 78 |
| Undeveloped Science | 64 |
| Art | 43 |

[a]Includes all projects with technical outcomes of "Met the Specs" and other higher degrees of success; see table 2-1.

[b]These definitions are more fully developed in the instrument, which is available from the author.

a lot of problems by experience and hunches. You can't get young people to do that today. They don't have the experience, so they want to use theories. That might be o.k., but most of our work just doesn't fit any theory very well. There are a lot of things you have to just try out. Things that worked one time may not work in another case." Interestingly, relatively few of the Art-type projects were classified as a "Complete Dud."

Except for the Well-Developed Science project types, the organizations generally recognized the difficulty of their projects before the efforts were initiated. Projects with low likelihoods of success or large marketing hurdles were identified and means for coping with these obstacles were planned. In general, the greater the difficulty of the project, the greater the quality and quantity of resources assigned to it. The most difficult projects were often accorded the higher priorities. The organizations generally postulated that, because of the difficulty of the project, if they succeeded they could reap many advantages over their less successful competitors.

In the case of Well-Developed Science projects, the managers and the project personnel too frequently glossed over important details. Well-Developed Science projects generated a mindset that the challenges were easier than they actually were. This mindset seldom occurred on Undeveloped Science or Art project types. Perhaps the lesson here is a variation of the old saying that familiarity breeds contempt. Don't assume that Well-Developed Science types projects are easy. The assumption itself can set up the conditions that lead to failures.

*Customer Attitudes and Success*

Do customer attitudes toward new products make a difference? The data in table 5-6 show that there is, indeed, a relationship between the degree of success and customer attitudes.[3]

The interview data showed that there were very few eager customers that were relatively unknown by the firm. In most cases, the firm's sales personnel had called on the customer many times. Moreover, various persons from the management, engineering, and marketing departments were acquainted with their counterparts in the customer firms. Quotes from the interviews at four firms indicate how deep these relationships often ran: "We have known them for so long we can pretty much tell them what they are going to need"; "They look to us to solve their problems"; "We always know what they're going to ask for next"; "They know we understand their operations." In many cases, these close relationships were further strengthened by personnel promotions. For example, when someone in the customer organization was promoted, this seemed only to foster stronger relationships higher up between the two organizations.

Thus, the lesson here is clear. Knowing your customer intimately and

Table 5–6
**Customer Attitudes and Project Success Rates**

| Customer Attitudes toward New Products[b] | Percentage Distribution of Commercial Success Outcomes[a] | | |
|---|---|---|---|
| | *Blockbuster* | *Above Expectations* | *Met Expectations* |
| Resistant | 8 | 7 | 85 |
| Indifferent | 44 | 32 | 24 |
| Eager | 49 | 40 | 11 |

[a]See table 2-1.
[b]These attitudes are more fully defined in the instrument, which is available from the author.

building long-standing trusting relationships can pay off handsomely for the new product developer.[4]

## External Influences on New Product Innovation

As noted in chapter 2 (figure 2-1), external environments were part of the focus of this study. Two external factors were found that exerted considerable influence on new product innovations: industry associations and government actions.

*Industry Associations*

Industry associations were frequently encountered. These associations were typically organized to protect the members' interests and facilitate nonproprietary information exchange. The associations carried out a range of functions including setting product standards, funding member-sponsored field tests, establishing minimum product safety requirements, monitoring industry health and safety practices and collecting information on pending legislation or congressional activities that could affect the industry.

The associations were quite active in setting minimum product standards. They worked to establish screening and performance tests for qualifying new products. Many of the associations also sought to obtain new legislation or eliminate old laws. Tests and standards were constantly being developed to detect product deficiencies. Many of the associations sought to establish their tests as the industry standards and to institutionalize these standards through federal laws.

Some product developers voiced the opinion that their associations sometimes inhibited innovation. The certification procedures were often viewed as highly bureaucratic. Some new product developers noted that the tests were capricious and unreliable. They questioned how an innovation could have an established test. The answer, of course, is that though it may be an innovation, the performance specifications it is trying to meet may in fact be well established and well known.

Many new product developers had developed tests they believed were superior to the industry association tests. Several of these tests had become accepted as the industry standards. In some instances, this effort came back to haunt them when their products failed to pass the tests they had designed!

Several new product developers feared that open testing of their new products in association tests could result in premature disclosure of their innovations to competitors. Some of the users of the new product innovations also felt that the associations were not necessarily advantageous to them. These customers thought that the work of the associations sometimes delayed the advent of new products that they needed. Some customers also felt they had very individualized needs that no industry-wide standard could adequately meet.

A number of cases were found where lengthy product testing and adherence to high standards was a very effective deterrent to foreign competition. Moreover, many new product developers who participated extensively in trade association activities were also the most innovative. They had the highest percentage of successful new product innovations (the nature of this statistic is elaborated in chapter 6). There seemed to be two reasons for this. First, those firms that were the most active in the associations were also the first to learn about new trends, new developments and new opportunities. Second, those who were the most active also had the highest image among the other association members. In some cases, the most active firms' personnel dominated the decision boards of the associations.

## Federal Government Influence

As table 5-7 shows, two types of governmental influences were found in the data base. In a direct influence, there is some type of direct contact between some government official and the firm's officers. In an indirect influence, the firm is affected by another firm's direct contact with government officials or by some general regulation.

Though many of the influences in table 5-7 are familiar, several are quite interesting. In one interesting case of a 1b type influence, the government intervened to assure the continued availability of a required raw material, thereby protecting the firm's new product development effort. Had this not happened, the firm would have terminated the development of this innovation due to lack of raw materials. An example of a 2a type influence was a

Table 5–7
Types of Federal Government Influences Found

| 1. Direct | 2. Indirect |
|-----------|-------------|
| a. Government restricted company's product | a. Government creates windfall opportunities |
| b. Government protected company's product | b. Restrictions elsewhere create calamities here |
| c. Government contracted for the work | c. Expired patents elsewhere create opportunities here |
| d. Government makes product the standard | d. Government policies augment demand |
| e. Government directly regulates the company | e. Government policies encourage new product features |
| | f. Government provides initiative to users |

federal mandate that a safety feature be installed in all new products. One firm in the data base had correctly anticipated this mandate and was therefore already ahead of its competitors with an acceptable product when the mandate appeared.

Examples of 2b types of indirect influence often appeared in the data base. In one of these cases, federal regulations caused an ingredient to be removed from the market. This led to the termination of a development that used the ingredient. A 2d type influence exists when government is a user, along with other nongovernment users. An example of a 2e type is the case where a firm develops a new product innovation in the hope that a pending government policy (such as recommended temperature settings in buildings to conserve energy) will make a particular product more attractive (an automatic thermostat). For a familiar example of a 2f type, consider the case of tax rebates that encourage the use of a particular product.

Thus, though this study was not primarily concerned with government or other external influences on innovations, these influences were important background variables. As indicated in table 5-7, government influences were found to be many and varied. Both promotive and restrictive influences were found. Some cases were found where government actions directly stimulated a new product innovation. Many more cases were found where various government actions *indirectly* stimulated innovations.

Within the rather general sample of projects and firms studied here, it cannot be said that government is either *directly* promotive or restrictive to innovation. Rather, particular firms are often indirectly influenced in particular ways, depending on their circumstances and technologies. One thing was clearly apparent, however. All the firms interviewed were alert to government actions as an influence on their innovation processes. This awareness commonly extended to the project manager level. It sometimes extended to surprisingly low levels of the organization, to the idea generator, creative scientist, or engineer working in the area. Today's scientists and engineers are apparently much more aware of the world around them than their predecessors were.

## Summary

In this chapter, a constellation of complex conditions and factors was found that influenced the success and failure outcomes of new product innovations. A high degree of understanding of the technical problems and the users' needs, a high degree of fit between the technology and the company's level of expertise, and high quality of resources were repeatedly found to characterize the most successful projects. Allocating too much money to a project was found to be more detrimental to its success than allocating too little.

Contrary to conventional wisdom, defensive efforts aimed at protecting a firm's current position were not necessarily found to have high success rates. There is a danger that project personnel will succumb to the common myth that such projects are easy, and thus become lulled into intellectual complacency.

There is a conventional wisdom that ideas from outside the firm are more likely to be successful than ideas from inside the firm. In particular, customers have been said to be a fertile source of new product ideas. Contrary to these tenets, internally-generated ideas were found to be more successful than outside ideas. Ideas originating from the firm's marketing personnel were the most successful.

One factor that consistently fostered the success of new product innovations was the degree of developer-customer interaction. The most successful new product developers maintained very close interpersonal relationships with their customers, at all organizational levels. One mechanism used for maintaining this close customer contact was participation in the established industry associations. Involvement in industry associations also brought many other benefits to new product developers. These benefits included the power to influence and even dictate the industry's new product standards, and the power to buffer domestic competitors and forestall the entry of foreign products.

New product innovation projects succeed and fail for numerous complex reasons. However, several specific factors and conditions were found that fostered project success. Managers are well advised to try to maximize these factors and conditions.[5]

# Notes

1. A useful reference here is Robert G. Cooper's *Project Newprod: What Makes a New Product a Winner* (Montreal: Quebec Industrial Innovation Center, 1980).

2. For more background, see Yoram Wind's *Product Policy* (Reading, Mass: Addison-Wesley, 1982).

3. This instrument, number 16-1, is available from the author.

4. See Thomas J. Peters and Robert H. Waterman, Jr., *In Search Of Excellence,* (New York: Harper & Row, 1982).

5. The results in this chapter are generally consistent with other studies. The reader may wish to consult Booz, Allen & Hamilton's *Management of New Products* (New York: Booz, Allen & Hamilton, 1968). The reader may also consult Roy Rothwell and Morris Teubal, "Sappho Revisited: A Re-Appraisal of the Sappho Data Base," *Innovation, Economic Change and Technology Policies,* K.A. Stroetmann, ed. (Basel: Brinker Verlag, 1977), pp. 39-59, and A.H. Rubenstein, et al, "Factors Influencing Innovation Success at the Project Level," *Research Management,* XIX, no. 3 (May 1976), 15-20.

# 6

# Organizing for New Product Innovation

> Great innovations will not be forced by slender majorities.
> —Thomas Jefferson, 1808

I s there one best way to organize for innovation? The results of the analyses in this chapter will show that the answer is no. However, the analyses will also show that some ways of organizing are definitely better than some others. Moreover, some ways of organizing are best for some circumstances. Still others are best for other circumstances.

## Methodology

As noted in chapter 2, the methodology used here resulted in the collection of the latest five-year population of new product innovation projects at 53 firms. The degree of innovativeness of each of these firms was measured in terms of the percentage of their new product innovation projects that met or exceeded the project's commercial expectations (see table 2-1). The "most innovative firms" were then defined as the top 12 firms on this statistic, or approximately the top 25 percent of the 53 firm sample. These 12 firms, as well as the remaining 41, were then intensively studied and compared to determine the characteristics that set them apart.[1]

## Qualities of the Most Innovative Firms

Seven unique qualities were found that consistently characterized the most innovative firms. These seven qualities are listed in table 6-1. Each quality responds to some hurdle or challenge that is typically raised by innovations.

The willingness of an organization to accept change is fundamental to successful new product innovations. The development and introduction of a new product often involves changes in the established authority patterns, decision-making behaviors, information needs, and distribution channels. This means that comfortable old behavior patterns, conventional relationships,

**Table 6–1**
**Seven Characteristics of Innovations and the Corresponding Qualities of Innovative Organizations**

| *Seven Characteristics of Innovations That Raise Hurdles* | *Corresponding Qualities of Innovative Organizations Required to Cope with These Hurdles* |
|---|---|
| 1. Disruptiveness; they create high sociobehavioral costs | 1. Willingness to accept change, altered behaviors, and disruptions |
| 2. Involve relatively high research, development, and commercialization costs | 2. Long-term commitment to technology |
| 3. Require time for idea germination, gestation, and maturation | 3. Patience in permitting ideas to gestate and decisiveness in allocating resources to those ideas having the greatest commercial prospects |
| 4. Carry high risk and uncertainty | 4. Willingness to confront uncertainties and accept balanced risks |
| 5. Timeliness | 5. Alertness in sensing environmental threats and opportunities and promptness in responding to them |
| 6. Involve combinations of various technologies that may exist inside and outside the firm | 6. Openness of internal, cross-departmental communications; diversity of internal talents and cultures; existence of many external contacts and information sources |
| 7. Involve the talents of many individuals who collectively possess interdisciplinary know-how | 7. A climate that fosters the natural confrontation and resolution of interdepartmental rivalries and conflicts and the development of reciprocal role-persons |

and accustomed ways of doing things will be challenged. The most innovative firms in the data base appeared to be highly willing to accommodate new patterns and changes.

Another requirement for successful innovation is an organization that fosters long-term commitments to technology. The most innovative firms in the data base exhibited a quality of patience in permitting ideas to germinate and gestate. However, this was not the "let them alone and something good will happen" philosophy applied to many American R&D laboratories during the 1950s. Rather, there was a definite decisiveness in controlling the amount of time ideas spent gestating. After a reasonable time, decisions were made and some ideas were selected while others were abandoned.

The most innovative firms had well-developed project selection systems (see chapter 8). These systems effectively communicated the firm's needs to the idea generators, fostered decisiveness in distinguishing good ideas from bad ideas, and promoted consistent policies for allocating resources. This avoided the on-again/off-again climate of starting and stopping projects due to cyclical budgets and indecisiveness in goal-setting that often characterized the less effective firms. This climate not only disrupted the progress of the projects, but it often demoralized the innovators and squashed their spirit (see chapter 7).

Innovations are inherently risky and uncertain. Willingness to accept risk and uncertainty is a requirement for dealing with innovations. However, this does not mean that successful innovators gamble more than non-innovators. Rather, the most innovative firms in the data base were more willing to look hard at risky opportunities and to confront them. They also appeared to be more able to accurately assess the degree of risk of a project. These firms frequently handled risky projects by balancing their portfolios with less risky projects.

The most innovative firms in the data base had the ability to sense threats and opportunities in a timely fashion. Their top managers were committed to environmental scanning, technological forecasting, and competitive analysis.[2] They had a constant awareness of where they stood vis-à-vis their competitors. Open communication channels and a diversity of subcultures often characterized the most innovative organizations. These qualities enabled them to move quickly into various roles and adapt to changing market needs. The open communication fostered many contacts with scientists, customers, and others outside the innovating firms. These contacts were frequent sources of new ideas, suggestions, and know-how.

Interdepartmental conflict can be a severe barrier to innovation. Goal conflicts, communication problems, and a lack of openness often characterize the relationship between R&D and other departments. Yet, a complete lack of such conflicts does not seem to make an organization innovative. Rather, the fashion in which such conflicts are handled is highly important. Sweeping conflict under the rug does not work. A willingness to confront and resolve conflicts was a salient climate for the most innovative firms in the data base. In fact, these firms seemed to be constantly in search of discontent and constructive frustrations which they could creatively resolve. The process of resolving these conflicts often led to new product ideas and a more receptive organizational climate. (See chapters 10 and 11 for more details on this aspect.)

The most innovative firms in the data base had several individuals who played various reciprocal roles. There were persons who generated ideas. There were other individuals who championed these ideas. Still other individuals helped to implement or otherwise link these ideas to the existing organizational goals. (See table 1-3 for a list of some major innovation roles.) Organization structures and climates that foster the development of these collaborative roles appear to foster successful innovations (see chapter 7).

## Principles of Innovative Organization

The above results may be formulated as a set of principles of organizing for innovation. In order to emphasize these principles, let us compare them to the classical principles of organizing. The classical principles epitomize the extreme case of non-innovative behaviors. Unfortunately, many organizations are founded on these classical principles.

The classical principles of organizing emphasize rigidly specialized behaviors and rational economic decision making. The emphasis is on the one best way to routinely perform repetitive tasks, to achieve the minimum cost and the maximum efficiency. The classical school views management's role as closely directing and controlling others to ensure that they conform to the established policies and rules. Authority is vested in a single person at the top of the organization, and there is a rigid linear chain of command from that person down through the hierarchy. The organization is structured into functionally specialized units like production and finance. Efficiency is maximized and conflicts are minimized by keeping these functions independent and non-overlapping. This idea is extended to subdividing individual jobs; one person drills the hole in a sheet metal panel, another inserts a bolt, a third person puts a nut on that bolt, and so on.

By contrast, innovative organizing principles avoid bureaucratic rules and policies. Horizontal, colleague-based relationships are stressed, in contrast to the vertical boss-employee relationships of the classical approach. The purpose of management is to foster harmony and change, and to adapt the organization to evolving needs. Authority is decentralized, participation of members is sought, and the organization is viewed as having many sources of power and influence. Cross-departmental teams, autonomous groups, and matrix structures are common. These concepts recognize that there is a natural overlap between jobs and functions that can be a source of synergism and creative outputs. This synergism is preserved by assigning shared responsibilities, like making both marketing and research jointly responsible for new products.

These principles are summarized in table 6-2. Note the considerable differences in the ways in which the classical and innovative principles view the human element. The classical principles view employees as simply another resource, to be managed in whatever way best achieves short-run organiza-

Table 6–2
Classical versus Innovative Organizing Principles

| Classical | Innovative |
|---|---|
| 1. Jobs are narrowly defined and subdivided into rigid, small units | 1. There is constant adjustment of tasks through the interactions of the organization members |
| 2. A narrow definition of authority is attached to the individual's job | 2. A sense of responsibility replaces authority and there is a commitment to the organization that goes beyond the individual's functional role |
| 3. There are many hierarchial levels and a strict hierarchy of control and authority; the bosses order things to be done | 3. There is a low degree of hierarchy of control and authority; things get done through a mutuality of agreement and a community of interest |
| 4. Communication is mainly vertical, between superiors and subordinates; these communications consist of instructions issued by superiors | 4. Communication runs in all directions between people of different ranks, and it resembles consultation rather than command |
| 5. There are many rules and policies, and loyalty and obedience to superiors are required | 5. Emotional commitment to the achievement of tasks and the expansion of the firm is highly valued |
| 6. Economic efficiency is the goal | 6. Newness and creativity are sought and growth is the goal |
| 7. Top-down authority-centered management is the mode | 7. Horizontal, expertise-centered influence is the mode; teams, task forces, and project management methods are used |

tional efficiency. This severely constrains behaviors. The innovative principles view the employee as a wealth of creative talent that can be used for the benefit of everyone within the organization.

## Organizing Principles and Project Outcomes

This is all very nice. But does it really make a difference for project outcomes? Can't innovation projects succeed under classical principles?

To answer these questions, respondents at each firm in the data base used the instruments developed for this study to rate the degree to which classical principles were present at their firm.[1] The ratings were then averaged within

Table 6–3
**Classical Principles That Were Statistically Significantly Negatively Correlated with Degree of Innovativeness[a]**

| |
|---|
| Degree to which jobs are perceived to be narrowly defined |
| Degree to which authorities are perceived to be narrowly defined |
| Degree to which information flows and communications are perceived to be top down only |
| Degree of loyalty and obedience to superiors perceived to be required |
| Degree to which rules, policies and hierarchical organizational levels are perceived to characterize the organization |

[a]Significant at the 95 percent confidence level.

each firm and compared with the degree of innovativeness of that firm. The five items shown in table 6-3 were found to be statistically significantly *negatively* correlated with the degree of innovativeness (at the 95 percent confidence level). That is, when these five principles were present to a high degree, a low degree of innovativeness occurred. When they were present to a low degree, a high degree of innovativeness occurred. These results indicate that principles of organizing do indeed make a difference to project success rates.

But just exactly how are principles and organizing philosophies translated into behaviors that influence project success rates? The interviews shed considerable light on this question. For example, consider the following statements about rules, policies, and control over behaviors that were collected at four of the firms: "We feel like we have to follow the rules here"; "It wouldn't get me anything to go around the policies"; "You pretty well have to conform around here"; "I just don't have the freedom to do that."

The interviews also revealed how perceptions about top-down information flow and the narrowness of jobs influenced some individual's behaviors. The following comments were collected at five of the firms: "We pretty well work on what we are told to"; "This is not a highly participative environment"; "I'm not supposed to go over to that department and talk to them about it"; "This is where my job ends"; "Based on what I've seen, I wouldn't think management wants us to cross over the lines."

It has sometimes been argued that macro-level organizational design principles and philosophies are a bit like apple pie. No one is opposed to them, but it doesn't matter whether we have them or not. This argument is not supported by the above results. Philosophies and principles do indeed send signals that people interpret and use to guide their behaviors. Moreover the classical principles send signals that many individuals interpret in very narrow, behavior-restricting ways.

## Organizational Goals and Project Outcomes

Is it important to have innovation stated as an explicit goal? Don't innovation projects succeed when innovation is not emphasized as an organizational goal?

Respondents at each firm in the data base rated the relative importance of six goals within their organizations, using the instruments mentioned earlier. The ratings for each goal were then averaged within each firm and compared with the degree of innovativeness of that firm. The results of this analysis are presented in table 6-4. The goals of economic efficiency, annual profit maximization, and return on investment were statistically significantly *negatively* correlated with the degree of innovativeness. That is, the more these goals were emphasized, the lower the degree of innovativeness. And the less these goals were emphasized, the greater the degree of innovativeness. On the other hand, the goals of sales growth, market share growth, and innovation were positively correlated with the degree of innovativeness. Thus, the conclusion is a rather robust one: Goals do indeed make a difference.

These results must be viewed as an extension of the above findings about organizing principles. It is apparent that perceptions do, indeed, influence behaviors.

## Organization Structure Types and Innovation

As shown, organization structures can and do influence employee behaviors. The structures are perceived and interpreted by the employees, as a basis for their choice of behaviors. Having the "right" organization structure may not be sufficient to stimulate behaviors that achieve innovation. However, structures that are not based on the innovative organizing principles outlined in table 6-2 will discourage innovation.

Many different organization structures were encountered in the data

**Table 6–4**
**Organizational Goals versus Degree of Innovativeness**

| Negatively Correlated Goals[a] | Positively Correlated Goals[a] |
| --- | --- |
| Economic Efficiency (Cost Maximization; Process Optimization) | Sales Growth |
| | Market Growth |
| Annual Profit Maximization | |
| | Innovation |
| Return on Investment | |

[a]At the 95 percent confidence level.

base. However, most of them were classified into the four generic types of structures depicted in figures 6-1, 6-2, 6-3 and 6-4.

*Type I Structures*

The type I structure depicted in figure 6-1 is superior for handling routine problems and well-known technologies. It is also the appropriate structure

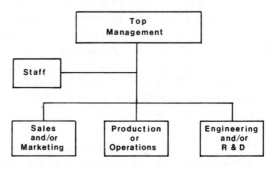

**Figure 6–1. The Type I Structure**

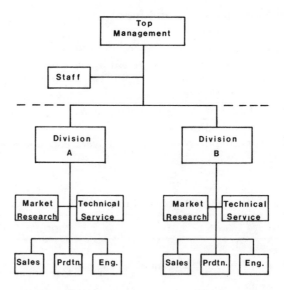

*Key:* Prdtn. = Production
Eng. = Engineering

**Figure 6–2. The Type II Structure**

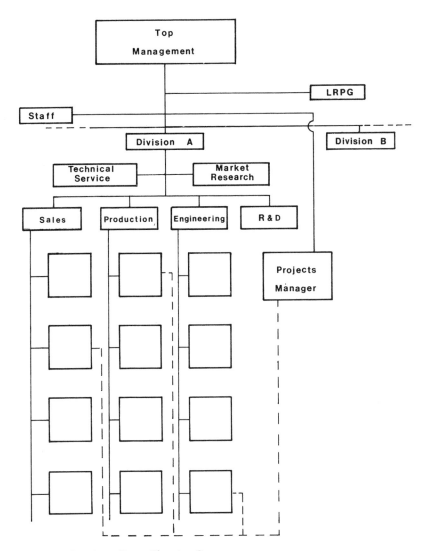

*Key:* LRPG = Long Range Planning Group

**Figure 6–3. The Type III Structure**

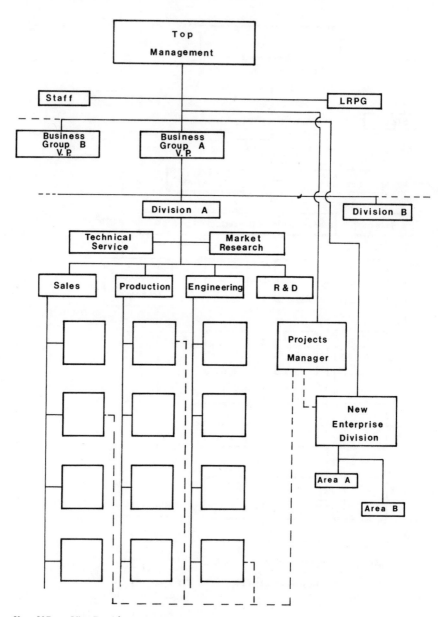

*Key:* V.P. = Vice President

**Figure 6–4. The Type IV Structure**

for handling stable environments, low product evolution rates, and well-defined markets. Decisions are centralized, lines of communication are short, and the various departments are clearly defined.

Type I structures epitomize the classical organizing principles listed in table 6-2. Thus, they lack the required qualities of innovative organizations listed in table 6-1. This is largely a result of the separation of the specialized functions of sales, production, and engineering in type I structures. This separation creates obstacles to joint collaboration and spontaneous interaction on new product developments. The specialization of the departments makes it difficult for personnel to appreciate anything beyond the work within their respective departments. No one department has the required broad focus needed for successful innovation.

Thus, the properties of type I structures that make them so effective for handling routine operations are the very properties that make them unsuitable for handling innovations. Even if top management in type I structures wanted desperately to innovate, this would be extremely difficult. The entire structure is set up to emphasize non-innovative, classical behaviors.

## Type II Structures

Unlike type I structures, the type II structure depicted in figure 6-2 is able to respond to diverse market needs and the desire for evolutionary product improvements. In type II structures, the division managers theoretically have the resources and authority to develop incremental innovations within their respective divisions. The purpose of the market research and technical service groups is to foster this orientation. The market research group identifies gaps in the performance of current products, and the technical service group produces the indicated product improvements or incremental innovations. Within the data base, the technical service groups carried various labels: R&D, development, technical service, product engineering. In all cases, their charter was the same: to maintain and improve existing product lines. This included cost and performance improvements, the expansion of current product lines, the development of related products, and the creation of other incremental innovations that could be produced and marketed by the existing departments.

Future growth is possible in type II structures by simply adding more divisions. For example, if the family of products becomes too large for any existing division to handle, a new division can be spun off from one of the existing divisions. However, this is only feasible for familiar products and familiar environments. Type II structures lack the ability to adapt to changing environments and to handle radical innovations. For example, suppose current customers suddenly decide they want a very different type of product. Or, suppose someone within the organization has a radical idea that does not fit into the existing product lines. Type II structures have no provision for handling anything more extreme than incremental extensions to current products. Type II structures are unable to cope with radical change. The pursuit of short-term profits and the need to maintain stringent return on investment criteria effectively keep type II structures within their current lines of business. Any new product or any product improvement that does not make an acceptable profit during its first year of existence is necessarily a wayward child. Unless top management severely bends the rules to permit losses, no operating division manager can tolerate anything that is not certain to make a profit. This is surely not a climate in which radical ideas and innovations can survive. Few real innovations can be expected to return profits during their early lives.

Type II organizations are thus only a small improvement over type I structures in terms of their friendliness to innovations. Type II structures are hidebound by their inherent short-term profit motive.

### Type III Structures

The type III structure depicted in figure 6-3 attempts to make up for the deficiencies of the type I and II structures. The long range planning group (LRPG), divisional research and development (R&D), and the projects manager function are added in an attempt to overcome the inherent problems of type II structures.

The purpose of the LRPG is to engage in market intelligence, environmental scanning, and other activities to sense strategic new opportunities and emerging threats to the organization.[2] The divisional R&D function develops new divisional products in response to the work of the LRPG. The projects manager's function is to develop corporate-wide technobusiness ideas that may be defined by the R&D groups or the LRPG. Generally, the projects manager is responsible for large, major new product efforts that involve the skills of several types of persons and resources. Completed projects may be transferred to divisional R&D groups or to the operating divisional personnel, or a new division may be added to handle the completed product. The latter option is a commonly used internal growth mode for many technology based firms.

The reader should note that a common variant of type III structures is to have a corporate R&D function in lieu of the projects manager. The corporate R&D function may thus behave identically to the projects manager, or it may play less active roles. For instance, corporate R&D groups often exist to investigate phenomena that may be of interest to the firm but would not normally be investigated by the more mission-oriented divisional R&D groups. When corporate R&D plays this role, it is important to have a projects manager function that can develop, translate, and transfer corporate

R&D products into the operating divisions. Otherwise, there will often be a large gap between the basic research outputs from the corporate R&D group and the apparent needs of the divisions.

Type III structures emphasize the development of interdepartmental interfaces, openness, and cooperation between departments. The operations of the LRPG, the divisional R&D groups, and the corporate projects manager intentionally overlap. Radical new ideas can originate from any of these sources and be transferred to their most appropriate locations. Personnel may openly communicate, move freely across the organizational boundaries, and develop close interrelationships. The number of projects undertaken by the projects manager can increase or decrease in response to changing diversification strategies or competitive needs. A variety of personnel can be drawn from throughout the firm and assembled into a project team under the projects manager. This is indicated by the broken lines from the projects manager's box in figure 6-3. When the project is completed, personnel may return to their functional areas or transfer to other projects.

Type III structures theoretically achieve the required qualities for innovation listed in table 6-1. They conform to many of the principles of innovative organizations listed in table 6-2. Unfortunately, type III structures often create more problems than they solve. The diversion of resources from the divisions to the projects runs the risk of constraining the divisional R&D and hurting the current operations. Enormous management time may be taken up deciding how to balance resources between the short-range (current product) divisional efforts and the long-range (future product) project efforts. In fact, top management's time may be completely absorbed in mediating quarrels between the divisional managers and the project managers, leaving no time for strategic decision making. And strategic decision making is precisely what type III structures are supposed to catalyze!

In such an environment, there is considerable danger that the corporate projects manager's efforts will be relegated to a fire-fighting role for the divisions. Then, no innovation at all will occur. It is easy to see how this might result. Because of the projects, the divisions may find that their manpower has been reduced beyond a level where they can effectively handle routine customer requests and customer service. Top management may then have no choice but to reassign the project personnel back to the divisions. Under this outcome, the whole reason for the type III structure is defeated. Type III structures thus often contain the seeds of their own defeat.

An equally serious problem of type III structures is their inability to handle the implementation of innovations. They do not possess any implicit means for safeguarding fledgling innovations during their commercialization stages. Once a project is completed, where does the newly developed innovation reside until customers can be generated for it? The projects are only chartered to develop ideas. Moreover, projects seldom have the massive capital, equipment, and budgets usually required for start-ups and commercializations. The operating divisions, being profit-centered, are unwilling to spend money on such risky start-ups. Thus, type III structures make no contribution to the transformation of radical new technical successes into commercial successes.

### Type IV Structures

The type IV structure depicted in figure 6-4 integrates several aspects of type I, II, and III structures. Current products are grouped by business lines and business groups to facilitate efficiency. In this aspect, type IV structures resemble type I and II structures. Like type III structures, a projects manager system is used to foster the development of radical innovations. However, the unique component of the type IV structure is the addition of the New Enterprise Division (NED). The NED is a kind of friendly block home for undeveloped, embryonic innovations. The NED fills the need for an incubator between the projects manager and the business groups. New products that have not yet achieved a breakeven level of profit can be housed in the NED until they are fully developed and proven. At that time, the operating divisions may be more willing to accept them.

Thus, type IV structures integrate the need for steady-state efficiency with the need for innovation. Type IV structures have mechanisms for developing and implementing innovations, while maintaining the current profit picture of the firm. In this way, neither the steady-state operations nor the innovative efforts interfere with each other. The current operations or business group managers are free to optimize their short term concerns. The projects personnel can devote their full time to creating new products for tomorrow's profits. The NED personnel can devote all their energies to implementing and starting up new innovations, which may be transferred to the operating divisions once they become established. The continued flow of new product ideas is fostered by the highway stretching from the project organization to the NED, and on to the operating divisions and business groups. Top management is free to properly focus their attentions on the strategic planning and long-range growth of the entire firm.

However, type IV structures are no panacea. They depend on the cooperative behaviors of the personnel in charge of the various functions. The NED and operating division or business group managers must cooperate fully in order to achieve an orderly transfer of ideas and innovations. The NED manager must convince the business group managers to accept an innovation when it is ready for them. The projects manager must similarly sell his outputs to the NED manager. The projects and NED managers are jointly responsible for coordinating the transfer of completed projects. There may be many political, technical, and personal reasons why the various parties may not readily cooperate and accept the other's outputs. (See chapters 9 and 10 for more details.) These parties must carefully coordinate all their activities with the LRPG, which is constantly directing the firm to new opportunities, emerging customer needs, and potential threats.

Thus, type IV structures depend on dynamic cooperation, collaborative planning and responsive behaviors. The various individuals must be willing to take the initiative in working together as a team, in very flexible ways. Unless they have forgiving personalities, the necessary cooperative behaviors may not actually occur. It is never easy to forge a true team mentality at the strategic level while preserving the dedication to the individual functions that is required to make type IV structures effective. Each party must possess a strong dedication to making their own specialized functions successful, while at the same time be willing to give and take for the benefit of the whole firm. Chapters 10 and 11 give more details on how this can be achieved.

## Selecting the Best Organization Structure

As noted in table 6-5, stable organization environments are characterized by low needs for innovation. Customers are not eager for new product innovations and success in serving these markets is a matter of efficiency of production and distribution, along with close cost control. Type I structures and classical organizing principles are appropriate for firms operating under such environments. However, even in relatively stable environments, incremental innovations and product improvements are often needed. Type I structures become ineffective under these circumstances. The firm must therefore look toward some other types, like the type II structure.

In dynamic environments, product innovation and nonstandard behaviors are necessary in order to cope with change. Type III structures and innovative organizing principles may be appropriate under these circumstances.

**Table 6–5**
**Contingent Conditions for Each Type of Organization Structure**

| | Market and Technical Environments | |
| --- | --- | --- |
| *Level of Innovation Desired* | *Stable* | *Dynamic* |
| None | Type I | [a] |
| Incremental | Type II | Type III |
| Radical | [a] | Type IV |

[a]By definition, these categories do not exist.

They are capable of handling the periodic or episodic incremental innovations that may characterize some dynamic environments. They are also appropriate for firms that have modest goals. Thus, here are two circumstances where type III structures are the best choice. One is the case where the environment is dynamic, but only incremental innovations are required and these occur only episodically. Another is the case where the firm does not want to be the innovative leader of their industry. That is, the firm is reactive rather than proactive. The firm wants to defend its domain rather than aggressively capture new territory. Note that there can be some good reasons why a firm would rather be a follower than a leader. Being the leader brings many responsibilities and pressures. For example, competition, visibility to legislators and activist groups, constant pressures to remain the leader, and the overall cost of doing business will surely be greater for a leader than for a follower. On the other hand, many benefits derive from being the leading innovator. Not the least of these benefits is profits. However, there may be nothing inherently wrong with deciding that the risk and returns are not worth the cost of being the leader.

When the need for radical innovation is continuous, type IV structures are mandatory. Under these environments, technical ideas must continuously stream from R&D and be constantly nurtured and pushed to their fullest commercial potentials. This requires the creative cooperation and collaboration of cross-functional teams and task forces. At the same time, the organization must devote the necessary attention to maintaining their current products, market shares, and financial positions. The type IV structure is the only one capable of balancing these conflicting demands for linking and harmonizing long run and short run needs.

Table 6-5 summarizes these points. The nature of the firm's environments and its goals with regard to the level of desired innovation collectively determine the best type of organization structure.

## Summary

Seven qualities were found that distinguished the most innovative firms from the others in the data base. These qualities reflect a consistent set of principles for organizing which are diametrically opposed to the classical management principles that underlie many firms. The classical principles of organizing were found to be related to low success rates for innovation projects.

On the basis of the results from the data base, new types of organizations and principles are needed to cope with the demands of innovation. Type I and II organization structures and classical organizing principles function well under stable environments. But they are woefully inadequate to handle new product innovations within dynamic environments. Type III and IV organization structures and innovative organizing principles are needed to handle new product innovations under dynamic environments. However, only type IV structures have the integrative qualities to handle all phases of the development of radical new product innovations. Moreover, only type IV organization structures have the flexibility and adaptability to handle continuous innovations.

Continuous, radical new product innovations are certain to be required in tomorrow's business environments. Customers are becoming increasingly willing to accept new products and eager to try new things. New ideas spread more rapidly today than they did only a few years ago, and this trend is likely to accelerate in the future. Rapid change is inherent in modern cultures. In such an environment, exclusive innovations and proprietary knowledge have a short half-life. To remain first, tomorrow's successful firms will have to be effective at producing a continuous stream of radical new products with superior performances. Thus, it seems safe to predict that type IV organization structures will become increasingly important. It also seems safe to predict that, in the true spirit of innovation, new and yet unknown structures that improve on the type IV structure will evolve to meet tomorrow's challenges and needs for better organizations.

## Notes

1. These instruments, numbers 5-2, 5-12 and 8-20 from the total instrument package, are available from the author.

2. For more details on these methodologies see William E. Souder, *Management Decision Methods for Managers of Engineering and Research* (New York: Van Nostrand Reinhold, 1980), pp. 81–99, and William E. Souder, *Project Selection and Economic Appraisal* (New York Van Nostrand Reinhold, 1984), pp. 5-22.

# 7
# Climates That Stimulate Innovation

The risk of failure is the price of success.
—Sir Winston Churchill, 1944

A n organization's prevailing attitude, atmosphere or orientation is often referred to as its internal climate. Can climate influence innovation success and failure? Are some climates restrictive to innovation? Are others promotive?

There is a prevailing wisdom that the nature of an organization's climate is important for success with innovations. The results in this chapter strongly support this notion. Moreover, there are several things a manager can do to foster a climate that promotes innovation.

## Methodology

Subjects at each firm were asked to score the climate of their firm along several dimensions.[1] These scores were then compared to the degree of innovativeness of each firm. (The degree of innovativeness was measured in terms of the percentage of successful new product innovations. See chapter 6 for more details.) The five dimensions listed in table 7-1 were found to be statistically significantly correlated with degree of innovativeness.

## Project Climate Results

### Uncertainty and Conflict in Task Assignments

Uncertainties about jobs, roles, and assignments in the minds of the personnel were related to *low* degrees of innovativeness. Nothing is more inhibiting than uncertainty.

Each individual's roles and responsibilities should be clearly known to him. Moreover, each should also know the roles and responsibilities of the other team members. Each individual must know whom to seek out for various kinds of assistance, whom to collaborate with, whom to keep informed,

Table 7–1
**Statistically Significant Project Climate Dimensions**[a]

Uncertainty and conflict in task assignments

Role flexibility

Openness and trust

Managerial support

Communications

[a]All are statistically significantly (95 percent confidence) correlated with the degree of innovativeness of the field sites.

and whom to contact for various decisions. In effect, this result simply says that well-understood goals and purposes are essential for successful innovation.

### Role Flexibility

The firms with the highest degrees of innovativeness had several persons on each project who played multiple roles. (See table 1-3 for a list of innovation roles.) For example, the idea generators and inventors also often played the role of idea salesman at later points in the project's life. Persons who coached and counseled the idea generators at one point in the life of the project often became aggressive idea carriers and idea communicators at later points.

The important facet of this dimension is the ability of the project team to respond flexibly to dynamic situations. When the circumstances demanded, the project personnel quickly put on one of their other hats and comfortably slipped into one of their other roles. Note that this is not a variant of role uncertainty. In role uncertainty, the people involved do not understand either their own primary roles or their freedom to play other roles that are demanded by the situation.

### Openness and Trust

In the firms with the highest degrees of innovativeness, the personnel often openly discussed project matters as well as personal items with their bosses. Personnel expressed trust, professional regard, and confidence in both their superiors and their subordinates. Peers expressed trust in one another. There was an air of mutual trust and confidence about coworkers' character, judgment, and ability.

## Managerial Support

In firms showing the highest degree of innovativeness, the employees perceived that all levels of management took an active and genuine interest in them. Management made them feel individually important and valuable to the company. Employees perceived that management decisions reflected genuine concern for their welfare as well as immediate profits. There was a feeling that management was well aware of employee attitudes. As one respondent phrased it: "We always have known each other pretty well."

## Communications

Firms with the highest degree of innovativeness were characterized by perceptions of high-volume and high-frequency communications. The personnel felt that they consistently received frequent, timely, and accurate information from upper management. Internal technical communications were believed to be generally dependable and accurate. Work targets and milestones were freely discussed.

In contrast to this happy story, a variety of communication problems were cited in the firms with low degrees of innovativeness. These problems included a perceived lack of general communication, frequent misunderstandings, and inconsistency of information.

## Improving Project Climates

How does a project climate that is highly stimulating to innovation come about? What can management do to promote such a climate?

An analysis of the data showed that four factors appeared to account for the differences between high and low degree of innovativeness project climates. One factor was technical competency. Where innovativeness was high, *all* the management personnel were perceived as being technically competent. All had spent portions of their careers in R&D or engineering. All were technically up to date; project personnel often sought them for technical advice.

A second factor was interpersonal competency. The managers worked hard at maintaining interpersonal styles that inspired trust and openness and motivated the personnel. The managers frequently attended training courses in interpersonal techniques, and their conversations often turned to matters of personnel motivation and management styles. Top management evaluated their lower level managers in terms of their interpersonal abilities. In some cases, managers were moved out of new product development jobs solely because they were perceived as not having a suitable managerial style.

A third factor that appeared to account for climate differences was the sense of direction or decisiveness provided by the management ranks. In the most innovative climates, the managers appeared to know exactly where they were going and why. Note that there was often considerable uncertainty about *how* to get there. For example, it was not uncommon for the managers to converse openly about the fact that they did not know how to make something. But there was seldom much uncertainty about what the end item should look like and when they wanted it, or why they needed to have it then.

The fourth factor was the way decisions were made. Sometimes the managers at the highly innovative firms made very unpopular decisions. These occurred when projects were terminated early in their lives and when a proposal that was strongly favored by one group was declined for funding. These unpopular decisions occurred surprisingly frequently in the highly innovative firms. Yet, the disappointments did not last long and the complaining parties soon turned their attention to other challenges. This was a most interesting facet. Why did the project personnel and the sponsors not harbor regrets? They were often vocal and intense in pushing their proposals and defending their projects. Yet, once the decision was made, they seemed to accept it. Why?

The answer apparently has a lot to do with the employees' respect for their managers' expertise and decision-making style. The decisions were usually made in a very participative fashion, with everyone's viewpoints presented and openly discussed. There was never any doubt left in anyone's mind why a proposal was declined or why a project was terminated. For example, one engineer made the following comment about his project after it was terminated.

> I tell you, that damned near broke my heart. I can see why they didn't want to go on with it. I guess maybe I would do the same if I were in their shoes. I feel good that I had my say. I think the project got a fair trial. There was just nothing else we could have done. But, hell, I just wish I could have had another three months. Well, I really respect him for having the guts to kill it instead of letting it drag on. But it still hurts to lose a project that was so much fun and so challenging. Well, there will be others.

Thus, in spite of his deep devotion to the project and his lingering mixed emotions, this engineer was willing to accept the decision and move on to other challenges. This experience typified the highly innovative firms.

## Promotive versus Restrictive Total Organization Climates

In examining the data base, it was found that total organization climates also appeared to have considerable effect on the project outcomes. Most (69 percent) of the successful projects (those whose commercial outcomes met or exceeded their expectations; see table 2-1), occurred within organizations with the characteristics listed in table 7-2. The label "promotive total organization climate" was invented to describe this climate. By comparison, many (47 percent) of the failure outcome projects occurred within the "restrictive total organization climate" characterized in table 7-3. Thus, promotive climates encouraged innovation success, while restrictive climates inhibited success.

Within the promotive climates (table 7-2), growth and innovation were much talked about goals. From the top management level to the project level, personnel frequently cited these goals in discussing their jobs and their work. Top management spoke in terms of the new products they hoped to develop and market within the next few years. Acquisition and product diversification

Table 7–2
Characteristics of Promotive Total Organization Climates

Growth and innovation are institutionalized goals

Top management is eager for new products

The company is in a growth and diversification mode

The company desires to be the first in the industry in at least one technical area

Budgetary control is highly decentralized

No one department is perceived to be the major seat of company power

Employees perceive that the climate is non-threatening, but that there is a sense of urgency to develop new things

Decisions are perceived as being participative or decentralized rather than dictated by one level of management

There is a substantial amount of group-to-group cooperation, borrowing and lending of people and equipment, and pooling of funds

Table 7–3
## Characteristics of Restrictive Total Organization Climates

---

The company is large-volume oriented, not interested in small-volume or small-dollar products

The objective is slow, solid growth

The company is more production-volume oriented than sales or profit oriented

There is no strong devotion to being the first in the industry

Budgetary control is highly centralized

Employees generally perceive that the president and a few top-level people are the power seats and they make all the decisions

Either the sales or the production department is perceived to be the seat of power within the company

Employees perceive that management is aloof, formal, and impersonal

Employees perceive that there is a great deal of gamesmanship and palace politics

There is a proclivity for each group to jealously guard its own budget and turf

---

strategies were often mentioned as a means to prominence. When asked to rank their organization's goals, respondents in promotive climates consistently ranked growth and innovation ahead of market share maximization, profit maximization, and company stock price maximization.[1]

By contrast, in restrictive climates (table 7-3), market share, stock price, and profit maximization were often ranked ahead of growth. Moreover, there was no strong devotion to being first in the industry, and a production-volume mentality prevailed. It is important to note that there was seldom any consensus about goals among the respondents in the restrictive climates. By comparison, in promotive climates there was usually a strong consensus ranking of goals across all organization levels. This high degree of agreement was one of the most dramatic features of promotive climates versus restrictive climates.

Major differences were noted in budgetary powers, decision-making powers, and the loci of power between promotive and restrictive climates. As noted in tables 7-2 and 7-3, lower level managers were given much higher sign-off limits and discretionary spending powers in the promotive climates. Decision making was perceived as centralized in restrictive climates and decentralized in promotive climates. In promotive climates, no individual department was viewed as being the seat of power. By contrast, either the sales or production departments were generally viewed as dominating most decisions in restrictive climates. Interestingly, many of the personnel in restrictive climates saw nothing wrong with sales and production being the dominant departments.

Thus, substantial differences were found between the total organization climates that surrounded the success and failure outcome innovation projects. These differences are consistent with many of our conventional wisdoms. These results, once again, reinforce the need for upper management to properly set the stage for innovation.

## Encouraging Intrapreneurs

Many firms do not create climates that encourage internal entrepreneurs, or "intrapreneurs." Today's organization climates often discourage employees from the essence of intrapreneurship: demonstrating individual initiative, using intuitive thinking, taking risks, generating controversial ideas, and pursuing new ideas to commercialization against all odds. The intrapreneur is an essential ingredient in every innovation.

The successful intrapreneur is many things rolled into one. He or she may be a creative inventor, but this is not the essence of intrapreneurship. The intrapreneur does not care whether it is his idea or someone else's. He is motivated by the sheer excitement of trying to score a goal with an idea, irrespective of "whose" idea it is. The successful intrapreneur knows how to corral the human and nonhuman resources needed to get the ball all the way to the goal line. The intrapreneur may be a guerrilla warfare agent, fighting his way against all odds. But he doesn't have to be. Some successful intrapreneurs have very smoothing personalities that would hardly ruffle anyone. The intrapreneur, however, is steadfastly dedicated and singleminded in this pursuit. He will not stop until he has carried the ball or caused it to be carried all the way to the goal line. He lives for the sheer joy of seeing an innovation come to fruition.

An in-depth examination of the data base suggested seven things, listed in table 7-4, that managers can do to encourage intrapreneurship. In 79 percent of the projects that met or exceeded their commercial expectations, five or more of these seven items were present. By comparison, in 71 percent of the projects that failed, no more than three of these items were present.

**Table 7–4**
**Seven Things Managers Can Do to Encourage Internal Entrepreneurs (Intrapreneurs)**

Early identification of intrapreneurs

Development of other role-functions

Establishment of formal licenses

Care and feeding of the underground

Fostering angels

Optimizing organizational location

Promoting bounded autonomy

*Early Identification of Intrapreneurs*

Several of the firms in the data base made an effort to identify their intrapreneurs early in the lives of the projects. Some even tried to groom their own intrapreneurs. How did they identify them? How did they groom them?

The successful intrapreneurs were all well-acquainted with the end markets, familiar with the technology, known by many others throughout the firm, and well known throughout their industry. Several of the successful intrapreneurs were world-class experts. The intrapreneurs were generally viewed by others as "someone who gets right in here and works with us," "a guy who spreads the credit around," "a team player," "a fellow with good technical savvy," "a very practical problem-solver," " a person who is tough and demanding but also fair and reasonable," and "a guy who can tell you a lot about a lot of things." One personal characteristic was especially observable: the ability to dispel any fears that he was a self-serving empire builder. The successful intrapreneurs all had strong personal desires to see ideas implemented and to solve real user problems. They expressed strong, long-term dedications to science and engineering as the means to solving world problems. And they characteristically viewed all problems in a systems context. That is, a problem was never seen as a single, isolated event. Rather, it was viewed as a variant or an imbalance in a system that could be corrected in many different ways.

Several firms in the data base identified budding intrapreneurs by matching their behaviors and personalities against a list of characteristics like the ones just described. These firms encouraged their potential intrapreneurs by making them more aware of these characteristics and by coaching them to develop themselves along these lines. Job rotation, exposure to many different facets of the business, and intimate exposure to customer operations were used to foster the emergence of intrapreneurial behaviors. Someone once said that diversity is the fuel of innovation. This is surely true in the case of providing job diversity as a fuel for intrapreneurship.

## Development of Other Role-Functions

Several of the firms that had been successful in fostering intrapreneurship pointed out that intrapreneurs in isolation are of little value. For every intrapreneur, a team of other role-players is required. To support their intrapreneurs, the organizations surrounded them with coaches, deep technical idea creators, and idea carriers through various task force and team assignments.

A coach is a kind of grand old organization man who can counsel the younger intrapreneurs on the best ways to circumvent organizational obstacles and natural bureaucratic barriers. Deep technical idea creators are the technical specialists who have the basic scientific knowledge of the phenomena under application. In most of the firms studied here, the intrapreneurs were not deep technical idea creators though they were far from being technically ignorant. There are times when the highly specialized scientist is essential. He is often the only person who understands the underlying scientific principles of the relevant phenomena. He may be necessary for the solution of key technical problems that can arise at critical points in the project.

Many of the idea carriers in the firms studied here were the organization's suicide squads. These are the daring persons who will hurtle themselves into battle, against all odds for a cause. Intrapreneurs are seldom so reckless. Their lives are governed by taking calculated risks, by working through others, and by achieving legitimization. The idea carriers however, want to succeed at any cost. Sometimes, such persons become essential to an effort.

Understanding these roles and knowing when to put each one on stage appears to be a key ingredient in successful innovation. Blending the right mix of these roles in a timely fashion is a management talent that the most successful firms seem to have at least partially mastered.

## Establishment of Formal Licenses to Innovate

Licenses provide lawyers, engineers, teachers, and other professionals with a sense of legitimacy. This causes others to listen to them, agree with them and cooperate with them.[2] This is precisely what an intrapreneur needs. How does he get a license?

One way is for top management to appoint the intrapreneur to the formal position of project manager. It is a powerful license, in that the project manager is the topmost manager on the project. He or she usually has the responsibility for all aspects of that project. The position also derives power from its place in the organization hierarchy. Project managers often report very high up in the organization, to a vice president or to the president. This license is temporary and automatically ends with the completion of the project. Even so, the successful intrapreneur carries the aura of the prior formal license long after the project has been completed. Formal licenses can thus easily develop into strong informal licenses for the individual.

Another way is to appoint the intrapreneur as chairman of a new product committee. A product committee is sometimes suitable when a project cannot be clearly identified, where several departments are involved, where the effort is large or where it is desired to provide a training ground for the potential intrapreneur. The product committee chairman has a budget, the authority to call meetings and the power to direct the efforts of other committees and personnel. The product committee is usually chartered with overseeing all aspects of the new product development. Some product committees can be very large and involve large organizational commitments (see chapter 9 for more details).

A third license that management can confer is the task force leader. This is not a very powerful license. Task forces are often used to explore the potentials of an embryonic idea or the feasibility of initiating a formal project. The typical task force leader has no budget, the duration of the task force is usually finite, and the task is usually well defined. However, task forces often represent the early beginnings of a more formal project effort. The successful task force leader is often the most natural choice to manage the subsequent project effort.

### Care and Feeding of the Underground: The Informal License

Successful intrapreneurs always develop an informal license: an informal network of colleagues or an underground they use to assist them. Informal influence is the real source of power of the intrapreneur. It consists of the peer respect, personal magnetism, and negotiating power used by the successful intrapreneur to marshal resources.

Informal influence cannot be conferred by management. How then, can management foster it? The cases studied here indicated that individuals whose prior experiences brought them into close working contact with a diversity of other functions and persons often gained an informal license. Those who managed projects also acquired some informal license. Thus, it is apparent that managers who wish to foster intrapreneurship should try to guide the career paths of their candidates through as wide a diversity of experiences as possible, and delegate as much responsibility to them as they can handle.

Something else that management can do is to *not destroy* the natural underground that normally exists within any organization. Provide enough personal and financial freedom for individuals to "smuggle" a little work. Give them time and money to work on their own ideas. Build enough slack into the official projects so that "interesting" things that arise can be pursued. Don't make the personnel formally apply for time off or write proposals to get the money or time to work on their own ideas. The whole spirit of the underground lies in the thrill of doing something that seems a little sub rosa. The forbidden fruit no longer becomes a heady attraction once management says it is not forbidden!

*Fostering Angels*

The data base repeatedly showed that one-man intrapreneurial efforts seldom succeeded. (See also the topic of one-man shows in chapter 9.) This may deeply disappoint budding young intrapreneurs, who generally want to be able to say "I did this all by myself." The data base suggests that it is important for the success of an intrapreneur to have an "angel." An angel is someone higher up in the organization who can sponsor or otherwise provide championship and funds when they are needed at critical points.

The very fact that the effort is championed by someone higher in the organization can sometimes be enough to obtain the funds, the equipment, or the required cooperation of some other department. Several cases were found where angels provided critical funds at various points, aided the intrapreneur in shouldering risks, and sanctioned efforts that did not fit the firm's usual operations. A vivid example of how an angel can help an intrapreneur was provided by one case in the data base. This intrapreneur had been assigned the chairmanship of a new product development task force. Chosen because of his informal authority, he worked through his network of friendly peers and outside-the-firm contacts to collect several bits of important market intelligence. But this information was not consistent with other information held by the firm's marketing research department. This immediately became a stumbling block; the marketing department vehemently disputed the validity of the intrapreneur's information. This critical hurdle was overcome by the project's angel, the senior vice president. He announced that the firm would proceed on the basis of the intrapreneur's information. He added a critical qualifier: "I'll take the risk of any failures here."

Several interesting cases were found in which the angel was not a top manager, but a middle manager. In one of these cases, a middle manager kept the project concealed during its early stages. This was done so that it would not prematurely excite top management and trigger a massive funding that would not be appropriate or warranted at the embryonic stage of the idea. The company had a history of propelling innovations into the marketplace too quickly on the basis of top management over-interest.

Alert managers can help the intrapreneur by making sure that one or more angels are available, perhaps at several organizational levels. A combination of angels would seem to be the most potent formula. Middle managers often have both the funds and the physical resources to develop embryonic ideas in their most natural environments. They can play the role of midlevel angels. Top management has the total organizational perspective for handling the ideas once they have succeeded beyond the development stages. Top management angels can amass the total organizational resources, as well as resources that may be needed from outside the organization, such as new capital. However, it is important that these massive and powerful resources be saved for the time when the project is ready for them.

## Optimizing Organizational Location

Analyses of the data base indicated that there is no one optimum location within an organization for intrapreneurial activities. However, one effective rule of thumb may be to locate the activity at the lowest level consistent with the needs of the project, the license of the intrapreneur, and the demands of the organization. For example, a project that depends on the close collaboration of the marketing and research departments should report to the lowest level officer with the authority over both departments. Any higher level might place this project in unfair competition with others.

To illustrate this rule, consider the following case from one of the firms. The intrapreneur, a person from the firm's R&D department, was assigned to report to the firm's marketing vice president during one phase of the work. This turned out to be a very appropriate place for the project. By placing the project at this high level, the R&D person had a direct line to the potential customers. This was something he could not achieve from his R&D department home. Moreover, the R&D manager suspected that the marketing personnel were not devoting sufficient attention to this project. Under this reporting scheme, the R&D manager had his man in a position to observe and verify or refute his suspicions! As it turned out, the involvement of the R&D person helped the marketing personnel communicate with the prospective clients, encouraged the marketing personnel to become more interested in this project, and generally fostered an increased sense of teamwork. This story has a happy ending: the project became a blockbuster (see table 2-1 for a definition).

Placing a project at too high an organizational level can create many problems. In several cases in the data base, projects suffered from lack of attention because the offices to which they reported had other, more pressing projects. In some cases, communications with important lower levels became awkward when the projects were located too high in the organization. In still other cases, the lower level personnel found it very difficult to translate their technical details into words that were fully understood by the nontechnically trained top managers. The high level visibility afforded these projects was offset by the inability of the high level executives to provide technical leadership, and by the lack of morale that resulted.

The data base also suggests that as projects evolve and mature it is important to relocate them carefully. Abrupt transfers were seldom effective. Personnel who will inherit the project should be used as consultants and liaison persons early in the life of the project (see chapter 13 for more details). When this was done, the eventual success and implementation of the project's outputs was considerably enhanced.

### Promoting Bounded Autonomy

How much autonomy does the successful intrapreneur need? No simple answer was found to this important question.

One approach is to provide the intrapreneur with enough autonomy, authority, and financial discretion to perform the first phase of the project. If that appears to be successful, and the next phase of the project also has a high probability of success, then the intrapreneur's autonomy can be gradually extended. The license for each subsequent phase can be decided in this same fashion, at the completion of the immediately preceding phase. Unfortunately, this piecemeal approach is often precisely what the intrapreneur does not want. He often feels that such a tight rein signals management's lack of trust. How can this dilemma be resolved?

The answer is perhaps contained in one of the cases in the data base. Recognizing the potency of budget discretion as a symbol, the intrapreneur was given a two-part budget. One part was for the main work on the project. The other was for "emergencies". The intrapreneur was permitted to define emergencies in any way he wanted. But once his emergency budget was used up, no more emergency monies were available. This simple solution permitted the intrapreneur to have some bounded latitude for making discretionary budget decisions. This does not meet the intrapreneur's desire for complete control, nor does it completely meet management's same need. But it may be an effective compromise for both parties.

Another approach used by one of the firms in the data base also has many attractive facets. In this approach, the intrapreneur was given several angels, scattered throughout the organization. Each angel was a source of funds, resources, or solutions to different types of problems. For instance, one angel stood ready to provide equipment if it was needed by the intrapreneur. Another angel was prepared to provide manpower. Still another angel was a source of political power. The intrapreneur also was permitted to combine the angels in various ways. If he needed resources beyond those provided by the equipment angel, he could appeal to his management through both his equipment angel and his political angel. This system had other advantages.

It brought the intrapreneur in contact with several top-level officers and helped him to build many valuable future alliances. And it encouraged the intrapreneur to develop important negotiation and communication skills. This particular intrapreneur matured into a very potent contributor for the firm as a result of these experiences.

## Summary

This chapter has shown how project climates relate to new product innovation success and failure. Project climates that were characterized by role uncertainty, lack of management involvement, restricted communications, and lack of openness and trust were associated with high degrees of project failure. Four factors were found that led to these deleterious project climates. They were: lack of technical competency among the management personnel, poor interpersonal skills among the management personnel, lack of decisiveness and direction from management, autocratic decision processes.

Three things were suggested to avoid such deleterious project climates. First, the managers responsible for the project should be chosen for their technical abilities. Projects should not report to managers who do not have a detailed understanding and appreciation for the jargon and the daily technical details. An ideal situation exists when both the first and second level managers over the project have previous careers in the project area. Second, openness, participativeness, and decisiveness should characterize the interpersonal styles of the managers who are responsible for the project. Interpersonal style is as important as technical competency in selecting a suitable organization location for the project to report. Third, good strategic planning and directing are essential. The first and second level managers who are responsible for the project must have a clear picture of where the project is going, what the new product should look like and why. Any uncertainty in these regards will soon be sensed by the project personnel, resulting in their diminished enthusiasm and emotional commitments.

Total organization climates were also found to relate to project success and failure. Total organization climates provide the background for the project climates. The most favorable total organization climates were those where innovation was an explicit company-wide goal reached by consensus, where decisions and budgetary control were highly decentralized, and where no one department dominated the strategic decisions and resource allocations.

Based on the data base, seven specific recommendations can be made for encouraging internal entrepreneurs, or intrapreneurs, within organizations. These seven are: early identification of intrapreneurs, development of complementary role-functions, establishment of formal licenses, encouragement of an underground, fostering angels, optimizing the organizational location of the entrepreneur and promoting bounded autonomy. Those firms in the data base that followed these recommendations were the most successful innovators.

## Notes

1. Copies of the instruments used here, numbers 2-1 through 5-1, are available from the author.

2. I am indebted to R. W. Avery for suggesting the concept of a license.

# 8
# Picking Winners

> As the births of living creatures at first are ill-shapen, so are all innovations, which are the births of time.
>
> —Francis Bacon, 1625

Success in new product development would seem to begin with the choice of the best projects. The dilemma is how to consistently pick winners. Do firms with high new product success rates approach project selection differently than less successful firms? Are they "smarter" about selecting projects? As this chapter shows, the most successful firms are not necessarily smarter. But they do indeed have unique approaches to project selection. And this seems to give them an edge in selecting better projects.

## Five Approaches to Project Selection

Five basic approaches to project selection were encountered in the data base. As shown in table 8-1, these five approaches were: committee, campaign, system, proactive, and reactive.

In the committee approach, project ideas are continuously proposed through a series of standing committees and task forces. Considerable inter-firm variations were encountered in the way the committees were organized, the number of committees and their formality. The essence of the committee approach was the emphasis on collectives of individuals across several levels and departments within the organization to assemble, review, evaluate, and judge candidates and select the best ones.

In the campaign approach, there is an annual campaign or solicitation for project ideas. Many variations were found in the solicitation procedures. In some cases the solicitation was part of the annual budget exercises. In other cases, annual off-site meetings were held to develop lists of candidates. In still other cases, annual suggestion programs were used. The collected ideas are then discussed in a series of top management meetings. Additional project ideas and proposals may arise from these meetings, the lists may be trimmed and modified, some proposals may be eliminated and some proposals may be replaced by new ideas. Through these discussions, the choice of the best projects emerges.

**Table 8–1**
**Approaches to Project Selection**

| | Sources of Project Proposals | |
|---|---|---|
| Frequency of Activity | Single Source[a] | Multiple Sources[b] |
| Continuous | Proactive | System, Committee |
| Discontinuous | Reactive | Campaign |

[a]One department, group, or person within the organization has the major responsibility for generating project proposals.
[b]Several departments, groups, or persons within the organization have the major responsibility for generating project proposals.

In the systems approach, project selection is viewed as only one component in a total system of activities. This system consists of business planning, budgeting, idea generation, project selection, project funding, and project control. As might be expected, considerable variation was found in the rigidity and types of planning processes used. In some cases, a rigid management-by-objectives (MBO) approach was followed. In other cases, the strategic plan was the basis for the technology objectives which gave birth to the project ideas. However, all the variations were characterized by the existence of a hierarchy of plans that guided the generation of project ideas and the selection of the best ones. Moreover, in all the systems approaches, projects were suggested from a variety of sources all year long. Whenever an ongoing project is completed, funds are freed for a new project to replace it. The queue of project ideas is thus always kept full. A backlog of ideas is quite naturally maintained because personnel know that there will come a time when their ideas can be funded. The selection of specific project ideas is often made on the basis of several project selection models and criteria that constitute a total system of decision-making aids.

In the proactive approach, one person or some group of persons is formally responsible for the generation of new project ideas and proposals. At some firms, the creative scientists were depended on as a major source of project ideas. In others, the marketing department was the major source. In still other firms, a new products department was expected to generate the bulk of the project proposals. In the proactive approach, project ideas are screened and selected by top management.

In the reactive approach, the organization waits, remains ready and reacts as quickly as possible. In this approach, the generation of project ideas and the selection of the best one are combined. Each threat or opportunity that arises is immediately worked on. Selection problems only arise when more opportunities or threats exist than can be worked on due to limited resources. In general, whatever most seriously threatens the near term profits is the highest priority. The choice of which idea to work on is often made by the persons or departments that are the most affected. For example, if the threat is to an existing product, then the sales department influences the choice. If the threat is production cost, then the decision may largely be dominated by the production personnel.

Many combinations of the five approaches were encountered in the data base. The most prevalent were combinations of the systems and committee, systems and campaign, and committee and proactive approaches. The classification of particular approaches into the five basic types was made on the basis of their most prominent characteristics.

## A Discourse on Project Selection

Every approach to project selection may be considered to consist of two aspects: idea flow and idea judging. Idea flow includes idea stimulation and submittal, idea documentation, idea handling, and idea screening. These activities are conducted to acquire and prepare the candidate projects. Judging includes the analyses and decision procedures used to select the best candidates.

The above five approaches used very different idea flow and idea judging processes. Before examining these differences in the next section of this chapter, it is important to understand the nature of idea flow and idea judging. Following is a short discourse on this.[1]

### Idea Flow

Idea generation sessions and generation group meetings have become popular within the past few years. Formal groups or teams are often assembled for brainstorming, big dream, Synectics, or other creativity exercises to generate project ideas. A wide variety of environmental scanning, competitive intelligence, technical forecasting, and technology assessment techniques have also come into popular use for identifying emerging new technologies and collecting ideas from outside the firm. The viability of these approaches often depends on the composition of the teams and the ways in which the teams are managed.[1,2]

However, the major obstacles to idea flow usually do not involve encouraging personnel to collect or generate ideas. Rather, convincing the personnel to let go of their ideas is often the real challenge. Two typical fears that keep personnel from submitting ideas include the fear that their ideas will not be fairly judged, and the fear that their ideas will be considered inferior and this will reflect badly on them. There are also fears that no one will take appropriate action on their idea, it will languish, and they will not receive the proper credit.

Proper idea documentation and handling are therefore very important. Every project idea must be correctly described, communicated, and recorded in order to accurately preserve its details. This is no trivial matter. Ideas often arrive in various states of undress. Idea documentation usually involves working with the submitter to develop the idea and provide more complete documentation or descriptions. It is not unusual for good ideas to be declared useless because their documentation was poor and they were misunderstood. This costs the firm much more than the loss of one good idea; it also costs the firm one very disillusioned idea submitter. As a consequence, the flow of future ideas from this person may be severely constrained.

Because the ideas that are initially collected in any system are usually of varying quality, some initial screening is warranted before the final selection of the best candidate is undertaken. Screening serves three purposes. First, it sorts out the most relevant ideas, thus economizing on the decision making efforts. Second, it familiarizes the judges with the candidates. Third, screening can provide important opportunities for the submitters to present and defend their proposals to the judges. The ensuing discussions and interactions can provide many opportunities for communication. The submitters can communicate their ideas, and the screeners can broadcast their selection criteria. The open discussions may lead to new ideas that both the submitters and the screeners favor.

### Idea Judging

Once the candidates that survive the screening exercises are assembled, the task of deciding which are best can begin. This judging can be done by one individual, several individuals, a group or a staff. Because groups take advantage of collective wisdom and thought processes, they may be superior to one individual.

The decision process itself may take many forms. Scoring models, economic index models, cost/benefit methods, mathematical programming models, discounted cash flow techniques, and other formal mathematical models may be used. Structured and unstructured discussions may be used, and the idea submitters may be requested to respond to various questions. The proposals may be judged by a panel and a consensus vote may be sought. Or the process may be much less formal, with no actual voting and a group sense of agreement being sought. Decision making processes usually closely reflect the decision making style of the firm's officers. Thus, considerable firm to firm variation can exist.[1]

## Idea Flow Characteristics of the Five Approaches

Each of the five approaches listed in table 8-1 used quite different idea flow subprocesses. These differences are summarized in table 8-2.

### Committee Approach

In the committee approach, every department was chartered with the responsibility for generating project ideas, and each viewed idea generation as a normal part of their daily work. Thus, the responsibility for generating ideas was highly decentralized among numerous departments and several individuals. The committee members were often sought for advice and counsel by the individual idea submitters. There was an unwritten but well-understood rule that key committee members should review all important new ideas before they were formally submitted.

The techniques used to stimulate project ideas within the committee approaches were many and varied. Gap analyses methods were commonly in use. In these methods, ad hoc teams of interdisciplinary personnel were assembled to examine current product performances and determine their shortfalls. Technology forecasting techniques were also in common use by various ad hoc teams, and ideas for projects or programs were often based on their results.[1] These techniques were all oriented to the identification of problems, opportunities, and gaps as a basis for proposing new product projects. At some firms, extensive efforts were placed on environmental monitoring, environmental scanning, and competitive analyses as bases for suggesting new projects.[1] Ad hoc idea generation groups were commonly used, and brainstorming or Synectics techniques were also in common use.

**Table 8–2**
**Characteristic Idea Flow Subprocesses Used**

| | Idea Flow Subprocesses | | |
|---|---|---|---|
| Approaches | Idea Generation | Idea Handling | Idea Screening |
| Committee | 1 | 1 | 1 |
| Campaign | 1 | 0 | 1 |
| Systems | 1 | 1 | 1 |
| Proactive | 1 | + | 1 |
| Reactive | 0 | 0 | + |

*Key:* 1 = These aspects were highly formalized
 + = These aspects were sometimes formalized
 0 = These aspects were not highly formalized

In addition to these methods for the inside-the-firm generation of ideas, the committee approach also had very active and well-defined procedures for utilizing external idea sources. These approaches included the use of commercial idea banks and consultants. Standing or ad hoc committees often interfaced with trade groups and professional associations, and many ideas came from these sources. One firm had a very sophisticated network of external contacts that they continuously used to give them a running picture of their environment, as a basis for suggesting new product ideas. They carefully briefed their employees to observe various items at technical conferences and off-site locations. Sometimes these procedures resulted in a surprisingly accurate mosaic of information about emerging technologies and competitive behaviors.

The committee approach had the most sophisticated and well-developed procedures for idea handling. Ideas were systematically cataloged to ensure that they did not simply vanish within the organization. The idea originator's and submitter's names were recorded and preserved along with the documentation of the idea. Periodic progress reports were made to the idea submitters, showing the disposition of each idea to date and the progress that was being made on it. Several firms defended their large investments in idea handling in terms of the high payoffs that could be obtained if only one idea became a big success. The investment was also defended in terms of its perceived impact on employee morale and the continued flow of high quality ideas.

Idea screening was very detailed within the committee approach. Ideas were first screened by a crude or coarse screen to filter out the obviously irrelevant or low priority ideas. Surviving ideas were then screened with a more detailed set of criteria and a more precise set of rating scales. This process was repeated until the queue of ideas had reached a small enough number to be handled in a decision-making setting.

## The Systems Approach

The systems approach used many of the same idea flow techniques and methods as the committee approach. The major differences were in the formality of the methods and their integration with the formal planning processes that characterized the systems approach.

In the systems approach, the responsibility for generating ideas was usually left to the individual. Suggestion committees were seldom used. The generation of project ideas was more a part of the overall planning system. Ideas were submitted as part of the MBO (management by objectives) documents or some other planning report. Unlike the committee approach, project ideas in isolation seldom existed. Ideas were codified and closely connected with objectives, goals, plans and mission statements. However, like the committee approach, project ideas could arise from any source and were in fact expected to arise throughout the organization.

Like the committee approach, external ideas were sought and environmental scanning techniques were used. Informal networks and contacts were emphasized. But formal planning techniques were also in use. For example, the committee approach would assemble ad hoc task forces to study a rumor that competitors were constructing a new production facility. The systems approach would also assemble a task force, but it would be a part of some staff planning group.

Like the committee approach, project ideas were also tracked carefully within the systems approach. However, this tracking was not focused on the ideas themselves; ideas were tracked as part of the planning process. This tended to emphasize the purpose and rationale for the existence of the idea. Thus, there was a kind of idea screening implicit in this process. Idea submitters were expected to submit only ideas that met the established criteria, thereby affording the idea a good chance of being accepted. By contrast, the criteria were much more nebulous and open to interpretation in the committee approach.

### The Campaign Approach

In the campaign approach, the emphasis was on getting project ideas for a particular need, an annual budget, or an annual wellspring. Consequently, the personnel were free to use whatever methods they desired. Moreover, the sources of the project ideas, and whether they came from outside or inside the firm, were of little concern. In some cases departments or persons were appointed to assist personnel in generating ideas. In other cases, consultants were employed to instruct the personnel in the use of various techniques. But more often, the organization simply issued a campaign for ideas without any further instructions on how the ideas were to be generated. This is not to say that criteria were not supplied. In all the campaign approaches, ideas were requested to meet certain stated requirements. Some requirements were rather specific: ideas to solve a particular customer problem or ideas for a product that would meet a list of performance requirements. Thus, the campaign approach was often used where there was a specific need for a particular type of new product idea.

Campaigns were often used within R&D departments or the technical functions within the firm. Moreover, campaigns were often designed when management felt the idea queue was running low. Thus, campaigns did not necessarily occur every year.

The procedures for utilizing the collected ideas from a campaign were seldom well prescribed. Those firms that used the campaign approach did not usually have well-developed procedures for the coding, storage, handling, and disposition of the collected ideas. Screening methods were also seldom highly developed in the campaign approach. Even though some campaigns appeared to be directed at a specific need or end application, most of the screening processes were very heuristic in nature. Screening meetings were characterized by unstructured discussions of each candidate, with a consensus sometimes emerging from these discussions and sometimes not.

## The Proactive Approach

In this approach, one or more departments were charged with the responsibility for generating project ideas. In some cases, this was the R&D department. In other cases, it was the marketing or new products department. In still other cases, the long-range planning and R&D departments were jointly responsible. In most cases, these departments were truly proactive: they aggressively sought new ideas from within the organization and from outside the firm. In a typical proactive approach, one or more persons were formally designated to engage in prospecting, scanning or searching activities related to ideas for new businesses. These persons were often located in R&D, corporate planning, and new product departments.

The proactive approach used many of the same techniques as the systems approach, such as gap analyses, technological forecasting, and creativity techniques.[1,2] However, the proactive approach generally did not have the degree of sophistication that characterized the systems approach. The activities were not so explicitly dovetailed with the organizational goals, objectives, and planning processes.

In the proactive approach, the idea handling procedures were nonstandard. Every firm did it a little differently. In some cases, generated ideas were held in a queue for later processing. In other cases, the ideas were processed as they were generated. In still other cases, the firms were proactive only for a specific purpose at a specific time, i.e., to find a new product idea in a narrow technical specialty. In some cases, the idea handling processes were truly haphazard. Collected ideas sometimes became lost or simply were shelved for later action. These later actions sometimes never occurred because the organization became involved in a higher priority prospecting operation and literally forgot about the previous one.

Idea screening was also highly variable under the proactive approach. Some firms had elaborate screening protocols comparable to those used in the systems approach. Others did not. In some cases, the search was so specific that as soon as the first acceptable idea was found it was immediately selected. Work was started on it and further searching was abandoned.

## The Reactive Approach

In the reactive approach, crises or unexpected events caused the organization to mobilize its idea generation and new product initiation activities. The most prevalent cause was the advent of a new product or a new technology by a competitor. Because firms that exclusively used a reactive approach did not have sophisticated environmental scanning or competitive intelligence systems, it was not uncommon for them to be totally surprised when a new threat arose. Panic reactions sometimes then set in as the organization rapidly mobilized to counter the threat.

Different departments or persons sometimes brought the threat to the attention of the organization. In some cases, it was the R&D department that called the threat to the attention of the rest of the organization. In other cases, it was the marketing department. In still other cases, top management sensed the threat and reacted to it. In some cases, the threats were sensed quite late in their occurrence.

Why would any organization be reactive? Why would they wait and let competition or technologies overtake them? There are several good answers. Some organizations saw themselves as the only viable supplier—precisely the role they had enjoyed for many long years. Other organizations were truly surprised by the advent of unexpected new technologies. In a few cases it simply never occurred to management that a traumatic event might disrupt the status quo. Some organizations intentionally waited for market or technical uncertainties to clarify themselves—and waited too long. In other cases, the reactive posture was a conscious part of a low-risk, follower strategy. As noted later in this chapter, this was generally a poor strategy for new product innovations.

As one might expect, the reactive approach used varying idea flow methods. One firm virtually stopped work and assigned all its personnel to full-time idea generation jobs for one week in response to the advent of a new product by a close competitor. Other firms appointed task forces in response to their threats. In still other cases, the firms assigned designated persons to a short-term think tank. A popular approach was to assign the most affected party to devise a defensive strategy. For example, if the threat was a radical new technology, R&D was assigned to respond. If the threat came from innovative new market strategies, the marketing department was assigned to respond.

Idea screening was also highly variable within reactive approaches. However, no cases were found where the organization had systematic screening processes comparable to the committee and systems approaches. Typically, screening was spontaneous and extemporaneous. The organization usually simply searched until a suitable first response to the threat was found. As one participant-observer vividly described it: "We sort of muddled around and discussed the situation without any agenda, until somebody suggested an idea that we all felt pretty warm about. And that was the idea that we picked up and ran with."

## Idea Judging Characteristics of the Five Approaches

Table 8-3 summarizes the types of idea judging decision processes used by the five approaches. As noted in the table, under the committee approach, the committee members collectively made most of the decisions about which project ideas to select. Management guided these decisions and made sure that they conformed to the established budget guidelines, but the committees were largely responsible for the ultimate decisions. The committees sometimes requested analyses from the staff personnel within their organizations or asked them to collect some needed data on various projects. In some cases, staff personnel were asked to make various recommendations. In a few cases, top management asked their staff to recommend or make a decision on some unresolved issue that the committees could not complete.

In the campaign and proactive approaches, the line managers or teams of managers often made the decisions on which project ideas were to be pursued and how much was to be spent on each of them. Sometimes, the line managers sought inputs from personnel at the lower levels of the organization. Staffs of creative scientists were sometimes called on to carry out some of the screening. But in all of the campaign and proactive approaches, the ultimate decisions about which project ideas to select and how much to spend on them were made by the line managers.

**Table 8–3**
**Decision Processes Used for Judging Ideas**

| | Types of Decision Processes | | |
| --- | --- | --- | --- |
| *Approaches* | *Individual* | *Staff* | *Group* |
| Committee | 0 | + | 1 |
| Campaign | 0 | 1 | + |
| Systems | + | 1 | 1 |
| Proactive | + | 1 | + |
| Reactive | 1 | + | 0 |

*Key:* 1 = This type was often used.
    + = This type was sometimes used.
    0 = This type was seldom used.

In the systems approach, a combination of staff and decentralized group decision making was used. Individuals at all levels made some decisions about the types of project ideas they would submit, based on well-publicized criteria and organizational goals. As one respondent noted: "If you properly communicate the company's goals to the people at the bench, then a lot of the whole project selection thing takes care of itself. You can count on getting relevant ideas that respond to the published goals." Ad hoc groups were often used to evaluate the ideas and make recommendations. Various levels of management also reviewed the ideas and discussed them with the submitters. This was usually a part of the goal setting and milestone reviews.

This was in vivid contrast to the reactive approach, where one person often made all the project selection decisions. Sometimes, various levels of management were consulted and other levels of personnel were asked for information or opinions. But the final decision was usually made by the highest level manager concerned with the types of projects being considered.

Thus, in the committee and systems approaches the criteria for distinguishing good project ideas from bad ones were very explicit. The decision processes were very open, many opinions were generally sought, and they were seriously considered. The decision processes involved the collective wisdom of all the interested parties, and the final decisions about which project ideas to select or reject were arrived at very democratically. It was relatively easy to track these processes and record the decisions that were made at each stage. It was clear how the decisions were made and why particular project ideas were rejected and others were accepted.

The reactive and proactive decision processes were much less visible. It was difficult to document them and to measure how and why they traveled their various courses. Many decisions were made by one or two persons in isolation of the project proposer or other concerned parties. Curiously, many of the personnel who experienced these systems did not complain greatly about them. Consistent with this, the reactive and proactive approaches did not generate the kind of enthusiasm that was typical of personnel who worked under the systems and committee approaches. Under the systems and committee approaches, the personnel appeared to be enthusiastic about project selection. They generally worked hard to generate many good ideas and to document them extensively, and they openly expressed many opinions about their project ideas.

The decision processes used in the campaign approach were somewhere in between the extremes of the systems and committee approaches, and the reactive and proactive approaches. There was some openness and some enthusiasm. But the fact that it was a periodic campaign seemed to diminish any lingering enthusiasm once the campaign was over. The decision makers openly discussed some ideas and proposals. But since the ideas were often responses to a specific solicitation, there was sometimes little to discuss. The ideas either met the criteria or they did not. In cases where only one project idea was to be chosen from among several submittals, managers were often able to make that selection on the basis of their interpretation of how well the established criteria were met.

## The Use of Formal Decision Models

A large number and variety of formal mathematical models have been developed in the literature as project selection aids. There have always been questions about the utility of these models. Surveys have consistently reported very low usage. Though there are some noteworthy exceptions, evidence indicates that these models are not widely used.

Thus, it was somewhat surprising that many firms in the data base made considerable use of some of these models. Table 8-4 summarizes the utilization patterns found.

### Checklists

Table 8-5 illustrates the types of checklists found to be in use. The campaign and proactive approaches were the primary users of checklists. This is consistent with their need for some way to rapidly and inexpensively screen the large volumes of ideas often generated by these approaches. Checklists are admirably suited to this task.

The committee and systems approaches sometimes used checklists, but for a different purpose than the campaign and proactive approaches. Their

**Table 8–4**
**Decision Models Used for Formal Project Selection**

| | Types of Project Selection Models | | | |
|---|---|---|---|---|
| *Approaches* | *Checklists* | *Scoring Models* | *Prioritizing Models* | *Portfolio Models* |
| Committee | + | 1 | 1 | 0 |
| Campaign | 1 | + | 0 | 0 |
| Systems | + | 0 | 1 | + |
| Proactive | 1 | + | + | 0 |
| Reactive | + | 0 | 0 | 0 |

*Key:* 1 = This type was often used.
+ = This type was sometimes used.
0 = This type was seldom used.

Table 8–5
**Example of a Checklist for Proposed Project X[a]**

| | Ratings | | |
|---|---|---|---|
| *Dimensions* | *Good* | *Acceptable* | *Poor* |
| Capital Requirements | | | ✓ |
| Return on Investment | | | ✓ |
| New Equipment Costs | | | ✓ |
| Availability of Personnel | ✓ | | |
| Quality of Personnel Needed | ✓ | | |
| Patent Likelihood | ✓ | | |
| Technical Success Likelihood | ✓ | | |
| Commercial Success Likelihood | ✓ | | |
| Competitive Advantage | | ✓ | |
| Market Penetration | | | ✓ |
| Profitability | | ✓ | |

*Conclusions:* Project passes this initial screening because of good success potentials, high patentability, and low personnel requirements. More detailed analyses are needed to confirm suspected high capital costs and narrow market potentials.

[a]For more examples and discussions of these types of models see William E. Souder, *Management Decision Methods for Managers of Engineering and Research,* (New York: Van Nostrand Reinhold, 1980) and William E. Souder, *Project Selection and Economic Appraisal* (New York: Van Nostrand Reinhold, 1984).

applications were more ad hoc. For instance, they were often used to introduce some rigor into the discussions and deliberations on some project ideas or to make distinctions between project ideas that were difficult to judge informally. More often, the committee and systems approaches used the more sophisticated scoring, prioritizing, and portfolio models.

*Scoring Models*

Table 8-6 presents an example of a scoring model that was found in use at one firm. Note that only the committee approach made extensive use of scoring models (table 8-4). Scoring models often helped the committee members in their recommendations. The committees generally had adequate manpower to collect the detailed information required to use scoring models. Thus, the detailed data demanded by scoring models was not a deterrent, and

**Table 8–6**
**Example of a Scoring Model for Proposed Projects Y and Z**

| Criteria = | Profit Potential | Patent Potential | Chances of Success | Weighted Score[b] |
|---|---|---|---|---|
| Weights = | 3 | 2 | 1 | |
| | | Criteria Scores[a] | | |
| Project Y | 5 | 10 | 10 | 45 |
| Project Z | 9 | 8 | 8 | 51 |

*Conclusion:* Reject project Y in favor of project Z. Project Y's unweighted score (25) is the same as project Z's, but its weighted score demonstrates the importance of its poor profit potentials.[c]

[a]Scale: 10 equals excellent, 1 equals unacceptable

[b]Weighted score $_i$ = $\sum_j$ (Criteria Score$_{ij}$ × Weight $_j$), for the $i^{th}$ project on the $j^{th}$ criterion

[c]For more examples and discussion of these types of models see William E. Souder, *Management Decision Methods for Managers of Engineering and Research* (New York: Van Nostrand Reinhold, 1980), pp. 137–62 and William E. Souder, *Project Selection and Economic Appraisal* (New York: Van Nostrand Reinhold, 1984), pp. 39–85.

the time and effort needed to construct and apply them was generally available.

*Prioritizing Models*

Table 8-7 presents an example of one prioritizing model that was found to be in use. In prioritizing models, each project is given a unique rank relative to all the others.

The committee and systems approaches were the primary users of prioritizing models (table 8-4). This was because these approaches were oriented to examining and analyzing lists of candidate ideas. However, the committee and systems approaches had very different motives for using prioritizing models. In the committee approach, it was perceived necessary to compare all the ideas and obtain a relative priority in order to demonstrate a thorough analysis. Moreover, the committees generally believed that even low priority ideas could catalyze other good ideas if they were explicitly analyzed. In addition, such analyses and documentations were perceived to be an effective way to demonstrate the types of ideas desired.

By contrast, in the systems approach the emphasis was on retaining every

## Table 8–7
## Example of a Prioritizing Model[a]

Project Priority, $P = (r \times d \times c) \times (E/A + M)/2$

where

$r$ = probability of research success on a scale from 0.0 to 1.0

$d$ = probability of development success on a scale from 0.0 to 1.0

$c$ = probability of commercial success on a scale from 0.0 to 1.0

$E$ = present value of all future expected net profits if the project succeeds

$M$ = technical merit rating or value for the project, on a scale from 0.0 to 1.0

$A$ = target maximum value for $E$ for projects of this nature

High Priority:     $1.0 \geqslant P \geqslant .70$
Medium Priority:   $.69 \geqslant P \geqslant .30$
Low Priority:      $.29 \geqslant P \geqslant .0$

[a]For more examples and discussion of these types of models see William E. Souder, *Management Decision Methods for Managers of Engineering and Research* (New York: Van Nostrand Reinhold, 1980), pp. 137–62 and William E. Souder, *Project Selection and Economic Appraisal* (New York: Van Nostrand Reinhold, 1984), pp. 39–85.

idea. It was felt that lower priority ideas might be shelved now but they might also be reactivated at a later point in time. It was noted by several firms that priorities change over time, and today's low priority ideas were often tomorrow's high priority projects. Priorities set at one level of the organization sometimes conflicted with priorities at other levels. In order to make these conflicts visible, it was necessary to have a complete list of prioritized projects to discuss.

### Portfolio Models

Portfolio models are the most sophisticated project selection aids. They involve mathematical programming and operations research methods. As table 8-4 shows, only the systems approach used portfolio models. Even then, the majority of the organizations studied here did not use anything this sophisticated.

It is interesting to note the way in which portfolio models were used by the systems approach. The models were not used to define portfolios or courses of action that should be implemented. Rather, they were used to explore alternatives, to conduct simulations, and to experiment on paper with various decisions and budget allocations before putting them into practice.

As one respondent noted: "It's a kind of learning experience. It helps clarify a lot of options. We sometimes discover options we never thought of by running the model. But we almost never do exactly what the model tells us to. After all, it's only a model."

## The Most Successful Approach to Project Selection

Not surprisingly, the reactive approach was not effective. None of the most innovative firms (chapter 6) used it. The reactive approach appears to be a lingering dinosaur. Being reactive is simply not sufficient to compete successfully in a dynamic world of aggressive innovators.

Which of the other four approaches yields the most successful new product innovations? Unfortunately, an intensive review of the data base did not result in any obvious answers to this question. It could not be said that either the proactive, campaign, committee or systems approaches were necessarily best. This is not surprising. Selecting the very best project does not guarantee success. The best project in one time period may not be the best project in the next time period. There are many uncertainties and unknown events that can derail even the best project during its life cycle.

However, there is one important question that can be answered: Which project selection approach is more appropriate under various circumstances? Does the culture of the organization, the nature of its new product development process, the nature of its organization structure or other factors have any bearing on which approach is better? Now we will turn our attention to these questions.

### Some Important Factors to Consider

In selecting an approach to project selection, two very important factors to consider are organization size and structure. If the organization is large and the structure is either type III or IV (see chapter 6), then either the committee or the systems approaches are suitable. In large, decentralized organizations, the systems and committee approaches may be the only suitable alternatives. Other approaches simply do not fit the nature of the organization. On the other hand, the committee approach may also be too cumbersome and unwieldy. The number of committees may exceed the ability of the managers to control them.

The effective use of the systems approach requires very sophisticated management. This approach assumes that the firm has a highly developed strategic planning system that is integrated with all the other planning activities throughout the firm. For the systems approach to be effective, the firm should have highly developed and routinely used MBO, project planning, operations planning, market planning, product planning, and forecasting systems.

The campaign approach is suitable for use along with any of the other approaches. An occasional campaign can sometimes liven up one's daily routines. But in order for the campaign approach to be effective, there must be a real need and this need must be fully communicated. Nothing is more frustrating to employees than to respond with an idea that seems to meet the requirements, only to be told that management did not like the idea. To be useful to the submitter, the response to each idea must be crystal clear. The submitter must know why his idea did not fit the requirements if he is expected to respond correctly to the next campaign.

The proactive approach is most suitable when management is highly specialized. Organizations that are run like the military, managements that are highly autocratic, firms that expect their professionals to behave like staff consultants—these are the firms that can best use the proactive approach.

## Some Contingencies

The systems and committee approaches produced more blockbusters (see table 2-1) than any of the other approaches. But it cannot be said that this is because the systems and committee approaches were used. It can, however, be said that these approaches were an important part of the contingent conditions that allowed the users to become the most innovative firms.

Many of the firms that used the systems approach also had type III and type IV organization structures (see chapter 6). Several of these firms had very well-developed strategic planning systems. They had promotive organization climates (see chapter 7). They had clear definitions of the user's requirements, high technical expertise in the project areas and relatively high quality resources. They did not have any projects that were flooded with funds, and they exercised good project control (see chapters 4 and 5). Most of their projects were of the strategic expansion category and most of their innovations arose internally. Both well-developed science and undeveloped science projects were undertaken by these firms. These firms successfully handled customers whose attitudes toward new products were variously eager, indifferent, and resistant (see chapter 5).

In effect, firms that used the systems approach were the "blue-chip innovators" of the new product arena. The project selection approaches they used were only a part of a contingent set of things that management did. Supporting their successes was a corporate culture, a company ethic and a depth of knowledge about their technologies and their customers. The firms that used other approaches to project selection either did not have refined planning systems, well-developed organizations, a command of their technologies, or an in-depth knowledge of customer wants comparable to the blue-chip new product innovators. For example, firms that used the committee approach often lacked the blue chip innovator's well-developed planning systems and promotive organization climates. In many cases, they seemed to be using the committees to overcome these inherent weaknesses in their organizations.

Thus, firms that used the campaign and proactive approaches were doing some things that were totally consistent with their outlook on life. They focused on excellence in one or two aspects, while the blue-chip innovator appeared to think in more conceptual, systems terms. The blue-chip innovator developed a balanced system of organizations, technologies, customer knowledge, plans, goals, and participative decision making. Thus, it may be said that the approach to project selection that one is likely to take will reflect one's outlook on life. But some outlooks are more effective than others.

*Selecting the Best Approach*

Figure 8-1 is a guideline to the choice of the most suitable project selection approach under various conditions. Note that the reactive approach is not one of the choices available in figure 8-1, since it was not deemed to be an acceptable approach.

The "decentralized innovator" in figure 8-1 is typically a multidivisional, decentralized firm. It may also be a consortium or a joint venture of several firms. In order for the parties to cooperate and collaborate on new innovations, it is necessary to have several standing committees or task forces.

The "centralized innovator" in figure 8-1 may be a relatively small firm or simply a firm in which top management dominates all major decisions. In these cases, the proactive approach to project selection is the only one consistent with the prevailing corporate style.

The "intermittent innovator" firm in figure 8-1 creates new product innovations periodically or intermittently. This case could occur where the users are reluctant to accept new things, where the industry grows slowly, where new products endure for long periods or where products become obsolete very slowly.

## Implementing Project Selection Processes

Too many firms have initiated project selection systems for the wrong reason: to create the ultimate device for decision making. Typically, the organization enthusiastically jumps into the use of project selection models to eliminate the subjectivity in decision making. This is a naive belief that can only lead to disappointment.

Project selection is basically an opinion-gathering process. It cannot be

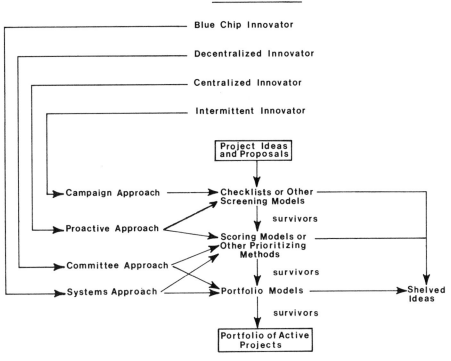

Figure 8–1. Guidelines for Choosing the Most Suitable Project Selection Methods

made significantly more objective. It will always be subjective. It can, however, be made more systematic. And that can bring many benefits. But these benefits are quite subtle, and they can easily be missed by an inattentive organization.

Figure 8-2 tracks the typical changes in the enthusiasm of an organization that seeks to develop or apply a project selection system. The organization typically begins with the pie-in-the-sky hope that a project selection system will make all their hard choices for them. As time goes by and they gain more experience with the system, it dawns on them that this is not happening. In fact things appear to be getting worse. They find themselves collecting elaborate information and some "data" to run the models that are pure guesswork, i.e., items like the probability of success of each project. What is more, there are suspicions that personnel have begun to inflate or deflate their numbers to achieve better scores on their pet projects. The data are so subjective that few other persons are able to seriously challenge the validity of submit-

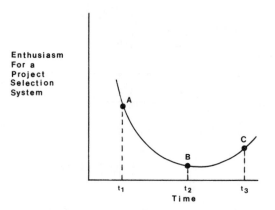

**Figure 8–2. Enthusiasm versus Time**

ters' numbers. The specter that the submitter will soon become the only one able to evaluate his project looms even larger each time the system is used. As a result, everyone soon becomes disillusioned. Their enthusiasm falls precipitously from point A to point B in figure 8-2. At this point, the organization hopelessly abandons the effort, swears never to get involved with any such thing again, and this bad experience is long remembered.

Yet a movement to point C in figure 8-2 is very possible. Point C represents a more realistic viewpoint of what a project selection system can and may be expected to do. It cannot select projects. But it can facilitate communication. It can induce the firm to keep better records. It can cause the firm to collect better data for decision making. Most important, it can provide a management decision laboratory for testing decisions and asking "what if" questions. It can do this *before* management implements policies that may have very long-reaching consequences. There is almost no other source of this kind of management laboratory. Project selection models do some very useful things. But these things sometimes are not what the organization originally thought it wanted. Point C in figure 8-2 represents a whole different set of accomplishments than point A. The key to using project selection processes is the recognition of this fact.

There is another important caveat to consider. It does not seem to matter so much what specific types of models are used. The process is more important. Any model that opens communication and moves the organization toward an honest and open discussion of its options and its strategic technical plans is an effective model. It meets the necessary, but not sufficient, conditions for getting to point C in figure 8-2. The sufficient conditions are: a willing and patient group of users who are able to put in the time to make it work. The time and devotion required to make a project selection process succeed are analogous to those required in any other new product development effort.

## Summary

This chapter has attempted to answer several questions about methods for selecting the best new product innovation projects. It was shown that there is no one best project selection approach. However, project selection was shown to be part of an important set of contingent factors that managers can specify. How they specify these contingencies can strongly affect new product innovation success rates.

Project selection is a very subjective information sharing and participative planning process. The most effective project selection processes take advantage of the collective wisdom of the entire organization. They achieve consensus on the basis of the best information and an open dialogue. If the project selection process is effective, personnel will remain committed to the selected projects throughout their duration. Management will provide the appropriate project resources in a timely fashion. And the completed projects will be enthusiastically accepted by the marketing and production personnel. Indeed, project selection is an important component of management's system for fostering and promoting innovation.

Thus, effective project selection processes involve open communication, since judging projects is ultimately a subjective process. Mathematical models and decision aids are only helpers to the process. They can help communication and thinking. But they cannot replace the need to develop personnel within the organization who are able to judge each other's efforts and understand each other's specialized areas. No employee should be permitted to fall into the trap of doing work that no one else can judge. To do so invites obsolescence of the employee, the work and the firm. It will result in an organization engaged in projects that only the suggester understands. At that point, the organization loses its entire reason for being: a mechanism for achieving synergism. The organization becomes powerless to guide its personnel, to distinguish good projects from bad projects, and to terminate wayward efforts. In effect, the inventor becomes his own worst enemy if he alone becomes the only one capable of judging his own work.

One might be inclined to think that organizational goals must be clearly defined before any useful project selection processes can be initiated. However, effective project selection processes can aid the organization in determining its goals and objectives. It is seldom possible to divine an all-encompassing set of goals and objectives and then to apply these in selecting the optimum set of projects. With each new project proposal, new goals or modified goals are often suggested. Like a pinball machine, ideas bounce off of each other and the stated goals, only to generate even better new ideas and new goals.[1]

Thus, the systems approach to project selection is indeed the ultimately "best" approach. But it may not be the immediately attainable approach for the type of organization, management style or other factors that characterize the firm at its current stage of development and growth. In the long term, any firm can strive to reach a level of maturity and sophistication where it can handle the systems approach to project selection. In the short run, there are several good alternatives: the committee, campaign, and proactive approaches. But they necessarily will not produce the potent results of the systems approach and its contingent conditions.

## Notes

1. For more details, see William E. Souder, *Management Decision Methods for Managers of Engineering and Research* (New York: Van Nostrand Reinhold, 1980); and William E. Souder, *Project Selection and Economic Appraisal* (New York: Van Nostrand Reinhold, 1984).
2. A good handbook on these methods is A. B. VanGundy, *Techniques of Structured Problem Solving* (New York: Van Nostrand Reinhold, 1981).

# 9

# Managing New Product Innovation Projects

Beware that you do not lose the substance by grasping at the shadow.

—Aesop, 550 B.C.

I s there one best way to manage new product projects? This chapter shows that there is no *one* best way. Rather, there are *several* good ways, depending on the nature of the technology and the nature of the markets for the new product.

## Methodology

One important dimension considered in selecting the 289 projects in the data base was the type of project management method used. Attempts were made to include about equal numbers of five different methods: top-down management methods, project manager methods, one-man shows, new enterprise departments, and teams. However, it was quickly recognized that there were many more methods than these five. Ultimately, the 10 methods listed in table 9-1 were encountered.[1]

Selecting the 289 projects in such a way as to obtain a balance of project outcomes across 10 management methods in a randomized design was not an easy task. As a result, small samples occurred in some breakouts of the data, as noted later in this chapter. However, the original objective of a balanced design was met surprisingly well. A total of 256 projects in the data base had sufficient data for the analyses in this chapter.

## Ten Project Management Methods

Table 9-1 shows the percentage of projects within each of the 10 methods that successfully met or exceeded their commercial expectations. Though these percentages may seem high for new product innovations, it must be

Table 9–1
**Percentage of Project Successes by Management Methods Used**

| Methods | Project Success Rates: Percentage of Projects That Met or Exceeded Their Commercial Expectations[a] |
|---|---|
| Top Down Structures | |
|    Commercial Line Management | 43 |
|    Technical Line Management | 25 |
| New Project Structures | |
|    New Products Department | 45 |
|    New Ventures Department | 33 |
| Project Management Methods | |
|    Commercial Project Manager | 73 |
|    Technical Project Manager | 32 |
| Taskforces and Teams | |
|    New Product Committees | 72 |
|    Dyads and Counterparts | 43 |
| One-Man Shows | |
|    Commercial One-Man Show | 27 |
|    Technical One-Man Show | 23 |
| Average of All Methods | 46 |

[a]Rounded to nearest whole percentage; see table 2-1. Sample sizes ranged from 23 to 28 projects in each of the 10 methods listed here.

kept in mind that these projects are the survivors of screening and project selection decisions conducted by the firms (see chapter 8).

As table 9-1 shows, the new product committees and commercial project manager methods had the highest project success rates. Some other methods that were expected to have above average rates did not, namely, new products departments and new ventures departments. Why? What factors account for these results?

## Top-Down Structures

### Commercial Line Management

In the commercial line management method, a top marketing person had the ultimate authority and responsibility for the entire life cycle of the project.

This person was usually the vice president of marketing or an equally high-ranking company officer. Projects were managed by the marketing line management structure. The line managers had the full responsibility and authority for planning, organizing, directing, and controlling the projects. As table 9-1 shows, the percentage success rate for this method was about the same as the average of all the methods.

The reasons for the relatively low success rate of this method reveal a great deal. Many of the products were technically deficient and the firm consequently "Took a Bath We Won't Forget" (table 2-1). These deficiencies were often traceable to communication problems with R&D. Attempts to go up the organizational chain of command and back down through the technical chain of command to bring R&D into the project were not very successful. The long chains of command, the involvement of so many parties, and the long waiting times for decisions often distorted the information flows. For example, there were several cases where the user's specifications were constantly changing throughout the life of the project. The time lags in information were so long that the latest changes reached the lower organizational levels at about the same time as the previous changes, thus causing considerable confusion.

It is noteworthy that in all the commercial line management projects that met their expectations, few technical inputs were needed. Cases were found where R&D in fact preferred not to be involved: the technical details were perceived to be too simple. In some other cases, the marketing departments included personnel who were sufficiently technically competent to guide the technical aspects. Thus, the commercial line management method appeared to be effective only where few technical inputs were needed.

### Technical Line Management

In this approach, R&D generated the project idea, defined the project and managed it throughout its entire life cycle. As the statistics in table 9-1 testify, this approach exhibited low project success rates.

Some of the technical line management projects were completed but their outputs were shelved because there was no mechanism available for proceeding further. In some cases, marketing personnel responded to the completed project with indifference. In several cases, the marketing department could not foresee any market for such a product, did not understand how the product fit into the existing line, and did not understand how the product could help the customer. In other cases, the product did not appear to perform as well as others on the market and marketing therefore saw no reason to invest in a full-scale trial.

Some of the technical line management projects were never completed because essential information was lacking. This included the following information: the precise performance specifications needed by the customer, the optimum trade-off design between cost and performance and the design features most useful to the customer. In several cases, laboratory personnel attempted to meet with customers to collect such data. Though they succeeded in some instances, they were generally unable to communicate effectively with the customer or otherwise gain the needed information. Even when armed with a final product and the necessary information, it was seldom feasible for R&D to directly market their completed projects.

## New Products Structures

### New Products Departments

In the new products department method, a single department that is separate from both the R&D and marketing functions was responsible for the idea from its inception until its establishment in the marketplace. Though many variations were encountered, all the new products departments reported to either top divisional or top corporate management. As the statistics in table 9-1 show, the new products department method was about an average performer.

Several differences were noted between those projects that successfully met or exceeded their expectations and those that did not. In all the successful projects, the personnel were technically qualified. They all held engineering or science degrees and all had spent some portions of their careers in R&D. By contrast, in many of the unsuccessful projects, the personnel did not have technical degrees and had not spent any time working in a technical function. In most of the successful projects, the new products department personnel had developed a network of company-wide interpersonal contacts that spanned the entire firm and transcended the departmental boundaries. Many members of this network considered themselves to be in-house radicals who could bring about great change. They occupied a position of high power status in the eyes of their R&D and marketing peers, and they were often sought for their experience and opinions. Moreover, in the successful projects, the new products department personnel, marketing personnel, and R&D personnel frequently visited customers as a three-party team.

On the other hand, considerable conflict often developed between the new products department personnel and the sales personnel. The new products department personnel were often placed in the awkward position of promoting something that would replace the existing products. New products department personnel were therefore viewed by the sales staff as adversaries.

These experiences suggest several things that management can do to make new products departments more effective. New products departments should be staffed with personnel who have a track record of success in R&D, and who have earned the respect and regard of their peers. Department members must be familiar with the end markets, appreciate the customer's needs, and understand the customer's way of operating. Management must be willing to live with some revolutionaries and some underground activities. New products departments naturally engender conflicts and hostilities that top management must be prepared to handle. Conflict resolution becomes a major job for an organization with a new products department. Moreover, management must endow the new products department with status by showing approval for jobs well done. Of course, this can pose very hard choices for management when their sales department becomes upset over the perceived loss of status. Staffing the new products department with long-term company employees who have earned the regard of both the R&D and sales personnel can lessen the frequency of such conflicts and reduce the need for management to make these hard choices.

### New Ventures Departments

As the data in table 9-1 show, new ventures departments did not perform especially well. Only about one-third of their projects met or exceeded their expectations. This is a surprising result. Conventional wisdom and empirical evidence suggest that new ventures departments are highly effective for creating successful innovations. How can this surprising result be explained?

The answer is that nearly all of the new ventures departments studied here suffered from the too-small/too-big dilemma. Their projects were either too small or too big. When the project is too small, it does not command the appropriate management attention. Moreover, divisional managers often reason that a small project can easily be handled within their own organizations. Thus, when the new ventures managers invested in relatively safe, small projects that minimized their technical risks and maximized their box score of success, it was perceived by the other managers as an infringement into their proper domain. It became difficult for top management, even if they deeply believed in this strategy, to override the other managers objections when allocating budgets and resources.

In the too-big case, the new venture projects are viewed by management as too risky, too large, and too uncertain. Typically, projects that are labeled too-big involve radical departures from the firm's basic technologies or are perceived as pushing the firm into unknown areas. It is interesting that risk taking is the usual reason given by management for having a new ventures department. Yet, when actually faced with the prospect of funding such efforts, many of the managers in this study were unwilling to accept them. When this happened, the venture managers retreated to safer projects, which brought them into criticism for taking a too-safe approach!

Thus, it appears that new venture organizations are self-contradictory. One top manager described the situation as follows. "It is difficult to sit still and watch negative cash flows year after year, never knowing when your innovation will pay off. Most new ventures fail anyway. So, how can you justify a crap shoot like that to your shareholders when your current products and operations have immediate needs? It is an impossible dilemma. I would like to see the new venture idea work, but I don't see how it can."

Alert readers may sense that these results contradict those in chapters 6 and 8, where new venture/type IV and systems organizations were found to be the most effective. However, the results in chapters 6 and 8 are not strictly comparable. For example, the type IV organization structure discussed in chapter 6 *combined* new venture, project management, and other highly effective methods discussed below. Here, the effectiveness of the methods are analyzed *independent* of each other. The effects of combinations of methods is discussed in the last section of this chapter.

## Project Management

### Commercial Project Manager

In this method, a formal project manager was appointed from the marketing department. He was given a budget for the entire project and he became the top-level manager for the duration of that project. Project members were drawn from several departments, returning to their home departments after the completion of the project. In all the successful cases studied here, the commercial project manager had been either a brand manager, a product manager, an area manager or a product planner.

As the statistics in table 9-1 show, the commercial project manager method gave the highest project success rates. Why? Is it because the marketing department is the best equipped department to manage new product innovations?

On the contrary, it wasn't so much that the marketing department was the most able department. Rather, it seemed that when the project manager came from the marketing department, all the "right" things happened. For example, in those projects that met or exceeded their expectations, top management was involved in the selection and legitimization of the commercial project manager. One company canonized the project manager in a letter from the president to every concerned person in the company. The tone of the letter made it undeniably clear that this was a vitally important project and everyone was expected to cooperate in its timely completion. At another firm, the top management introduced the project manager at a mass meeting in which the project was fully explained to everyone in great detail.

In the most successful projects ("Blockbuster," see table 2-1), the project managers were well acquainted with the end markets and the customers. They were familiar with the technology, technically competent, and well-known to the R&D personnel who worked on the project. The project managers were tough-minded persons who maintained tight budgetary control, demanded hard work and attention to detail from their staffs, and expected superior performance from their personnel. Even so, there was a definite participative ambience about the projects. Personnel at all levels often made presentations, attended high-level meetings and contributed to the decision-making. For example, it was not uncommon for technicians to visit customer facilities. Interestingly, these most successful commercial project managers were often viewed by their personnel as "a fellow who spreads the credit around," "firm but fair," "a person who works you hard but gives you a feeling of achievement," and "a real team player."

Surprisingly, there were frequent eruptions of conflict within the most successful projects. However, these conflicts were brought out and openly resolved. The conflicting parties were assembled by the project manager and the issues were openly discussed (sometimes heatedly). No conflict was permitted to grow for very long. In the less successful projects ("Below Expectations," see table 2-1), conflicts were often left to fester or they were simply unilaterally overridden by an edict from the project manager.

## The Technical Project Manager

In this method, the project manager was drawn from the technical (engineering or R&D) department. As the data in table 9-1 show, the technical project manager method was not very effective: the project successes rate is among the lowest in table 9-1. Why?

The answers are not appreciably different from those given for the technical line management method discussed above. In several cases, the marketing personnel did not feel involved and therefore did not contribute. There were many refusals by marketing to accept the completed project. There was no joint agreement as to how the R&D and marketing parties would divide their roles on the project, and marketing personnel were seldom involved in setting the product specifications.

Top management often commented that R&D "wandered off" or "went off on tangents a lot" in the cases studied here. In two of the failure outcome projects, the R&D project team closeted itself for the duration of the project. Their resulting products were far from those originally desired by the marketing department. It may be noted that careful selection and legitimization by top management was not a part of the technical project manager method. Rather, in most of the projects the researcher with the idea automatically became the project manager. He was sometimes announced as the project manager by the R&D director, though more often he was not publicly announced in any ceremonial way.

*Optimum Choice of a Project Manager*

On the basis of these results, it might be concluded that the project manager should not be chosen from the R&D department. This conclusion *cannot* legitimately be drawn from the data. Rather, the results tell us that the successful project managers owed their success to two aspects: their legitimization by top management and their personality profiles.

Department managers cannot effectively confer status on a project manager whose authority must range across several departments. Only top management can confer such status. This is why top management legitimization is so essential. The major problem faced by most of the technical project managers was obtaining support from other departments. They simply did not command the license and legitimization to obtain the required cooperation. (See chapter 7 for more discussions about licenses and legitimization.)

The successful project managers all possessed a similar set of personality attributes and skills. They were experienced at commanding nonhuman resources and motivating human resources to high performance. They combined a sense of tough-mindedness and participativeness in their management styles. They simultaneously exercised close project control and a "one of the boys" style. They were technically astute and at the same time well-informed about customer needs. The typical successful project manager was 30 to 45 years old, had spent 5 to 12 years in a technical function and worked for 4 to 10 years in a marketing or sales function. Several of the successful project managers had the broadening experience of working for at least one other firm.

It is interesting that most of the technical project managers did not see themselves as having either the requisite managerial talents or the desire to manage their projects. They wanted to see their ideas move ahead and be part of the team effort that did this. But they were not enthusiastic managers. Then, why were they chosen to fill those roles? The answer: management did not feel the ideas merited a full-blown project level effort at that time. In some cases, it was a matter of priorities: the more capable managers were assigned to higher priority projects. Sometimes the projects were pushed ahead by the research director before either the projects or the organization was ready for them.

## Task Forces and Teams

*New Product Committees*

As the data in table 9-1 show, new product committees were highly effective. A large variety of new product committee structures were encountered. All these varieties were characterized by some combination of standing committees and ad hoc task forces. Variations in the forms of these arrangements, number of members and powers of the committees were common.

Typically, the new product committee consisted of a standing top level council that developed strategic plans and coordinated the efforts across the departmental boundaries. For example, in one new product committee, the council consisted of the company president, the vice presidents of marketing, research, production and finance, the R&D task force leader and the marketing task force leader. They met monthly and on other occasions when issues required their joint decisions. The council membership and the marketing and R&D task force memberships changed as the project evolved. During the later stages of the project, an engineering task force leader replaced the R&D task force leader on the council. Later a production task force leader was added to the council. This approach follows the core task force model of internal technology transfer discussed in chapter 13.

The new product committee was used primarily when the project was very costly, risky, radical, or time consuming. It was also used when customers were resistant to new things or their wants were ill defined. Some other reasons for using product committees included the interdisciplinary nature of the project, the number of different skill specialties involved in the effort, and the perception of a high regret for failure. The results here thus suggest that interlocking hierarchical team efforts may have an important role to play in new product development. The new product committee was revealed to be a powerful organizing device.

However, the power of the new product committee carries many disadvantages and hazards unless it is properly applied. First, it is important to note that new product committees were used sparingly, and then only on selected projects and developments. The committees described here were cumbersome giants that required enormous efforts to make them work. Something else should be noted: sometimes, the product committee brought in a failure. And when it did, it was a big one! For example, in one new product committee effort, an attempt was made to increase the funding by nearly 50 percent on one phase of the project in order to bring it back on schedule. This resulted in considerable confusion because new personnel were assigned to the project and additional managers were appointed whose jobs overlapped. Factions formed and commitments were prematurely made to directions that were not soundly based in technical reality. The poor organization of the task forces left several jobs and spans of authority unclear. Decisions made at one level were often reversed by another level, while other important decisions were overlooked. The combination of technical confusion, emotional distress, and lack of direction resulted in an end product that was inadequate for the customer's needs. Warranty costs on the product breakdowns in the customer's shop soon accumulated enormous losses. In this case, once the project began to falter, the enormous structure of the new product committee made it more difficult to quickly alter the project's course.

### Dyads and Counterparts

A dyad is a strong interpersonal alliance between two persons. The case of Mr. M and Dr. R, from the data base, illustrates the formation and workings of a dyad.

Both Mr. M and Dr. R were hired into the company at about the same time. Mr. M, a graduate engineer, was hired "to upgrade the technical ability of our field sales force." Dr. R, a Ph.D. scientist in a highly specialized area, was hired "to provide some modern technology in our aging lab."

After two years in the field, Mr. M. was brought into the home office. Management felt he was good at analyzing problems, but he was not an effective salesman. He was assigned to conduct product and market analyses on product A, a product whose future was in some doubt due to a declining market share and sales volume. Mr. M soon began to feel that his career was foundering. Meanwhile, Dr. R had been devoting increasing amounts of his own time to some nebulous radical ideas that management would not sanction. Dr. R was beginning to "feel the need for someone who had some customer insights and could give me a sympathetic ear about applications and possible uses. I was starting to doubt the value of continuing this work. I was even wondering about looking for another job." The stage was set for the emergence of a dyad.

Dr. R had accompanied Mr. M on a field customer visit during their first year of employment with the company. Each was impressed with the other's intense devotion to solving customer problems. With this memory, Dr. R made a phone call to Mr. M and surprisingly discovered he was now in the home office, a few miles away. They quickly developed a strong personal liking for each other, and their families developed close social ties. Dr. R and Mr. M took pleasure in continuously debating and challenging each other's viewpoints on many things: sports, politics, science, and work-related matters. Paralleling this social relationship, a deep professional respect also developed. Dr. R found intellectual stimulation from Mr. M; Mr. M was equally rejuvenated by his association with Dr. R.

Dr. R eventually reached the point in his experimentation where he could no longer continue to obtain useful data and make substantial achievements by bootlegging experiments in the laboratory. Similarly, Mr. M reached the point where he could no longer contribute ideas on the basis of his previous knowledge of customer and market conditions. Fortunately, their ideas were then sufficiently promising that one of the firm's vice presidents was able to provide funding for a project effort. This high-level champion or "angel" (see chapter 7) was an essential factor in the success of this innovation. Once the vice president's support was gained, the idea blossomed. Their efforts resulted in an advanced product that filled long-standing customer needs and catapulted the firm into leadership in that product area. It may be noted that Mr. M and Dr. R are presently working together on another radical innovation for the company. Both of their careers have prospered.

As the data in table 9-1 show, the dyads and counterparts methods were not highly effective. This was very surprising. It was expected that such a strong interpersonal alliance would be more effective. Why wasn't the dyads/counterparts approach more effective?

In some of the failures, top management did not market the product because it was "too small to bother with." In some cases, the product was abandoned for lack of inside support and a champion at high levels of the organization. In some cases, the product did not "fit" the company's way of doing things, i.e., a small specialty product in a large, production oriented firm. These results reinforce the notion that effective dyadic relationships are a powerful force during the early stages of the life cycle of a new product idea. But even the most powerful and effective dyads are seldom sufficient to overcome all obstacles.

It is clear that managers should be sensitive to the existence and emergence of dyads within their organizations. Alert managers can set the scene for potential dyads to form and quietly make funds available to them in a variety of ways, without asking the dyad to justify itself. Such funds will nearly always be modest; dyads do not spend much money on the exploratory portions of their work. Effective managers will sense the time when the effort is ready to be known. Then, a formal project effort can be commissioned and openly championed.

It may be noted that it is not unusual for the members of a dyad to become so friendly that they fail to challenge each other's judgments and therefore blindly follow their own bad advice. This was in fact observed within the data base here. More is said about this in the too-good friends syndrome discussed in chapter 10.

## One-Man Shows

### Commercial One-Man Show

In a commercial one-man show, one person from the marketing or sales function within the firm generates the idea, conducts the development work, and establishes the product in the marketplace. Since marketing and sales functions seldom have their own product development facilities, the commercial one-man show must contract any required technical development work with an outside laboratory or with the customer. The latter approach was commonly observed here.

As the statistics in table 9-1 indicate, the commercial one-man show was not very successful. Nearly three-fourths of the commercial one-man show projects failed to meet their expectations.

All the commercial one-man show projects that met or exceeded their expectations involved familiar technologies and customers known to the firm for many years. In many of these cases, the marketer was able to tell the outside contractor exactly how to fabricate or develop the item. The amount of research needed was small, and the effort was almost entirely a development operation. In all but one of the cases, the marketer had been a powerful force in the industry for many years and was the undisputed expert in that area. By contrast, where the output of commercial one-man shows was below expectations, the end product was much less well defined and required much more research. The marketer was much less of an expert, less established in the area and the customer's needs were not well understood.

Thus, it is clear that it is possible for one marketing or sales person to run the entire new product development alone. However, he or she must have significant organizational power and the command of significant resources. The person must also be recognized, trusted, and esteemed in the eyes of the customer. But that alone is not enough. There must also be several other conditions. The customer's needs must be well understood and the technology must be well developed. Otherwise, there will be technical uncertainties that cannot be resolved without considerable original research. If it can truthfully be said that "I know exactly what you want and I can have precisely that item made for you in exactly x days at z cost," then a commercial one-man show may be viable.

### Technical One-Man Show

The technical one-man show differs from the commercial one-man show in that the principal is from the R&D, engineering, or another technical function within the organization. As the data in table 9-1 show, this method was the least effective of all those studied.

Like the technical line management approach, the technical one-man show had no inherent means for placing the completed product in the marketplace. Moreover, a lack of market and customer information was a serious barrier. In some cases there were no apparent markets for the products that were developed. In other cases, the products failed to perform in the customer's facilities. In several cases, the products were too sophisticated for the customer. In still other cases, no products were ever actually produced because the technical person could not fully define the user's needs. Most of the technical one-man shows lacked a detailed understanding of the user's perceptions and underlying needs. For example, in one case, the one-man show attempted to distribute the product through independent wholesalers. But since this was not the normal route, the wholesalers were unable to provide the point-of-sale advice, product counseling, and warranty services which were traditional within that industry.

Nonetheless, as the statistics in table 9-1 show, one-man shows can succeed. One factor that was common to all the successes was the commitment of top management. Another factor common to all the successes was the prominence of the principal. He was the undeniable expert in this area, and customers sought him when they had problems. He had lived and worked with the users for many years, and was a well-known scientist in this area.

Thus, for a technical one-man show to succeed, the person and the performer organization must meet several criteria. The principal must be an exceptional individual: technically renowned and also competent in business functions. He (or she) must be a competent marketer who understands the user's requirements and knows how to serve the user's need. He must understand the market dynamics and have a sound awareness of competitive reactions to the new product. Organizational resources must be available to the principal when he needs them. Eventually, any project will require capital, know-how, and manpower beyond the principal's storehouse. Most one-man shows do not succeed because this unique combination of characteristics is seldom available.

## The Best Methods

### Technology and Market Environments

Respondents rated each project in terms of the degree to which its technology and the relevant markets were understood.[1] In a poorly understood technology, there is considerable trial and error within the project efforts because high degrees of prediction are not possible. Just the opposite occurs in a well understood technology: the phenomena are so well-known that great predictability is possible. Likewise, a poorly understood market environment is one in which the customer's wants and needs are not well defined. Therefore, a product to satisfy these needs cannot be developed without repeated trials in the customer's environment or its replica. In a well understood market environment, the customer's needs are apparent and products to satisfy these needs can readily be defined.

The 256 project data base used in assembling table 9-1 was broken out using the respondents' degree of understanding ratings. Two of these breakouts are shown in table 9-2. As may be seen from the data in table 9-2, the

Table 9–2
**Project Success under Various Technical and Market Environments**[a]

| Methods | Percentages of Projects That Met or Exceeded Their Commercial Expectations under Two Conditions[b] | |
|---|---|---|
| | Technology Well Understood and Market Poorly Understood | Technology Poorly Understood and Market Well Understood |
| Top Down Structures | | |
| Commercial Line Management | 60 | 17 |
| Technical Line Management | 0 | 60 |
| New Product Structures | | |
| New Products Department | 37 | 43 |
| New Ventures Department | 33 | 33 |
| Project Management Methods | | |
| Commercial Project Manager | 75 | 60 |
| Technical Project Manager | 25 | 50 |
| Taskforces and Teams | | |
| New Product Committees | 67 | 80 |
| Dyads and Counterparts | 50 | 50 |
| One-Man Shows | | |
| Commercial One-Man Show | 50 | 33 |
| Technical One-Man Show | 40 | 20 |

[a]See table 9-1 and table 2-1 for the definition of success rates and the project outcome scale used here.

[b]The percentages are computed within each condition, i.e., 60 percent means 60 percent of the projects experiencing this condition; the numbers are rounded to the nearest whole percent.

commercial project manager and new product committee methods show insignificant differences in success rates under both sets of conditions. Moreover, both methods have success rates well above the 46 percent average for all the methods (table 9-1). None of the other methods perform as well, under both sets of conditions. Some of the methods exhibit relatively high success rates under one set of conditions but not the other. For example, this was true of the commercial line management method.

Does it matter whether the technology or the market is the unknown? Which is more important? Table 9-3 responds to this question. In examining

**Table 9–3**
**Breakout of Project Success Rates from the Data Used in Table 9-1[a]**

| Methods | Percentages of Projects That Met or Exceeded Their Commercial Expectations Under Selected Conditions[b] | |
| --- | --- | --- |
| | *Technology and Market Well-Understood* | *Technology or Market or Both Poorly Understood* |
| Top Down Structures | | |
| Commercial Line Management | 62 | 31 |
| Technical Line Management | 43 | 18 |
| New Product Structures | | |
| New Products Department | 60 | 41 |
| New Ventures Department | 60 | 38 |
| Project Management Methods | | |
| Commercial Project Manager | 75 | 72 |
| Technical Project Manager | 51 | 29 |
| Taskforces and Teams | | |
| New Product Committees | 80 | 69 |
| Dyads and Counterparts | 49 | 48 |
| One-Man Shows | | |
| Commercial One-Man Show | 50 | 36 |
| Technical One-Man Show | 33 | 18 |

[a]See table 9-1 and table 2-1 for the definition of success rates and the project outcome scale used here.

[b]The percentages are computed within each condition, 60 percent means 60 percent of the projects experiencing this condition; the numbers are rounded to the nearest whole percent.

this table, the reader is cautioned that minor differences in percentages should not be interpreted as significant due to small samples in some of the breakouts. With this caveat in mind, several observations may now be made from tables 9-2 and 9-3. Specifically, the commercial line management and commercial one-man shows only produce above-average results (using the 46 percent average from table 9-1) when the technology is well understood. This is a reasonable result, since these methods specialize in marketing problems and are unable to handle technical problems. Analogously, tables 9-2 and 9-3 taken together show that the technical project manager method only produces above average results when the market is well understood. Again, this is reasonable: this method specializes in handling technical problems. But note the results for the commercial project manager, the new product committees, and the dyads/counterparts methods. These three methods recorded above average results under all the conditions in tables 9-2 and 9-3. Clearly, these are valuable and powerful methods.

Now let us turn our attention to table 9-4, where some of the pesky problems of small samples are eliminated by aggregating the individual methods into overall types. Table 9-4 shows that top-down types of structures only produce above-average results (46 percent; table 9-1) when both the technology and the markets are well understood. The same is true for new product types of structures. One-man shows only produce above average results when the technology is well understood. But note the results for the project management, and for the task forces and teams types of methods. These methods produced above average results no matter what the conditions of the markets and technologies. Thus, these methods are shown to be very effective and very powerful. No matter which uncertainty prevails, markets or technologies, these types of methods show above average effectiveness. Of course, the results in table 9-4 are aggregates for individual methods whose effectiveness may differ considerably, as noted in table 9-1. But the results in table 9-4 are very revealing when examined along with those in tables 9-1 through 9-3.

**Table 9–4**
**Additional Breakout of Project Success Rates from the Data Used in Table 9-1[a]**

| Methods | Percentage of Projects That Met or Exceeded Their Commercial Expectations Under Various Conditions[b] | | | |
|---|---|---|---|---|
| | Both Technology and Market Well Understood | Technology Well Understood But Market Not | Market Well Understood But Technology Not | Both Poo Understo |
| Top Down Structures | 53 | 27 | 36 | 10 |
| New Product Structures | 60 | 31 | 39 | 43 |
| Project Management Methods | 63 | 50 | 54 | 48 |
| Taskforces and Teams | 58 | 58 | 70 | 47 |
| One-Man Shows | 42 | 64 | 27 | 8 |

[a]See table 9-1 and table 2-1 for the definition of success rates and the project outcome scale u here.

[b]The percentages are computed within each condition, 60 percent means 60 percent of the proj experiencing this condition; the numbers are rounded to the nearest whole percent.

*Implications of These Results*

The above results show that when customer wants are poorly understood, special methods are needed to guide the new product development effort. On the other hand, when customer wants are well understood, the end product can readily be specified and its development can proceed. In such a case, efficiency in the performance of well-known product development activities is needed. This is something several of the methods do very well.

When the technology is well understood, it is also a relatively straightforward task to prescribe what is to be done and who should do it. But when the technology is not well understood, then considerable experimentation and exchange of a diversity of opinions is required. The new product development process must proceed in a very nonlinear and heuristic fashion. Special methods are needed for assembling the right personnel to perform these tasks.

When both the technology and the markets are poorly understood, this puts great demands on the management methods. It is not enough to assemble one team that is good at discerning user needs and another team that is good at perfecting technical things and bring them together. More than this is required. The integration of these two teams is mandatory. Whatever the market team learns must be immediately fed into the technical decisions. Whatever the technical team discovers must be immediately fed into the market decisions. The parties must all work together in a totally integrated fashion, combining their data, impressions, and perceptions. This is no small order. The key is to create a synergistic output: something more than the two teams could create if their individual outputs were simply linearly added together. This synergism is the key to new product development when both the technical and market environments are poorly understood. Synergism is an essential ingredient for success. Very special methods are thus required under these circumstances.

*Rules for Selecting the Best Method under Each Circumstance*

Table 9-5 summarizes the lessons learned. Three methods were found to be universally effective under all technical and market environments. These three are: the commercial project manager, the new product committees, and the dyads and counterparts methods. Managers can be assured of selecting the universally most effective methods when they choose any of these three. The other methods require considerable intelligence about the surrounding technical and market conditions in order to make a wise choice among them.

If both the technical and market environments are well understood, man-

**Table 9–5**
**Successful Methods under Four Environmental Conditions**[a]

| Market Environment | Technical Environment | |
|---|---|---|
| | *Well Understood* | *Poorly Understood* |
| Well Understood | Commercial Project Manager | Commercial Project Manager |
| | New Product Committees | New Product Committees |
| | Dyads and Counterparts | Dyads and Counterparts |
| | Technical Project Manager | Technical Project Manager |
| | Commercial Line Management | Technical Line Management |
| | New Products Department | |
| | New Ventures Department | |
| | Commercial One-Man Show[b] | |
| Poorly Understood | Commercial Project Manager | Commercial Project Manager |
| | New Product Committees | New Product Committees |
| | Dyads and Counterparts | Dyads and Counterparts |
| | Commercial Line Management | |
| | Commercial One-Man Show[b] | |
| | Technical One-Man Show[b] | |

[a]Those methods with project success rates greater than 46 percent; see table 9-1 and table 2-1.

[b]This method is only highly effective under special circumstances beyond those indicated in this table. See the text for more information.

agement has many options. As table 9-5 shows, in addition to the three methods just named, four other methods can be expected to lead to above-average project success rates. They are: the technical project manager, the commercial line management, the new products department, and the new ventures department methods. A fifth method, the commercial one-man show, may also lead to high success rates. But several prerequisite conditions must exist, as discussed above under the section "Commercial One-Man Show". If these prerequisites are not present, then the commercial one-man show should not be used here.

When the technology is well understood but the market is not, then the commercial line management method is an appropriate choice, in addition to the three universally applicable methods. The commercial one-man show and the technical one-man show are also listed in table 9-5 as acceptable choices under this set of conditions. However, care must be taken to be sure that several prerequisites are present if either of these two methods are to be used. The prerequisites are discussed above under the sections Commercial One-

Man Show and Technical One-Man Show. It may be noted that one could question the wisdom of using the relatively ineffective commercial line management and one-man show methods (see table 9-1). But, with the technology well understood, the major challenges are market related. Hence, the commercial aspects become the major challenges. This is precisely where the commercial line management and commercial one-man show methods are appropriate (see table 9-2). Why then is the technical one-man show appropriate here? The technical one-man show may be uniquely effective when the technical person has great market savvy with regard to a special market clientele (see Technical One-Man Show above).

If the technology is poorly understood and the market is well understood, two methods are appropriate, in addition to the three universally applicable ones. As shown in table 9-5, they are: the technical project manager and the technical line management methods. One might wonder why these two otherwise relatively weak methods would be effective under these particular conditions. Since the markets are well understood, the challenges are primarily technical in nature. These types of challenges are precisely the ones that these two methods are most adept at handling (see table 9-2).

If both the technology and market environments are poorly understood, then this is a very challenging situation. If management wants to maximize their success rates, there are only three appropriate choices. As table 9-5 shows, the three universally applicable methods are the only feasible choices. These three are: the commercial project manager, the new product committees, and the dyads and counterparts methods.

## Costs and Other Factors

*Relative Costs of the Various Methods*

Managers must always consider the costs of selecting and employing an appropriate method for managing new product development efforts. Costs include the time burden and drain on management talents, the recruiting and training of qualified staff, and any increased levels of conflicts caused by the methods. The commercial project manager method was observed to be the most expensive method. It required the most patience, skill, and management attention and the most serious recruiting efforts. It also caused the most organizational strains. On the other end of the cost spectrum were the one-man show and line management methods. The relative cost-effectiveness of the methods are portrayed in figure 9-1. The figure shows a range of relative costs for each level of capability in order to indicate the variations that might be encountered from one organization to another.

Thus, a rational approach to the selection of the "best" method for man-

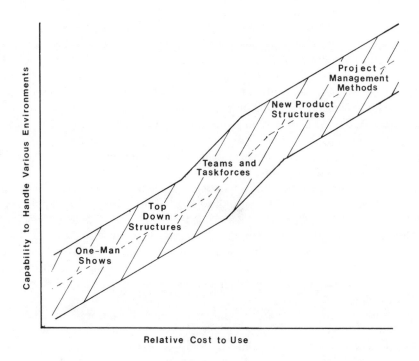

**Figure 9–1. Relative Cost-Effectiveness of Various Methods**

aging new product development projects must consider both the incremental benefits and the incremental costs. The most potent methods are the most costly; the least potent are the least expensive. Potency has its price. More potency than required should not be used. Where alternative methods are equally effective, consideration should be given to the least costly one. For example, the commercial line management method (a top-down structure) and the commercial project manager method are about equally effective when the technology and market environments are both well understood (tables 9-3 and 9-5). But, all other things equal, the commercial line management method might be used under these conditions since it is the cheaper alternative (figure 9-1). Again, it must be stressed that this rule only holds when both the technology and market environments are well understood. A different set of conditions would lead one to different conclusions about the most cost-effective alternative choice.

## Life Cycle and Organizational Considerations

A project that begins its life in a poorly understood state must naturally transition itself into a well understood state if it is to succeed. This suggests that the management methods ought to be correspondingly changed over the life of the project. For example, a project might begin as a technical one-man show, transition to the commercial project manager method, later move into a new ventures mode, and finally end up in a commercial line management mode. However, too frequent changes may be counterproductive. Thus, managers must consider the main thrusts and the more general trends in the uncertainty of the technology and the markets in switching from one method to another.

Project management methods must be kept consistent with the overall organization structure and management philosophy of the parent firm. For example, it would be more difficult to achieve success with the project management methods in a type I (classical, top-down) organization structure than in a type III or IV structure. Similarly, a line management structure would not be completely effective at the project level unless there are corresponding elements of the type I structure at the total organizational level. Thus, much of what has been said about innovative total organization structures also applies at the project level. (See chapter 6 on structures.)

## Management Discretion

In practice, managers may have much less discretion to select the particular type of new product management method than has been implied here. Organization structures often evolve over long time spans. They also tend to endure even longer, in spite of efforts to change them. Human behaviors and institutionalized ways are often surprisingly resistant to change!

One-man shows and dyads are very natural phenomena that often emerge in spite of any purposive management design. Managers can, however, set up conditions and climates that foster their birth and growth. Alert managers who see such natural phenomena forming can encourage them and assist them to become institutionalized modes of behavior. Thus, although some of the methods described here may not be completely discretionary, managers can often influence their use under the appropriate circumstances.

Managers often inherit organizations, people, and other resources that are largely fixed in the short run. This may be especially true for project managers, who often complain that their ability to develop successful products is shackled by the inconsistent resource limitations their bosses have placed on them. Having personally experienced this situation, this author is very sympathetic with this complaint. The results throughout this book support the position that many things must be consistent in order to achieve new product innovation success. Perhaps the results herein will help increase top management's awareness of the need to maintain such consistencies. On the other hand, this book has also shown that there may be many more alternatives than the project manager recognizes. These alternatives should be exhaustively explored before the project manager seeks more radical changes.

## Combinations of Methods

A very large number of combinations of the ten methods discussed here are possible. Some combinations may have synergistic effects, in which their combined effectiveness far exceeds the effectiveness of either method alone. Other combinations may be less effective than the individual methods alone. It is possible for some methods to enhance each other, while others depreciate each other in combination.

It is not possible or informative to try to study all of these combinations indiscriminately. Clearly, some are more interesting than others. Chapter 6 examined two combinations: the type III and type IV structures. The type III structure was a combination of project management, task force methods, and top-down methods. The type IV structure was a combination of all these three plus a new ventures method. These combinations were found to be highly effective.

Thus, it is apparent that the choice of a "best" method is, indeed, a very complex decision. Though this chapter has provided several important and useful guidelines for managers, it has only provided a starting point for more sophisticated research and study.

## Summary

This chapter has shown that the choice of the optimum method for managing new product development efforts is not a simple matter. There is no one best method. There are in fact several good and several bad alternative methods, depending on the prevailing technological and market conditions. Rules were prescribed for selecting the best methods under each condition.

The choice of the most appropriate method is influenced by many different considerations, some of which go beyond the prevailing technical and market conditions. It must be noted that even the optimum method cannot guarantee success, since many other nonmanagerial and uncontrollable factors may come together to determine a project's outcome. However, this chapter has shown that the choice of the most appropriate project management method facilitates new product development success. The use of inappropriate methods was shown to foster failure.

## Note

1. For more details on these dimensions the reader is referred to the instrument package, which is available from the author.

# 10
# Managing the R&D/Marketing Interface

Hope is a good breakfast but it is a bad supper.
—Antoninus, 180 A.D.

Research and development (R&D) and marketing personnel are dependent on each other for the creation of new products and processes. Their cooperation and collaboration are vital to the success of innovation processes. Yet R&D and marketing departments commonly have many misunderstandings and conflicts.

## Common Misunderstandings between R&D and Marketing

Marketing personnel frequently do not comprehend why R&D can not immediately change their product designs in response to changing customer needs. They have problems understanding why R&D cannot be more flexible and responsive. As a result, marketing personnel frequently view R&D as unresponsive, oversophisticated and overexuberant about impractical ideas. On the other hand, R&D personnel often do not comprehend why marketing must have products so quickly or how a less-than-perfect product can be acceptable. They have problems understanding why customer needs can not always be precisely predicted and new product specifications can not be rigidly fixed before the work begins. As a result, R&D personnel frequently view marketing as simplistic, superficial, and short sighted. In short, both parties often have inadequate comprehensions of the other's roles and purposes and the nature of the other's discipline.

This chapter examines the R&D/marketing interface conditions found within the data base. The incidence of different types of problems between R&D and marketing are discussed and the effects of these problems on project outcomes are analyzed. Recommendations are made for increasing project success rates by improving conditions at the R&D/marketing interface.

## Methodology

The 289 project data base was examined for projects exhibiting disharmony between R&D and marketing. Three mild disharmony states were observed and accordingly labeled: lack of interaction, lack of communication, and too-good friends. Two severe disharmony states were observed: lack of appreciation and distrust. Projects were then classified as exhibiting primarily one of these states or no significant disharmony, depending on their most prominent characteristics.

## Mild Disharmony States

### Lack of Interaction

As illustrated in table 10-1, in this state of affairs the R&D and marketing parties did not feel any motivation to interact. This was more a matter of neglect than the result of any strong animosities. In some cases the neglect was a natural result of work deadlines and pressures. As one subject noted: "You get busy and you don't stop to think about whether or not they should know about this or that . . . . when you have to get your part of the job done . . . and you know that talking to them takes valuable time." Another respondent said: "If you don't get used to seeing each other you don't miss each

**Table 10–1**
**Mild Disharmony: Lack of Interaction**

| Behaviors | Attitudes |
|---|---|
| There are few informal meetings between R&D and marketing personnel | Marketing feels they cannot afford the time to get involved in details with R&D |
| There are few formal decision meetings between R&D and marketing personnel | R&D feels there is little value in becoming intimately involved with marketing |
| Neither party attends the other's staff meetings | Both parties are deeply concerned with their own narrow specialties and neither sees any reason to learn more about the other party |
| Working documents, salesperson's call reports, and progress reports are not circulated between the R&D and marketing personnel | Neither party sees the need for interaction; R&D expects marketing to use whatever they give them, and marketing expects R&D to create useful products |

other, and if you don't think about each other you don't make any effort to get together. And you always have to make an effort."

Several projects that evidenced lack of interaction occurred in classical type I and type II organization structures of old-line firms that were attempting to develop new product innovations. These firms had no history of substantial R&D/marketing interaction.

## Lack of Communication

As illustrated in table 10-2, in this state the two parties purposely maintained verbal, attitudinal, and physical distances from each other. This was an intentional behavior, resulting from some experience or feeling that was collected at a prior point in time. Note how this differs from the lack of interaction syndrome. In the lack of interaction state, the two parties simply neglected each other. Here there were some negative feelings that kept the parties apart. One (or both) did not want to talk to the other.

Though various causes were observed, two factors appeared to lead directly to this problem. One factor was perceived theft of credit. When either party took what the other thought was undue credit for meritorious project achievements, this inevitably led to a lack of communication problem. The impression that the other party had taken unfair advantage was long remembered. Another factor was top management accolades. If top management praised one party and did not praise the other, rivalry invariably shut off some future communication. As one subject noted: "If we don't tell them anything, they can't go to management and take credit for it."

**Table 10–2**
**Mild Disharmony: Lack of Communication**

| *Behaviors* | *Attitudes* |
| --- | --- |
| There is some communication between the parties, but potential problem areas are glossed over and there is no real depth of communication between them | Neither party sees any reason to inform the other of their activities |
| Marketing is not fully informed of the new technologies that R&D is working on until very late in the life of the technology | Neither party feels that the other has any information of special value |
| R&D is not fully informed of the market need and the rationale for the new product | Neither party feels any need to give the other any detailed information or explanations |

**Table 10–3**
**Mild Disharmony: Too-Good Friends**

| Behaviors | Attitudes |
|---|---|
| Neither party challenges the other or questions the other's judgments and assumptions | Neither party wants to hurt the other's feelings |
| Both parties avoid entering into conflict with each other or arguing over details | Each feels that the other has his own turf and they should stay off of each other's turf |
| The R&D and marketing individuals appear to be "good friends"—they see each other socially, they occasionally make joint visits to customers, they go to lunch together and they meet with each other frequently | R&D relies exclusively on the marketing personnel for judgments and information about the marketing aspects |
| | Both parties feel the other's advice will always be accurate and beyond reproach |
| | Both parties have enormous regard for each other |

## Too-Good Friends

As illustrated in table 10-3, in this state of affairs the R&D and marketing personnel were too friendly with each other. A kind of complacency developed that inhibited the parties from challenging each other's judgment and information. Important information and subtle observations were overlooked and project success was inhibited as a result.

What factors led to this type of problem? Surprisingly, past successes sometimes led the team members to become too-good friends and to fail because of it. Teams of R&D and marketing personnel who had worked together successfully for long periods of time sometimes became complacent. Their potency appeared to decline once they had achieved complete harmony. It was as if they needed some conflicts or the challenge of building harmonious relationships to maintain their alertness.

A related factor was a kind of blind faith in the correctness of the counterpart person. As one respondent observed: "You are always sort of reluctant to challenge and question what your colleague tells you. He's the expert in that area. And you don't expect that he'll play politics with you, so there's no reason to question his integrity. And you figure he's the best man you've got, so he probably won't steer you wrong."

The reader may wonder how this syndrome relates to the dyad method discussed in chapter 9. Some dyads were observed that did in fact fall into the too-good friends trap. But the successful dyads always challenged and

## Table 10–4
## Severe Disharmony: Lack of Appreciation

| Behaviors | Attitudes |
|---|---|
| Marketing sometimes purchases its R&D work outside the firm rather than use the in-house R&D group | Marketing feels that R&D is too sophisticated in their approaches |
| Rather than consult marketing concerning new product ideas, R&D independently moves ahead with its own ideas | R&D feels that marketing is too simplistic in their approaches<br><br>Marketing feels that R&D should not visit customers because they will "talk over their heads" |
| Marketing attempts to exercise close control over R&D whenever they work together | R&D feels that marketing does not really have a good grasp of the kinds of products that are needed |
| R&D sometimes attempts to by-pass marketing and directly market their new ideas | R&D feels that the marketing function is generally unnecessary |

penetratingly questioned each other. They appeared to enjoy and thrive on this aspect, sometimes with impish good humor. When one partner found a gap in the other's logic, both partners were suddenly energized to close that gap. Such experiences invariably only further strengthened the dyad. The partner who committed the logic gap never seemed to suffer any prestige loss in the other's eyes. Rather, the ambience was described by one partner as "a climate where we look for flaws, and it's not important who committed the flaw. We just want to find it and work together to fix it." This is clearly a different climate from the too-good friends syndrome.

## Severe Disharmony States

The severe disharmony states were characterized by deep-seated attitudes and distrust that stood in the way of collaboration. Typical of these is the lack of appreciation problem illustrated in table 10-4.

### Lack of Appreciation

What caused the lack of appreciation? No single cause was identified. Some cases had long remembered histories of ineffectiveness by one party. For example, in one case, R&D failed to develop the promised product. In another case, marketing failed to correctly identify the market. Sometimes, the organization climates fostered a lack of appreciation. For example, several respondents indicated that they "never see any signals from top management

**Table 10–5**
**Severe Disharmony: Distrust**

| Behaviors | Attitudes |
|---|---|
| Marketing attempts to dictate exactly what, where, when and how to do the project, allowing no room for rebuttal and no tolerance for suggestions from R&D | Marketing feels they lose control when R&D gets involved; the project disappears and they never see it until it is completed, at which point it is seldom what they wanted |
| R&D initiates many projects and keeps them secret from the marketing personnel | Marketing feels that R&D cannot be trusted to do what they are instructed to do |
| Marketing brings R&D into the picture only after they know exactly what they want done, so that R&D will not have any reason to argue for their own ideas | R&D fears that marketing wants to liquidate them |
| | R&D does not feel they can trust marketing to accurately tell them what the customers really want |
| Marketing and R&D personnel purposely avoid each other, sometimes refusing to sit down together at the same table | R&D feels they are blamed if products fail, but marketing is credited if products succeed |

that collaboration is desired" and that "management has not indicated that we are expected to cooperate with them." It is interesting that top management must make a special effort to encourage cooperation: it does not seem to be automatic.

In many cases, the organization of R&D and marketing into separate departments with separate budgets and operations fostered a lack of appreciation. For example, consider the following sampling of statements from several firms in the data base: "We don't have any inputs into their plans and budgets"; "They have their own operations and so do we"; "We get our rewards from doing our thing and they get theirs from something else"; "No one is responsible for how it all comes together"; "We just go our separate ways."

### Distrust

Distrust is the extreme case of negative attitudes and behaviors, as illustrated in table 10-5. Deep-seated jealousies, negative attitudes, and hostile behaviors characterized this syndrome. What caused the distrust problem?

No single cause was found. But several important contributing factors were isolated. All the distrust cases began as either a lack of appreciation or a lack of communication problem that evolved into the distrust state. Many of the distrust cases were characterized by personality conflicts that top management had allowed to exist. In some cases, these conflicts were so institutionalized that even personnel who were not involved harbored feelings of distrust. Note the following quote from one respondent, referring to his counterpart in another department. "He once did some things to us. I'm not sure what they were. It all happened before I came into this group. So, you see, you really have to watch out for him." This type of institutionalized distrust was found surprisingly often.

## Harmony and Disharmony: Some Distinctions

Though many projects were found in the above five mild and severe disharmony states, there were also many projects that did not exhibit any of these five states. Two types of harmonious situations were found: equal partner and dominant partner harmony.

### Equal Partner Harmony

In this state, each party felt strongly positive about the other. Typical quotes collected at several firms included the following: "We couldn't get along without them"; "We're on the phone with each other constantly"; "I feel like I've known them a long time"; "We've been through 'thick and thin' together." Each party felt they were on a par with the other in political, organizational, technical, and decision-making powers. New product ideas originated with about equal frequency from the R&D and marketing functions, and each party felt free to call joint meetings on almost any issue. These meetings were characterized by an open give and take of facts, opinions, and feelings. No issues were left unresolved and consensus was sought by everyone.

In all the equal partner cases the marketing personnel were technically trained. Most had prior careers in R&D. Personnel were often exchanged or rotated between R&D and marketing. Study committees and task forces with joint memberships were common, with the chairmanship rotated between the R&D and marketing personnel. A common feature characterizing all the equal partner cases was the early involvement of R&D and marketing personnel. Moreover, it was part of the equal partner culture to involve R&D and marketing personnel jointly in customer visits, customer follow-ups, customer service, new product planning and forecasting, and product strategy formulation.

### Dominant Partner Harmony

In this syndrome, one of the parties was content to let the other lead. For example, one R&D subject in a marketing-dominant case noted: "We have no idea at all what the market needs are. But if they'll tell us what they want

**Table 10–6**
**Incidence of Harmony and Disharmony**

| States | Percent of Projects Experiencing This State |
|---|---|
| Mild Disharmony | |
| Lack of Interaction | 7.6 |
| Lack of Communication | 6.6 |
| Too-Good Friends | 6.3 |
| Subtotal | 20.5 |
| Severe Disharmony | |
| Lack of Appreciation | 26.9 |
| Distrust | 11.8 |
| Subtotal | 38.7 |
| Harmony | |
| Dominant Partner | 29.1 |
| Equal Partner | 11.7 |
| Subtotal | 40.8 |
| Total | 100 |

and supply the specs we can sure make it for them." A marketing respondent in an R&D-dominant case said: "We can usually sell what R&D gives us. We don't really know what they are able to come up with. They know what it takes to make a good performing product better than we do."

## The Incidence and Severity of Disharmony

Is R&D/marketing disharmony a significant problem? Do R&D/marketing interface problems occur often enough that management should be concerned with them?

As table 10-6 shows, over half (59.2 percent) of the projects studied here experienced some type of R&D/marketing interface problem. Moreover, it is especially disconcerting to see that over one-third (38.7 percent) of the projects studied here experienced severe problems.

The lack of interaction, lack of communication and too-good friends problems were often overcome by modest efforts and changes in behaviors of the personnel at the firms. More frequent joint meetings, invitations to consult on proposed projects and increased sharing of information often ameliorated many of these types of problems. Moreover, though these types of problems often lowered the organization's effectiveness, they were not totally disruptive and they seldom led to major project failures.

By contrast, the lack of appreciation and distrust problems were much more severe. They usually caused operating disruptions and consumed many hours of managerial talent in moderating disputes. Because of this, key actions were often delayed, important decisions were not taken in a timely fashion and many project failures occurred. Unfortunately, the lack of appreciation and distrust problems were not easily overcome. Attempts by management to ameliorate them through negotiation, reorganization, bargaining, or personnel transfers often left deep scars and sowed the seeds for a renewed outbreak of similar problems elsewhere.

These results show that the incidence and seriousness of R&D/marketing interface problems are distressingly high. Moreover, many of these problems are chronic and disruptive. Still, we must ask one more question: Does harmony/disharmony make a difference with respect to project success/failure rates? This is the ultimate criterion for judging whether disharmony is a serious problem.

## Harmony, Disharmony, and Project Success Rates

In many of the projects experiencing the too-good friends problem, important information was overlooked that severely diminished the effectiveness of the end products. In many of the projects experiencing the lack of communications problem, the new products either did not match the market needs or failed to meet some important customer specification. In about half of the projects with lack of interaction problems, the end products either did not perform as originally planned or arrived too late to capture a rapidly changing market. Thus, the mild disharmonies generally depreciated the degrees of success of the end products but seldom resulted in dismal product failures.

By contrast, in a majority of the projects experiencing lack of appreciation problems the end products either failed to perform or they were not cost-effective. In many of the projects where distrust occurred, the products did not perform. Thus, the cases of severe disharmony resulted in a high frequency of rather dramatic failures.

Table 10-7 summarizes the relevant project outcome statistics. Note that the harmony state (dominant plus equal partner syndromes) resulted in some failures. However, the harmony state resulted in significantly more successful projects than either the mild or severe disharmony states. Thus, the data make it clear that R&D/marketing disharmony severely reduces new product development success rates.

## Guidelines for Promoting Harmony between R&D and Marketing

An analysis of the projects in the data base revealed several things that could alleviate R&D/marketing interface problems. Moreover, several of the firms in the data base suggested various practices for overcoming interface prob-

Table 10–7
**Distribution of Project Outcomes by Harmony/Disharmony States**

| | *Project Outcomes in Percentages[a]* | | |
|---|---|---|---|
| *States* | *Success* | *Partial Success* | *Failure* |
| Harmony | 52 | 35 | 13 |
| Mild Disharmony | 32 | 45 | 23 |
| Severe Disharmony | 11 | 21 | 68 |

[a]The following definitions are used, based on table 2-1:

| | |
|---|---|
| Success | = High plus Medium Degrees of Commercial Success (Blockbuster plus Above Expectations) |
| Partial Success | = Low Degree of Commercial Success plus Low Degree of Commercial Failure (Met Expectations plus Below Expectations) |
| Failure | = Medium plus High Degrees of Failure (Protected Our Position But Lost Money plus Took a Bath We Won't Forget) |

lems. The following eight guidelines were formulated from these analyses and suggestions.

**Break Large Projects into Smaller Ones.** Three-fourths of the projects with nine or more persons assigned to them experienced interface problems. By contrast, projects with five or fewer persons assigned to them seldom experienced problems. The smaller number of individuals and organizational layers on the small projects appeared to permit increased face-to-face contacts, increased empathies, and easier coordination.

**Take a Proactive Stance toward Interface Problems.** In those cases where potential interface problems were avoided and actual problems were overcome, the parties maintained a posture of aggressively seeking out and facing such problems head-on. They openly criticized and examined their behaviors. As one individual noted: "We don't treat it like a social disease and sweep it under the rug; if we got it, we want to know about it so we can get rid of it."

**Eliminate Mild Problems before They Grow into Severe Problems.** All the cases of severe (lack of appreciation and distrust) problems studied here began as mild problems at some earlier points in time. As noted above, severe disharmonies were extremely difficult to eliminate. Mild disharmonies were much easier to overcome. Thus, it is wise to eliminate mild problems while they are still mild.

**Make Open Communication an Explicit Responsibility of Everyone.** An illustration of how this can be done was provided by one of the firms in this study. This firm had a history of poor R&D/marketing relationships until the R&D manager established an "open-door" policy. This policy consisted of quarterly information meetings between R&D and marketing, day-long and week-long exchanges of personnel, periodic gripe sessions, and the constant encouragement of R&D personnel to visit their marketing counterparts. Every member of the R&D department was charged with the responsibility of playing a role in this open-door policy, and every member was judged on this as part of his annual performance evaluation. The open-door policy survived the initial skepticism that surrounded it, and the examples set by a few diligent individuals eventually spread. Significant improvements in new product development success rates were achieved as a result of these changes. Here is a policy that all R&D and marketing departments could emulate.

**Promote and Maintain Dyadic Relationships.** A dyad is a very powerful interpersonal alliance. An example was given in chapter 9 illustrating how individuals from R&D and marketing can become intensely committed to each other and forge a successful new product innovation. The dyad is strongly promoted by open-door policies. It is fostered any time persons with complementary skills and personalities are assigned to work together and given significant autonomy. The dyad is worth promoting not only because it encourages innovation in particular cases, but because it can become the kernel of a much wider circle of interrelationships between R&D and marketing. A successful dyad composed of an R&D person and a marketing person will draw other R&D and marketing personnel onto their bandwagon. These experiences can catalyze and institutionalize longer term interactions between R&D and marketing. The danger is that the dyad will fall into the too-good friends syndrome. This is why it is important for managers to thoroughly understand and closely monitor all dyads.

**Use Task Forces and Product Committees.** Examples of product committees were presented in chapter 9. To further illustrate how project-level task forces and top-level committees can be linked, consider the arrangement used at one firm in the data base. The top-level task force consisted of the company president, the vice presidents of R&D, marketing, and finance, the project coordinator, the R&D task force leader and the marketing task force leader. They met monthly to decide on strategic matters. The marketing and R&D task force memberships changed as the project metamorphosed over its life cycle. In the early stages of the project, phenomenological research work was carried out by Ph.D. scientists. Application oriented scientists gradually replaced them as the project aged. Finally, engineering personnel replaced them. This committee structure was repeatedly successfully used by this firm to foster R&D/marketing harmony and new product development success.

**Involve Both Parties Early.** Much has been said and written about the benefits from participation and early involvement of parties in decision processes. The results here reinforce the conclusion that when R&D and marketing are joint participants to all the decisions, from the start of the project to its completion, lack of appreciation and distrust are lessened.

**Clarify the Decision Authorities.** The decision authority is a kind of charter between R&D and marketing. It governs and guides the R&D/marketing venture by detailing who has the "right" to make what decisions, under which circumstances. For example, at one firm the policy specified that marketing had the sole authority and responsibility for defining the user's needs. R&D had the ultimate authority and responsibility for selecting the technical means to meet these needs. R&D and marketing were given the joint responsibility for deciding when an adequate product had been defined. Complaints and appeals to top management could not be made unilaterally by either party. Rather, top management would only entertain an audience composed of both parties. A decision authority policy, as well as the group process of developing such a policy, can contribute enormously to clarifying the roles between R&D and marketing. Well-developed decision authority policies were observed at several firms. They fostered a sound foundation for the avoidance of many time-consuming conflicts.

## The NIG Process for Fostering Harmony

The process of working toward consensus can often foster harmonious behaviors between R&D and marketing. This may be true even though consensus is not achieved. The structured process of interchanging perceptions can result in an enlightened appreciation of each other's worth. A method developed by the author called the nominal-interacting group (NIG) method has been repeatedly shown to be effective in this regard.[1,2,3]

### The Nominal-Interacting Group (NIG) Method

In the NIG method, key R&D and marketing personnel are asked to work together as a decision-making team on some task. The team begins their work with an individual or nominal study period. In this period, each member privately and anonymously documents their own thoughts and viewpoints. For example, if the task is to achieve consensus on a portfolio of projects, each individual would rank, rate, or prioritize the alternatives. Various ranking techniques, idea creation methods, or other exercises may be used to assist the individuals.[4] Each member is asked to write a rationale or justification for their choices and rankings. Note that this individual period should be

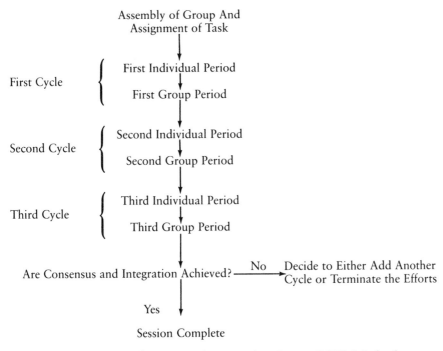

Figure 10–1. The Nominal-Interacting Group (NIG) Method

conducted in a group setting, with all the members seated around a table, so that they can see each other industriously working and feel the group ambience.

Each individual's completed work is collected and copies are distributed to all the members. However, no member's work is identified; anonymity of authorship is an important part of this process. The group is then left alone for a specified time period (usually 90 minutes) in an interacting setting. In this setting, the members are free to challenge each other, reveal their feelings, reveal their authorship, exchange information, or discuss their outputs. The only requirement is that they work toward group consensus. As shown in figure 10-1, one individual and one group period constitute an NIG cycle. Normally, three NIG cycles will achieve the maximum group consensus and R&D/marketing integration.

Consensus and integration may be measured in several ways. In one study, the task was to achieve consensus among marketing and R&D personnel on strategic guidelines for selecting projects.[2,3,5] The degree of member to group consensus was measured in terms of the number of similar guidelines and the degree of correlation between them. At the end of the first cycle, there was little consensus. At the end of the second cycle, several members had adopted a large number of the group-generated guidelines. By the end of the third cycle, high degrees of consensus were achieved for all the members. In this same study, the degree of integration was measured by questionnaires that tracked the extent to which each member felt he was a part of a harmonious, effective team. The degree of integration increased at the end of each cycle, to reach a high level by the end of the third cycle.

In general, the NIG method is based on the observation that groups naturally iterate between introspective individual (nominal) activities and socioemotional group (interacting) activities to reach consensus and integration. The nominal periods provide opportunities for quiet reflection and introspection. The interacting periods provide a forum for information exchange, personal value modification, and team building.

It should be noted that, unlike many team building and group facilitation methods, the NIG method improves strategic collaboration behaviors while retaining the specialized cultures of the team members. This is very important in the case of R&D and marketing parties. Joint collaboration is only sought at a strategic level of behaviors. We do not want to convert the marketers into researchers or the researchers into marketers.

### Example of the NIG Method

In this application of the NIG, five scientists, four engineers, six midlevel managers, and five marketing administrators were assembled to prioritize a list of proposed new product projects for the coming budget period. Each group member was assigned the responsibility of serving as an advocate for one or more of the projects. Problems had previously been encountered in attempting to come to agreement on the priorities for these projects.

To open the session, each member gave a brief presentation of their advocated projects, followed by a short question and answer session. In the first individual period, each attendee rated every project either very high, high, intermediate, low, or very low priority. In the first group period the attendees openly discussed the ratings, the merits of each project, the spread in the ratings for each project, and the possible rationales for assigning various ratings. The emphasis of the group was on information gathering and opinion sharing. Many questions were asked and a great deal of information was exchanged. When the group seemed to reach a level of comfort and no more questions were forthcoming, a second individual period was held. Figure 10-2 shows an example of the rating tallies for the first and second individual periods, for three of the proposed projects. The arrows in figure 10-2 show the changes in votes from the first to the second individual periods. A third cycle brought the group to consensus on all the projects but two, which were remanded to a subcommittee for further study and resubmittal. The group

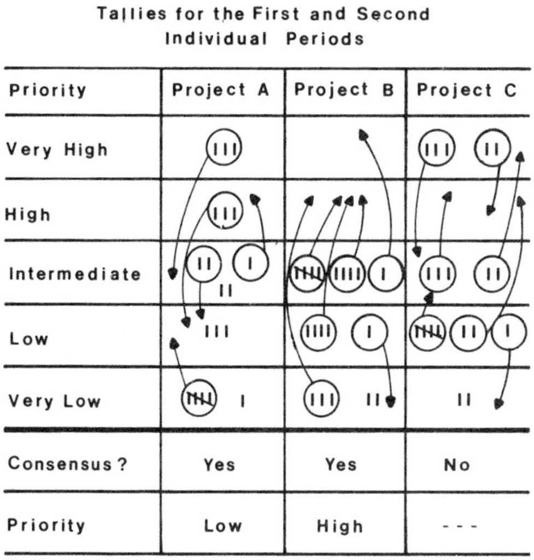

Tallies for the First and Second
Individual Periods

| Priority | Project A | Project B | Project C |
|---|---|---|---|
| Very High | (III) | | (III) (II) |
| High | (III) | | |
| Intermediate | (II) (I) II | (IIII)(IIII) I | (III) (II) |
| Low | III | (IIII) (I) | (IIII)(II)(I) |
| Very Low | (IIII) I | (III) II | II |
| Consensus? | Yes | Yes | No |
| Priority | Low | High | - - - |

*Note:* The arrows track the changes in voting from the first to the second individual periods.

**Figure 10–2. Example of Rating Tallies from the NIG Method**

then recommended that work be started on all projects with consensus ratings above intermediate priority.

The group members reported strong feelings of accomplishment and a strong sense of achievement. A strong sense of cohesiveness was reported, derived from the appreciation the parties gained for each other as a by-product of the NIG process.

## Understanding the Interdependent Roles of R&D and Marketing

*Traditional R&D and Marketing Roles*

Traditional marketing functions include the identification of potential customers, conducting research to determine customer needs, the definition of the demand and price-volume relationships for the potential product, the analysis of market trends, the analysis of competitive products, the determination of price strategies and forecasting market trends. Some traditional functions of R&D include the choice of the technical means to develop the product, the determination of the types of technologies to employ in developing the product, the R&D work on the new product, scheduling the development work within the established time allowed for its completion, and allocating the R&D resources used in the development work.

These traditional separations of roles can lead to serious obstacles to collaboration in the case of new product innovations. To innovate, a new approach is required. R&D and marketing must find ways to develop joint roles that transcend these traditional, institutionalized behaviors if they want to create successful new product innovations.

## Joint Roles and Responsibilities

In many organizations today, neither R&D nor marketing feels they are being well served by the other. Yet, when asked what they want from the other party, the responses are often either unclear or unrealistic. This is because neither fully understands what information each has, what skills each can bring to bear, what each can contribute and the various limitations in knowledge and skills that each has. Because of unrealistic expectations, marketing does not appreciate the technical problems of developing new products and R&D does not appreciate the difficulties of precisely defining the customer's requirements.

These problems are compounded by R&D and marketing's incomplete understanding of their own roles, and their occasional feelings of ineffectiveness. In today's world of rapidly evolving technologies, marketing cannot always expect to know what role to play, or to fully understand the customers' needs. Similarly, R&D cannot always expect to understand a new technology or to possess all the required skills to solve every technical problem.

The way to overcome these problems is easy to state but not so easy to do: the parties must play reciprocal roles. For innovations to occur, R&D and marketing must come to realize that they are jointly responsible for many things. This includes setting new product goals and priorities, generating and selecting new product ideas, researching and analyzing customer wants, setting product performance requirements and defining performance-versus-cost trade-offs. These joint functions must be completed before any other work proceeds. Once they are carried out, the appropriate individual roles will become apparent. R&D becomes individually responsible for all things having to do with how the new product development work is conducted. However, R&D must not carry out this function within a vacuum. Constant contact with marketing and continual sharing of information and perceptions are essential. Interactions keep R&D abreast of information that might have an impact on the technical aspects. More important, interactions maintain a harmonious and effective team. Marketing has an analogous responsibility for continually sharing customer information and market perceptions, in addi-

tion to their individual responsibility for all things having to do with customers and markets.

## Required R&D and Marketing Behaviors

By being involved as part of the team, R&D can supply a creative vision of
the product. By being involved as part of the team, marketing can assure that
R&D does not lose sight of the realities and create a useless product. In order
for this joint effort to be effective, give and take is needed. Each party must
be inquisitive and assertive. Each must have an intelligent viewpoint. Each
must be able and willing to listen to the other, to explore alternatives, to
extract salient features from the other's views and to build on them. This
requires negotiation, compromise, and creativity.

Though this may sound difficult, only two conditions are needed: the
two parties must talk to each other daily, and they must stay involved from
the beginning to the end of the project. Talking to each other daily means
sharing perceptions and feelings as well as factual data. People who work
together successfully have achieved a very important level of mutual understanding: they fully understand each other's thought processes and values.
There is truth in the old saying that one cannot work with another person he
doesn't really know. Sharing fundamental values and philosophies often re-
moves myths and builds mutual respect. Sharing project data and facts often
leads to creative synergism: each party contributes enlightened pieces of insights to the mosaic of innovation. Sharing information, data, and perceptions is the basis for the parties to define their roles, to determine which tasks
each is best able to perform and to agree on the division of labor.

Staying involved from start to finish is the second necessary condition
for effective R&D/marketing collaboration. Marketing should be involved in
the project from the point of idea generation. Similarly, R&D should stay
involved through the establishment of the product in the marketplace. This
is the only way that each can come to appreciate what the other does. And it
is the only effective way to maximize the long term contributions of the two
parties.

It is not clear that any detailed behaviors can be prescribed for either
R&D or marketing in the area of innovations. By definition, innovative behaviors are required to create successful new product innovations. Perhaps
only one cardinal rule can be postulated with confidence: the two parties
must maintain an open, eager, trusting, sharing, opportunity-seeking attitude
toward each other. This implies a willingness to play whatever roles and carry
out whatever tasks the situation appears to require.

## Summary

A lack of harmony between R&D and marketing is a common barrier to successful new product developments. Disharmonies often form between R&D and marketing departments. It is not uncommon for these disharmonies to grow into extreme climates of distrust or even open warfare.

Over one-half of the 289 projects in the data base experienced one or the other of the five types of disharmony examined in this chapter. The severity of disharmony was found to be related to the success/failure outcomes of the innovation projects in the data base. Eight guidelines and a nominal-interacting group (NIG) decision process were suggested for overcoming disharmonies. Since the data base showed that severe disharmonies were extremely difficult to overcome, it is essential to prohibit their formation.

The only effective means to permanently avoid disharmonies is for the R&D and marketing parties to fully understand and appreciate their reciprocal roles, and to play out these roles in a true team setting. The following chapter explores these aspects and suggests several behaviors for R&D and marketing personnel that will foster successful innovations.

## Notes

1. See William E. Souder, *Project Selection and Economic Appraisal* (New York: Van Nostrand Reinhold, 1984), pp. 78-83.

2. For the original work here, see William E. Souder, "Achieving Organizational Consensus with Respect to R&D Project Selection Criteria," *Management Science*, 21, no. 6 (1975), 669-91.

3. For an early application of the NIG method, see William E. Souder, "Effectiveness of Nominal and Interacting Group Decision Processes for Integrating R&D and Marketing," *Management Science*, 23, no. 6 (1977), 595-605.

4. See William E. Souder, *Management Decision Methods* (New York: Van Nostrand Reinhold, 1980), pp. 9-98 and 137-58.

5. See William E. Souder, *Management Decision Methods* (New York: Van Nostrand Reinhold, 1980), pp. 64-77 and 159-61.

# 11
# R&D and Marketing Roles for Innovation

> New opinions are always suspected and usually opposed without any other reason but because they are not already common.
> —John Locke, 1685

What roles should marketing and R&D play in order to achieve new product innovation success? Should marketing be responsible for setting the design specifications of the new product? Or should R&D do that? Should R&D participate in the market definition? Or should that be an exclusive marketing role? Should R&D lead marketing on some aspects, while marketing leads R&D on others?

A review of the data base indicated that there is no one answer to these questions. It all depends on the circumstances. The data base revealed several models that can guide R&D and marketing in selecting the appropriate roles for the circumstances.

## The Customer-Developer Conditions (CDC) Model

Two dimensions captured many of the situations found within the data base. The two dimensions are: the customer's level of sophistication and the new product developer's level of sophistication.

There were some customers who had very little awareness of their own needs. Others were very much aware of their needs. Some customers understood their needs but were unable to translate them into product specifications. Others were able to specify precisely what they needed. They could write a set of specifications for a new product innovation that precisely met their needs. Thus, some customers were highly sophisticated. Others were much less sophisticated.

Similarly, new product developers were encountered who were highly sophisticated. They understood the forms and specifications for most types of new products, and they had the know-how to make them. Understanding new product forms requires a depth of knowledge about the processes for developing new products and the processes of fulfilling customer needs. The know-how to make new products requires a depth of knowledge about science, engineering, and technical means. Thus, the most sophisticated product developers have a high level of product form sophistication, and a high level of technical means sophistication. Lower degrees of sophistication are common. For example, it is possible to know a lot about new product forms but to lack the technical means and know-how to make them. Similarly, it is possible to have high means knowledge or technical know-how, but to lack the ability to use it in developing useful new products. Many such situations were encountered within the data base.

A consideration of these aspects led the author to formulate the customer-developer conditions (CDC) model shown in figure 11-1. In this model, the customer's level of sophistication and the new product developer's level of sophistication are viewed as orthogonal variables. The customer's level of sophistication is a function of two other continuous variables: his awareness of his needs, and his ability to translate these needs into product specifications. The developer's level of sophistication is also a function of two other continuous variables. One is the depth of his technical know-how, or his technical means sophistication. The other is his breadth of knowledge of new product processes, or his product form sophistication. The combinations of these four variables create various sets of conditions, or cells. These conditions dictate the nature of the R&D/marketing interface that is required in order to achieve a commercially successful new product innovation within each cell.

It should be noted that figure 11-1 considers only 12 possibilities from among the many combinations of customer-developer conditions. In between the extremes of cells A and L are a universe of degrees of customer-developer sophistications.

## Cell A

Customers who fall into cell A of figure 11-1 know exactly what they want and can state precisely what will satisfy their needs. These customers are well aware of their own needs and can translate them into precise product specifications. These are highly sophisticated customers. They understand both themselves and the technology.

Similarly, the new product developers in cell A are also highly sophisticated. Once the customer informs the developer of their needs and the corresponding product specifications, the developer can immediately proceed to use his superior knowledge of the technical means to make the product.

In effect, cell A is the condition of no uncertainty. Under these conditions, there is no need for a traditional marketing function. Note that there is a need for some type of shipping, merchandising, or selling function. Someone must convey the product to the customer (make sure the product is shipped

*Customer's Level of Sophistication*

—— Increasing Level of Need Awareness ——

—— Increasing Level of Translation Abilities ——

| | Understands Own Needs and Can Translate Them into Product Specifications | Understands Own Needs But Can't Translate Them into Product Specifications | Does Not Understand Own Needs |
|---|---|---|---|
| Understands the Product Specification and the Technical Means to Develop New Products | A | B | C |
| Understands the Technical Means But Does Not Understand the Product Specification | D | E | F |
| Understands the Product Specification But Not the Technical Means to Develop It | G | H | I |
| Does Not Understand Either the Technical Means or the Product Specification | J | K | L |

← Increasing Level of Product —— Form Sophistication

← Increasing Level of Technical —— Means Sophistication

*Developer's Level of Sophistication*

**Figure 11–1. Customer-Developer Conditions (CDC) Model**

and collect on the sale). But there is no traditional marketing function. There may be marketing personnel in the act, but they are only communicators, facilitators, or conveyors. The product is defined by the customer and the developer makes it to his specifications with no uncertainty. That is the key: there is no uncertainty for either party.

Cell A is the classical technology-pull situation. Here is a case where R&D can naturally dominate marketing in a harmonious relationship. A technical one-man show in which the inventor also markets the product may be effective under these conditions. Technical line management methods may also be effective here (see chapters 9 and 10). Note that because the cell A customer is technically sophisticated, he will only purchase the product if it is truly performance superior and cost-effective. Thus, the developer must have a high quality, deep-science based R&D effort.

*Cell B*

Customers often fully understand their own needs but are unable to translate them into product specifications. Customers may be able to state that they want a product to do this or that or solve such and such a problem. But it is often more difficult for them to clearly state precisely how that product should look or how it should perform under various conditions. Similarly, even though developers may be very sophisticated, they cannot proceed without a set of product specifications.

A translator is needed. Someone must interact and dialogue with customers to translate their needs, as they perceive them, into precise technical product specifications. These are marketing skills, and a significant marketing function must be performed here. Highly specialized marketing skills and know-how are required. Note that this translation function is not a one-time undertaking. Rather, the customer's needs are usually only revealed through a series of translations and prototype product trials. A typical cycle of activities consists of need translation, development of prototype, customer trial of prototype, translation of newly discovered additional needs, development of modified prototype, trial of modified prototype, and so forth. The cycle may be repeated many times before the new product innovation is perfected. Thus, the required marketing function is significant and enduring in cell B. It is not a one-shot, one-time need.

Translating needs involves frequent communications and interactions between the R&D and marketing parties. However, most of this communication is one-way, from marketing to R&D. Thus, the project can still succeed, even if only a relatively weak R&D/marketing interface prevails in cell B. Here is a case where marketing can justifiably dominate R&D. Commercial line management, commercial one-man shows, or dyads (defined and discussed in chapter 9) may be effective under cell B conditions.

## Cell C

In cell C, the users do not understand their own needs and cannot therefore translate them into product specifications. This is not an uncommon situation. For example, consumers shopping for a new automobile may be aware that they have a need for economical transportation. Yet they may walk out of the showroom satisfied that they have the answer to their needs with a large, energy inefficient automobile. The customer discovered (and so did the salesman!) that they had other needs, including status and psychic gratification.

Cell C is a demanding case. Someone must help users understand their own needs and also translate these into product specifications. Thus, two significant and fundamental marketing functions must be carried out in cell C: need identification and product specification translation. There is no denying that, in theory, the developer may be able to perform all these feats. It is only claimed that these are marketing functions, regardless of who carries them out.

Cell C places much greater demands on the marketing function than does cell B, since the users do not understand their own needs. Research, study and introspection into the users' environments are needed. It may be necessary to observe the users' environments for long periods of time to ascertain their needs. Considerable dialogue and interaction may be needed to determine how they perceives their needs. Personnel trained in customer psychology are often needed to observe and interpret the users' needs.

Cell C can place heavy demands on the R&D/marketing interface. Close collaboration between marketing and R&D may be needed in order to fully understand the users' technical environments and to describe the users' feelings and motives. Sometimes the language and insights of both marketing and R&D are jointly required to fully define the users' problems. Thus, a strong willingness of the R&D and marketing parties to collaborate and communicate with each other is needed to succeed under the conditions in cell C.

## Cells D, E, and F

In cells D, E, and F developers have lower product form sophistication than in cells A, B, and C. They are technologically adept in the underlying sciences and skilled in the relevant engineering disciplines. But they are unsure how to use these to achieve a need-fulfilling product that meets the performance specifications that are detailed for them. For example, as an engineer, I know many different ways to design a high-pressure pump. But I would not necessarily comprehend the specifications for a pump to be used in outer space. Someone would have to explain why the various specifications exist and what they imply.

Thus, the conditions within cells D, E, and F are analogous to those within cells A, B, and C respectively, except that a greater degree of translation is required. In these cases, R&D and marketing must interact, question each other, and jointly work out definitions and specifications that each party understands. Marketing has a teaching function to carry out in addition to their translation function. They must teach R&D exactly what the specifications mean. But here is the salient point: they cannot do this teaching by themselves. R&D must teach marketing enough about their world that the two parties can arrive at mutually familiar grounds. For example, my marketing colleague may not be able to tell me why an outer space pump must perform in a certain way unless I give him enough knowledge about pumps that he can understand my dilemmas. We must both achieve the same level of knowledge about pumps. Only then will he be able to explain why these particular specifications are needed, in terms that I can understand and accept. And I will not produce a good pump for my marketing colleague unless I fully understand why he must have these particular specifications. Achieving this type of understanding is vital to creating a good product. And this type of understanding can only be achieved through a harmonious R&D/marketing interface (see chapter 10).

### Cells G, H, and I

The conditions in these cells are analogous to those in cells A, B, and C, except for one important difference. Here, the developers do not fully understand the means to be used to achieve the end product specifications. Simply put, the developers do not understand how to get there.

This is a very different situation from any of those in cells A through F. In all those cases, the developers understood the technical means. If the customers could tell the developers what they wanted, the developers could quickly select a means from their repertoires. For example, give a competent polymer chemist a list of desired performances in a new plastic hose and he can quickly specify which polymers to use and how to blend them. The ability to do this depends on technological know-how. Some know-how is not this well developed. This poorly developed know-how is the one referred to in cells G, H, and I.

But isn't this a technical function? What does this have to do with marketing? Indeed, in cells G, H, and I the developer needs to learn about alternative means. This is indeed a technical function. It requires experimentation and technical research. But more than this, the developer needs to learn which means are associated with which end performance specification. Learning to match means with end performances requires the joint intelligence of marketing and R&D.

For example, the marketing managers may discuss the end specifications they think are required. R&D personnel may ask what this implies and inquire whether this can be achieved by such and such a technology if it could be made so and so. This may suggest a whole new way of looking at the problem that stimulates new thoughts and product concepts. Alternatively, what the marketing department says may trigger a whole new way of thinking by R&D about the various means. As this dialogue continues, each department builds on the thoughts of the other, and still more creative thoughts and new understandings may emerge. This is the creative thought process in action. From these dialogues, R&D personnel may be able to formulate experimental research programs. They may do this, at first, on paper. Marketing can then react and provide further guidance to R&D. The next step may be a laboratory research program in which R&D creates prototype products for marketing to consider. From their reactions, R&D may learn a great deal about which means to employ to achieve the desired product performances. Ideally, they will advance their state of knowledge to the point of the above polymers example: they will understand the complete repertoire of means to achieve a complete spectrum of performances.

Thus, there is great need for considerable interaction and patience between R&D and marketing in cells G, H, and I. Typically, R&D will require substantial funds and time to learn. They will offer several prototypes which marketing and the customer must react to in order for R&D to build on their learning curve. This experimentation may not be highly palatable to marketing, who would like R&D to go directly to the best solution. But going directly to a solution is simply not possible under the conditions of cells G, H, and I. Thus, new product committee, commercial project manager, and dyad methods may be required under these conditions (see chapter 9). A strong, harmonious R&D/marketing interface is mandatory for success in cells G, H, and I (see chapter 10).

## Cells J, K, and L

In these cells, the developers lack both a depth of knowledge about the relevant sciences and the know-how to apply them. Therefore, the marketing roles which were so important in cells G, H, and I become even more important here. The need for R&D to engage in experimentation and learning are vital in these cells. Funding and time will be required for R&D to bring themselves up to date on the learning curve.

Note that cell L is the most demanding of all. Marketing must be a very effective discoverer of the customer's needs. Marketing must also be highly skilled at perceiving and translating these needs. And marketing must be a creative catalyst, helping R&D to learn the relevant means-product performance systems. New product committees, commercial project manager methods, and dyadic relationships are especially important in cell L. Harmonious R&D/marketing interfaces are essential in cell L (see chapters 9 and 10).

## Implications of the Customer-Developer Conditions (CDC) Model

It is vital for a prospective innovator or new product developer to understand which cell he will be operating within. The cell conditions define many of the roles which the R&D and marketing parties must play if a successful new product innovation is to occur. A knowledge of the cell conditions confronting a new product developer or marketer indicates the nature of the R&D/marketing interface and the management methods that are required (see chapters 9 and 10).

Cell A is the only one where a highly developed R&D/marketing interface is not required. The conditions in cell A do not appear to occur very often, at least not for innovations. Anyone who thinks they are in cell A would be well advised to verify that impression, since it is a relatively rare condition.

On the other hand, cell L may pose insurmountable obstacles. To succeed in cell L requires that the innovator acquire great knowledge of the relevant sciences, the application know-how and the user's needs. Achieving this requires a considerable commitment of time and funds, and is not a matter to be taken lightly. Innovators in cell L must ask themselves a fundamental question: Do we now have, or can we acquire quickly enough, the skills to succeed under these conditions?

The CDC model emphasizes the importance of accurate forecasting, thorough planning, and honest analyses. New product developers must accurately forecast which cell they will be operating in at the time they expect to market their innovations. That same customer who was in cell C last year may have moved up on his learning curve this year: he may now be in cell A. Every customer is a moving target. New product developers must therefore plan their work so that their actions are the appropriate ones, and so that they occur in a timely fashion. New product developers must also make honest assessments of their own strengths, weaknesses, and capabilities. Developers too often visualize themselves as having higher levels of sophistication than they actually have. They often see themselves in cells A, B, or C when in fact they are in cells J, K, or L.

## Testing the CDC Model

The CDC model suggests that top-down structures and technical one-man shows (see chapter 9) could successfully be used to manage projects within cell A. Moreover, the lack of appreciation and distrust syndromes between R&D and marketing (see chapter 10) may not inhibit project success within cell A. Just the opposite can be hypothesized for cell L, where such methods and syndromes would appear to be very deleterious to project success.

These hypotheses were tested by randomly sampling cell A and cell L type projects from the data base. The CDC model dimensions for each project were scored by the subjects at the firms as part of the data collections.[1] Unfortunately for this test of the CDC model, there were relatively few projects in cell L that used top-down structures and technical one-man show methods. But, this fact alone provides some support for the hypotheses: management correctly avoided these methods under cell L conditions. The results of the sampling and analyses are presented in table 11-1. In spite of some small sample sizes, the results support the above hypotheses.

Though this has been a very modest test of the CDC model, the results clearly support the model. Cell A conditions place few demands on the R&D/marketing interface, and sophisticated management methods are not required. Cell L conditions demand a very well-developed R&D/marketing interface, and highly sophisticated management methods are needed to cope with these conditions.

**le 11–1**

**C Model Cell Conditions, Management Methods, and R&D/Marketing rface Conditions**[a]

| | *Percentage of Projects That Met or Exceeded Their Commercial Expectations under Various Methods and Conditions*[b] | | | | |
|---|---|---|---|---|---|
| | *Methods* | | *Conditions* | | |
| *C Cell ditions* | *Top Down Structures* | *Technical One-Man Show* | *Lack of Interaction* | *Lack of Communication* | *Distrust* |
| A | 68 | 60 | 65 | 62 | 45 |
| L | 20 | 15 | 0[c] | 14[d] | 11[e] |

cept where noted, at least 20 projects were in each cell.
table 2-1.
ere were only four projects here.
ere were only seven projects here.
ere were only nine projects here.

## Perceived Opportunity Genesis Models

As discussed in chapter 5 (tables 5-3 and 5-4), the new product innovations in the data base came from several sources. The genesis of these project ideas was found to have implications for the behaviors of R&D and marketing personnel.

Three types of genesis situations were found. In one situation, model A, the idea for the new product was a technology push from R&D. In another type, model B, the idea for the new product was a technology pull from the marketing department. In the third type, model C, the idea was a suggestion by a third party outside the firm (supplier, customer, agency). Let us now look at each of these three models and their implications.

### Model A: Technology Push by R&D

Table 11-2 traces the typical sequence of activities for the case where the R&D department has a technology with new product potentials. This is the means-generated innovation situation (see chapter 1). The sequence of seven key activities shown in table 11-2 as model A were the ones most frequently observed within the data base for successful means-generated innovations. Thus, model A may be viewed as a kind of normative model or set of pre-scriptions to be followed in order to maximize the chances of success for a means-generated innovation.

Activity 1 in table 11-2, information seeking, is a very important activity. R&D personnel seldom have the special skills required to analyze the market potentials of a new technology. They must rely on marketing specialists for this information. The exception is the technical one-man show. However, as noted in chapter 9, few technical one-man shows succeed. Relatively few situations exist where R&D can successfully analyze the markets for their technologies. Unfortunately, this is not a widely held belief by R&D personnel. All too often, R&D either lacks faith in the marketing specialists or distrusts them. Unless these hurdles can be overcome, the typical means-generated project is doomed from the start of this first activity.

Activity 2, marketing response, is equally as critical as activity 1. The marketing specialist has a serious responsibility to respond to the best of his creative professional abilities. R&D personnel frequently complain that when confronted with a new technology their marketing specialists flippantly respond that no market exists. This result is often an artifact of the market research techniques that are used. For example, when asked if they would spend $1,000 for a five-inch round screen to receive movies in their home, consumers in the late 1940s and early 1950s generally said no. Thus, some marketing specialists concluded that there was no market for such a technology. If every product developer had accepted that conclusion there would be

**Table 11–2**
**Key Activities within Genesis Model A: Technology Push by R&D**

Activity 1. Information Seeking. R&D seeks market opportunity data for a technology from marketing specialists

Activity 2. Marketing Response. Marketing specialists suggest application opportunities

Activity 3. Agreement. R&D and marketing agree on a product or market plan

Activity 4. Product Development. R&D performs the work in collaboration with marketing

Activity 5. Product Testing. Marketing evaluates the product in collaboration with R&D

Activity 6. Product Modification. R&D optimizes and adjusts the product according to the test results from step 5 above

Activity 7. Implementation. R&D, marketing, and production collaborate to move the product into routine customer applications

no home television today. Fortunately, in this case there were some creative marketing specialists and product developers who tested other configurations of the basic technology, at other prices. In analyzing the potential markets for an innovation, several different concepts of that innovation should be tested in a variety of scenarios. Potential users of innovations often have limited awareness of their needs for such products (see the CDC model above). Thus, several different versions or concepts of the innovation must be tested with them. Unfortunately, there are far too many stories like the above five-inch television; the marketing specialist often has a serious credibility problem to overcome. Because of it, many R&D personnel would rather chance a one-man show than have their idea effectively killed by a hidebound marketing specialist, who declares to top management that no market exists for this technology. This can devastatingly demoralize R&D personnel, especially if they feel that marketing has the ear of top management.

Activity 3, agreement, is also extremely critical. R&D must be willing to compromise on their ideas. For example, a five-inch screen that costs $1,000 may indeed not have a consumer recreational market. Can't R&D make it bigger? Could it be made portable? Can't trade-offs be made between cost and performance? Marketing must also be willing to compromise, to take a more creative viewpoint. Is there another group of nontraditional users who might be interested in this five-inch screen product? Does it have uses in laboratory instruments where size limitation is a common problem? Does it have nonrecreational uses? None of this creative thinking will come to anything worthwhile if it does not lead to a plan for joint R&D/marketing action. The two parties must come to agreement on a joint action plan for the development and implementation of the technology.

Activities 4 through 7 emphasize the need for teamwork. R&D must be willing to submit their prototypes for market testing and willing to participate in these activities according to the established plans. R&D personnel must learn to overcome their natural reluctance to have their ideas and technologies evaluated. They must suppress their fears and apprehensions that their ideas will be unfairly tested. They need to develop a sense of trust and confidence in their marketing counterparts. Marketing must be equally willing and able to give advice and to be involved in the technical developments. They must behave in such a way as to earn the trust and confidence of their R&D counterparts. They need to overcome their reluctance to get deeply involved in the technical details. They must be willing to take the time to let the R&D personnel educate them in the technology. And they must be willing to share their thoughts and subject their opinions to scrutiny by R&D. Moreover, R&D and marketing must act as a team, collaborating in order to move the product into routine customer applications.

It is clear that all seven steps in model A require close cooperation and flexible behaviors by the R&D and marketing parties. The maintenance of harmonious relationships and the avoidance of the disharmonies discussed in chapter 10 are vital to the success of this model.

## Model B: Technology Pull by Marketing

Table 11-3 traces the typical sequence of activities for the case where the marketing department senses a market opportunity for a new product. This is the needs-generated innovation situation (see chapter 1). The sequence of seven key activities shown in table 11-3 as model B were the ones most frequently observed within the data base for successful needs-generated innovations. Thus, model B may be viewed as a kind of normative model or set of prescriptions to be followed in order to maximize the chances of success for a needs-generated innovation.

The only differences between model B and model A are in the first three activities in the sequence. However, these differences lend some unique aspects to model B. Specifically, in activity 1 of model B, marketing must have a sufficient understanding of the relevant technologies and the language to convey the opportunity to R&D. This is not a trivial barrier. It demands a high degree of competence on the part of the marketing personnel in accurately sensing a potential user need, translating that need into product specifications, and communicating that need to R&D.

In activity 2, R&D has a very serious responsibility to respond carefully to marketing's communication. A common complaint of marketing personnel is that R&D promises too much at this point. Too many R&D functions fail

Table 11–3
Key Activities within Genesis Model B: Technology Pull by Marketing

| | |
|---|---|
| Activity 1. | Opportunity Communication. Marketing communicates the opportunity to R&D |
| Activity 2. | R&D Response. R&D indicates capabilities and possibilities |
| Activity 3. | Compromise/Agreement. A product/market contingency plan or flexible compromise plan is agreed upon |
| Activities 4–7. | Same as Model A |

to appreciate their own limitations. There is a tendency for R&D to become overly optimistic about their capabilities, causing the firm to rush into things they cannot deliver. An equally common complaint is that R&D tends to reject the idea solely because it comes from marketing. There are some R&D departments that feel the only credible ideas are the ones they generate. Thus, the organization climates discussed in chapter 7 and the R&D/marketing attitudes discussed in chapter 10 become very significant in the case of model B.

To accomplish activity 3 in model B, considerable give and take, flexibility, and compromise are required. These needs are much greater in the case of model B than they are in the above model A. Why? Because in model B the technology is undeveloped. Uncertainty exists about its feasibility. No one knows for sure that the technology can actually be developed. By contrast, in model A, R&D has a technology in hand and there is a much higher level of certainty about that technology. Thus, in activity 3 of model B it is vitally important that the parties generate a set of contingency plans for the project. Key checkpoints must be prespecified over the life of the new product development plan. This is a very important aspect that must not be overlooked. At each of these checkpoints, the R&D and marketing parties must jointly meet to assess the progress to date on the project. They must be prepared to alter the project, based on their assessments at that time. This demands a true team spirit and mutual respect. A very strong R&D/marketing interface is thus a prerequisite for success in the case of model B.

*Model C: Technology Suggestion by an Outsider*

It is not unusual for customers, suppliers, vendors, independent inventors, or others outside the organization to suggest potential new product innovations to either R&D or marketing. This scenario is presented in table 11-4 as model C. Whether or not R&D or marketing actually become advocates for the outside suggestion may depend on the status and credibility of the suggester, and many of the other factors discussed in connection with models A and B.

**Table 11–4**
**Key Activities within Genesis Model C: Suggestion by an Outside Party**

| | |
|---|---|
| Activity 1. | Suggestion Is Made. An outside party suggests an idea to either R&D or marketing |
| Activity 2. | Joint Consultation and Evaluation. R&D and marketing meet to consult with each other to evaluate the suggestion; combination of activity 2 from model A and activity 2 from model B |
| Activities 3–7. | Same as model A. |

If R&D becomes an advocate for the suggested technology, then this situation becomes model A. If marketing becomes an advocate, then this situation becomes model B.

However, there are some major differences between model C and models A and B. In the case of model C, the advocates may feel less emotional commitment and enthusiasm for an outside idea than they would for their own ideas. This can make a significant difference. Emotional commitments are an important ingredient in many successful innovations.

Suggestions by an outsider may be meaningless if the firm knows little or nothing about that technology. Suppose marketing becomes an advocate for an outside idea where R&D feels incompetent. How will R&D react to this? Will R&D simply turn a deaf ear on a suggestion they don't understand or an area where they feel technically inadequate? Will R&D fear that admitting their incompetency lowers their status in the eyes of marketing? Will R&D therefore engage in tactics to hide their inadequacy? Will marketing pressure top management to initiate a new product development in the face of R&D's reluctance? This is sufficient discussion to show that many dynamic behavioral action/reaction scenarios can occur.

Thus, model C may induce more complex behaviors and create more difficult challenges for the R&D/marketing interface than either model A or model B. It appears that, because of these behavioral dynamics, success with outside ideas could be far more difficult than when the genesis of the idea is internal to the firm.

### Implications of the Genesis Models

It is important for the R&D and marketing parties to understand whether they are in a model A, model B, or model C situation. The models dictate the necessary roles and behaviors needed to achieve a successful innovation in each situation. Roles and behaviors that are important in one model may not be important in another. A complete understanding of these models by R&D

and marketing personnel should foster a better R&D/marketing interface and higher new product success rates.

## Organizational Settings and Task Activities

An organizational setting consists of a set of activities carried out in order to achieve an organization's goals. There is a corresponding set of roles to be played in carrying out these activities.

### Settings for New Product Innovation

Table 11-5 lists five organizational settings and their corresponding activities that were frequently found in the data base. In the service setting, a group or department responds to a request for information, materials, or actions. All groups and departments must necessarily devote some of their time and resources to an occasional service setting. The R&D/marketing interface is characterized by numerous, frequent service settings. R&D and marketing parties typically alternate in providing various services to each other.

In the problem solving setting, the department or group exercises its

**e 11–5**

**nple of Five Organizational Settings and Corresponding Task Activities**

| | Examples of Corresponding Task Activities for New Product Development | |
| --- | --- | --- |
| *nizational Setting* | *R&D* | *Marketing* |
| ce | Processing a request from marketing for laboratory performance data | Collecting and reporting sales estimates on candidate projects which R&D is contemplating |
| lem Solving | Selecting the best portfolio of projects | Determining the best strategy for the introduction of a new product |
| lopment | The development of a new floor tile resin | The development of a marketing strategy for a new floor tile |
| ctrination | Attempts to persuade marketing that an entirely new product idea or concept is needed | Attempts to persuade R&D that only a minor variation of an old product is needed |
| rol | Reallocating resources based on project status changes | Readjusting the timing of a planned new product introduction as a result of shifts in consumer demand |

power, autonomy, and authority to establish a policy concerning some resource under its control. This is one of the settings that many individuals and groups within organizations often enjoy. An aura of high status and perceived power tends to surround this setting. By contrast, the service setting is often viewed as implying a low status, passive, or dependent role. The development setting is generally perceived to be a high status item. Indoctrination can imply high or low status, depending on whether or not one is giving or receiving the indoctrination. Control can also take on high or low status images, depending on whether one is doing the controlling or being controlled.

### *Consequences of High and Low Status Settings*

It is unfortunate that high status and low status images have become so well established for these settings. These images often get in the way of R&D/ marketing collaboration. They represent sociopsychological barriers that R&D and marketing parties must overcome if they are to become an effective team.

These status images are more myth than reality. For example, it is often said that the service setting is a low status and low power setting. But how can such myths endure? The party doing the serving is, in fact, in a position of great power. Without the requested service, the recipient is severely hampered. Looked at in this light, service is a very powerful setting.

All this is a moot point within a true R&D/marketing team ambience. A true team recognizes that all the settings listed in table 11-5 are necessary. Effective team members stand ready and willing to enter into whichever setting is needed to achieve the team's goals.

## Task Level Conflict and Integration

Table 11-6 lists seven artifacts of organizations that were found among the data base. These seven repeatedly appeared as antecedents of conflict between R&D and marketing. Disharmonies and conflicts between R&D and marketing were often traced to one or more of these seven factors (see chapters 9 and 10).

### *Conflict Producing Factors*

Specialists are essential in modern organizations. Depths of expertise are vital to the establishment of the deep know-how required for innovation. Grouping specialists into separate departments maximizes organizational efficiency. It is also advantageous to the specialists to be grouped together in a cohesive

### Table 11–6
### Antecedents of R&D/Marketing Conflict

Technical specialization

Different time sense

Different motives and goals

Functional allegiances

Dissimilar jargon

Bounded sense of responsibility

Clique mentality

___

unit, where they can achieve a critical mass of effort and associate with like personnel of similar interests.

But problems arise when these specialists are requested to collaborate with other specialists. Then dissimilar jargons can lead to misunderstandings and communication failures. Different specialized groups naturally have different motives, different goals, and a different sense of time. For example, marketing's major concern is usually to get a working product into the customer's hands as quickly as possible. This often conflicts with R&D's objective of perfecting the technically best product.

The strong functional allegiances that specialists build for their home group or function often stand in the way of collaboration with other groups. This allegiance promotes a bounded sense of responsibility ("Our work stops here"; "We won't stick our necks out for you"). A clique mentality develops, in which only like specialists are privy to some types of information. This can result in the following pseudo-rationale: "You must accept the fact that we can't take the time to explain this to you, and you wouldn't understand it anyway." Under these circumstances, it becomes all too natural for one specialized group to lock out another from participating in their activities.

### *Achieving Task Integration to Overcome Conflicts*

The cases in the data base suggest that the specialized R&D and marketing parties must achieve task integration. This is a commonality of goals and purposes, but only for the task at hand. In task integration, the parties retain their specialized viewpoints, functional allegiances, and separate cliques. But they cooperate in those aspects necessary for the success of the new product development task, for the duration of that task. Otherwise, the specialized parties are free to go their separate ways. This is an important quality. Task integration does not ask the R&D personnel to act more like marketers, nor the marketers to act more like R&D personnel. It does not ask the parties to change their fundamental values or beliefs. Under task integration, the parties can continue to dislike each other, they can continue to think that the other is rather peculiar, etc. But they are expected to collaborate on matters essential to the successful completion of the project, which is in their mutual interest. Task integration is a partial collaboration, partial exchange, limited trading with the enemy or detente.[2]

How is task integration achieved? Four antecedents of task integration were found in the data base, as listed in table 11-7. All of these antecedents involve top management intervention. First, top management must set forth the task integration rules. These rules specify the areas where the parties are expected to collaborate and the areas where they need not associate with each other. Second, these rules must often be fortified by sanctions for non-compliance, including low performance ratings for those who do not follow the rules. Third, the establishment of a common enemy, the competition, may be necessary to further motivate task integration. The R&D and marketing parties can become very harmonious if top management convinces them that the firm's future health and their jobs are seriously threatened by a competitor's new product! Fourth, it is also very helpful if top management agrees to assume the risk for some errors that the groups may make. Just knowing that they will not be held responsible makes groups more inclined to take risks.[3]

The reader should note that the NIG method discussed in chapter 10 was aimed at achieving task integration. Though the NIG method does not specifically provide any of the four items listed in table 11-7, it does invoke a very effective spirit of task integration. For those parties who appreciate the need for task integration, the NIG method may provide the only inducements needed. When used with the four items in table 11-7, the NIG method can be especially powerful and effective.[4]

### When to Invoke Task Integration

Spontaneous, self-initiated cooperation and collaboration by R&D and marketing is the optimum condition for fostering new product innovation success. When this optimum is not available, when the two parties refuse to

**Table 11–7**
**Antecedents of Task Integration**

Establishment of task integration rules

Sanctions for non-compliance

Common enemy

Management risk absorption

cooperate, or when time does not permit the luxury of letting the two parties grow together, then top management must intervene. Task integration is called for.

Top management can foster task-only collaboration or task integration between R&D and marketing by invoking the four antecedents listed in table 11-7. This is preferable to top management dictating all the finite behaviors that must occur between R&D and marketing, or engaging in other attempts to destroy the separate R&D and marketing cultures.

Reorganizing in ways that break up the established cliques and commingle the specialists also destroys the advantages of these specializations. This can be a significant loss. Yet such reorganizations are commonly used in an attempt to bring R&D and marketing together. Moreover, at the end of the task, management will probably again reorganize and reassemble the specialized groups as they originally were! It would seem preferable to try to achieve task integration. It may be noted that task integration is the essence of an effective matrix organization or a project management team.[4]

## Summary

The success of new product innovation projects depends greatly on the collaborative roles played by the R&D and marketing parties. However, no one set of roles can be prescribed. The R&D and marketing parties must be flexible enough to play whatever joint roles or engage in whatever team behaviors are demanded by the situation.

This chapter has detailed several models of situations and the appropriate R&D and marketing roles corresponding to these situations. It is not possible to develop rigorous recipes and prescriptions of successful behaviors. At best, the models described in this chapter can only serve as guides to successful behaviors. They can be used as useful reminders of the behaviors and attitudes that R&D and marketing personnel should strive for. The models in this chapter all reiterate the importance of empathy: R&D and marketing must constantly strive to literally walk a mile in each other's shoes.

## Notes

1. For more details, the reader is directed to chapter 12 and chapter 13 and the associated discussion of difficult versus easy technologies and markets.

2. See William E. Souder et al., *An Exploratory Study of the Coordinating Mechanisms Between R&D and Marketing as an Influence on the Innovation Process,* National Science Foundation Final Report, August 26, 1977, chapter 2, pp. 2.1-2.35.

198 · *Managing New Product Innovations*

3. The classic work on this phenomenon is M. A. Wallach, Nathan Kogan, and D. J. Bem, "Group Influence on Individual Risk Taking," *Journal of Abnormal and Social Psychology,* 65, no. 2 (1962), 75-86.

4. For more on this, see William E. Souder, "Effectiveness of Nominal and Interacting Group Decision Processes for Integrating R&D and Marketing," *Management Science,* 23, no. 6 (1977), 595-605.

# 12
# Technology as a Determinant of Project Success

Half the failures in life arise from pulling in one's horse when he is leaping.

—Augustus Hare, 1834

What is a technology? Technologies permeate every aspect of our daily lives. Therefore, this should be an easy question to answer. Yet it is not.

This chapter presents some definitions of technology, develops a technology scale, and uses it to measure the technologies in the data base. These measurements are then used to examine the effects of the technologies on the success rates of the new product innovations. The results show that the nature of a technology can significantly affect the success or failure of an innovation project, no matter how well it is managed.

## Definition of Technology

One source of difficulty in defining and measuring technologies is their multidimensional nature. Technologies can exist in various levels of embodiment: as products, as processes, in different forms, in different shapes, or as embryonic ideas. Technologies may exist at several levels: applied, developmental, or basic. Technologies may have various characteristics: complexity, newness, riskiness, etc. Another source of difficulty lies in our colloquial use of terms like "high technology" and "low technology", which create the illusion of precise measurement.

Anything that increases one's knowledge or know-how may be considered to be a technology. Technologies thus include machines, tools, equipment, processes, instructions, prescriptions, recipes, patterns, devices, ideas, and other knowledge. Accordingly, all technologies are ultimately reducible to some kind of knowledge. Technology is therefore the knowledge to make machines, invent patterns, solve problems, develop things, and conceive new ideas. Thus, a technology is any storehouse of knowledge that can lead to still more knowledge.

Consider the following three kinds of technologies: conceptual technology, implemental technology, and practice technology. Conceptual technology is the capability to create new concepts, forms, shapes, and theories. Implemental technology is the capability to create useful devices and other technologies from conceptual technologies. Practice technology is the capability to routinely use these devices and other technologies.[1]

Conceptual technology creates theories. Implemental technology reduces them to practice. Practice technology guides their routine application. Conceptual technology provides the basis for implemental technology, which is the basis for practice technology. Abstract theories (conceptual technology) give rise to applications (implemental technology), which give rise to routine use (practice technology). High degrees of implemental technology enable us to apply theories and abstract concepts through some device or know-how. High degrees of practice technology enable us to make repeated use of this device or this know-how in a successful fashion. For example, Einstein's theory of relativity is a conceptual technology. It is theoretical, conceptual, and abstract knowledge. Controlled nuclear fission is an example of an implemental technology that is based on Einstein's conceptual technology. The procedures used to routinely operate a nuclear power plant are an example of a practice technology that is derived from conceptual and implemental technologies.

The three kinds of technology are closely interrelated and interdependent. For example, many theories are purely conceptual technology. But theories and concepts are also derived in part from observations about some event or device (an implemental technology) or some routine practice (practice technology). Various facets of all three kinds of technologies are used in our daily lives. To develop his theory of relativity, Einstein drew on several existing conceptual and implemental technologies in physics and mathematics. It is common to use a particular implemental technology to develop a new conceptual technology from an old one.

## Characteristics of Technologies

Because conceptual technology (CT) is associated with theories and conceptual knowledge, it affords the power to predict. A high degree of CT permits high predictability about phenomena. Whether the theory or concepts are based on abstract ideas like the theory of relativity or on years of observations, a theory provides predictability. Given a high degree of CT, it can confidently be stated that something will behave or happen in a certain fashion. High CT is a quality that all sciences strive to achieve: the ability to predict confidently the outcome of an action that is carried out on the system.

Implemental technology (IT) is associated with the ability to respond to a problem or opportunity in an appropriate fashion. Having a high degree of IT enables one to respond appropriately. High IT is indicated when one has a large repertoire of alternative responses, problem solutions, or means to an end, and when one can appropriately match these to the situation. For example, I have a large response repertoire for a stormy day. I can wear boots and a raincoat, carry an umbrella, drive my car instead of walking, and so on. Each is an effective response. Each will achieve my goals every time. Which of these responses I actually select will depend on the severity of the storm. But the point is, I have several known alternatives that I can choose if the weather is stormy. And they will effectively keep me comfortable. Whatever the weather, I can take a known action. Thus, I have a good repertoire of responses. I have high IT for weather.

Practice technology (PT) is associated with the ability to develop routines. Having a high degree of PT allows one to be sure of repeating the same act with equal effectiveness. A recipe is a good example of a PT. By following the steps in the recipe, one can be reasonably certain of achieving the same results each time. A plan is another kind of PT. For example, when it rains, I plan to drive my car instead of walking to the university.

CT, IT, and PT are interrelated in several ways. For example, where I happen to live, the weather is not very predictable. I am able to remain comfortable only because I have a large repertoire of responses. If weather forecasting involved better predictability (a higher degree of CT), then I could easily get by with a smaller repertoire (a lower degree of IT). I could also remain comfortable with fewer contingency plans (a lower degree of PT). On the other hand, it is possible for the weather to be highly predictable, and for one to have a large repertoire of responses but still be uncomfortable. In that case, there is something wrong with the way in which the repertoire is being used, based on the prediction. There is something wrong with the way the CT-IT chain is being reduced to practice. Thus, it is entirely possible to have situations where one or two of the three types of technologies are well-developed while the others are not.[2]

## CT, IT, and PT as Measurable Dimensions

A technology may be pure CT, IT, or PT. Or a technology may consist of some combination of these characteristics. For example, a particular technology could have relatively high CT and IT contents but a relatively low PT content. This suggests the use of some type of scale for measuring the CT, IT, and PT contents of technologies, as illustrated in figure 12-1. Technologies may score either high (at the extremes of the three axes) or low (at the origin of the three axes) on any one of the three characteristics CT, IT, or PT. A technology that scores high on the CT axis has a high degree of conceptuality.

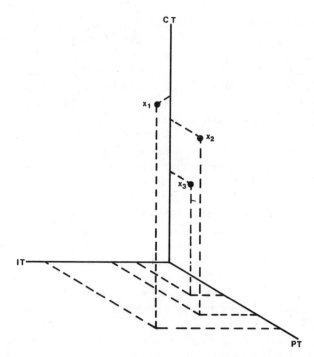

**Figure 12–1. Illustration of CT, IT, and PT Relationships**

Such a technology provides the holder with a high degree of understanding of some system and a corresponding high degree of ability to predict events and outcomes within the system. For example, the currently poor predictive powers about weather patterns suggest that this is not a high CT technology.

A technology that scores high on the IT axis has a high degree of response repertoire. Such a technology provides the holder with many alternative solutions, means, or avenues of action to use in the face of threats or opportunities. For example, it may be said that though the weather sciences have low CT, their IT contents are relatively higher. Temperature, humidity, and atmospheric pressure measurements are highly refined and exact. Based on only one two-digit number, a person can quickly judge the kind of clothing to wear to remain comfortable.

A technology that scores high on the PT axis has a high degree of routine practice about it. Such a technology provides the holder with the ability to repeat an operation or some action with the same consequences or outcomes each time. But the CT content of a technology can affect its PT. For example, a standard prescription when driving an automobile into a tornado is to stop, get out and lie in the ditch beside the highway. This is generally an effective recipe for avoiding personal injury. But it certainly may not be very effective if the tornado suddenly changes direction, by-passes the highway, and comes roaring down the ditch. Here is a case where the low CT of meteorology affects the PT of tornado avoidance. Because of the low CT, the available PT is of limited effectiveness. If tornado behaviors were better understood, more effective recipes and prescriptions could be developed that would reliably avoid them.

Figure 12-1 demonstrates the use of the three-coordinate CT-IT-PT model for characterizing technologies. A new claw hammer would be represented as point $x_1$ in figure 12-1. The claw hammer is based on well-understood principles and theories of physics (CT). If any surprises should occur to a developer of a new claw hammer, there are a large number of actions that can be taken to solve the problems or overcome the obstacles to its successful development. There are many known alternative materials, designs, and configurations that can be used effectively (IT). Failing these, the users of claw hammers have well-defined practices that may allow them to overcome some product deficiencies (PT). For example, I can use either an aluminum, steel, or wooden handled claw hammer with about equal dexterity. Thus, here is a technology that scores high on all three axes.

In contrast, synthetic beef would be represented by point $x_2$ in figure 12-1. There are theories governing the chemistry of synthetic foods. However, they are not as well-developed as the theories for a claw hammer. Food chemists have alternative ways of using these theories and rearranging molecules to create potentially acceptable products. But, most of this has not yet been reduced to routine practice at this time.

Many other examples can be cited and plotted in figure 12-1. An example of a technology with low CT and low IT but relatively high PT is gear oil additives technology. This technology is shown as point $x_3$ in figure 12-1. There are few well-developed theories on the universal behavior of gear oil additives. Yet manufacturers have long been successful in making additives to enhance the performance of gear lubricants. Based on trial and error and observation, they have developed rules that effectively guide them.

Thus, technologies are complex to describe and define. They are multidimensional and multifaceted. The model captures only a few of the salient dimensions. It takes the rather narrow position that technologies are bundles of knowledge. However, this model has the advantages of simplicity and usefulness. It may be said that what the model lacks in CT it makes up in PT.

## A Scale for Measuring Technologies: An Application of the CT-IT-PT Model

### Q-Sort Exercise

To perform a Q-sort exercise, give each person participating in the exercise a deck of cards, with each card bearing the name or other identification of a technology. Each person is then requested to sort the cards sequentially into five priority levels according to the following four steps.

Step 1: Divide the deck into two stacks, one representing a high priority and the other a low priority (the stacks need not be equal).

Step 2: Select out the medium-priority technologies and stack them separately

Step 3: Select out the very-high and very-low priority technologies and stack them separately.

Step 4: Survey all five stacks and shift individual cards until the classifications are satisfactory.

The Q-sorting exercise illustrated in figure 12-2 was conducted with 25 common technologies (internal combustion engine, suspension bridge, radar, etc.) A panel of managers, engineers, and scientists served as subjects in this exercise.[3]

The objective of the exercise was not to obtain Q-sort data. Rather, the objective was to obtain scale descriptors for each of the resulting Q-sort categories. At the completion of the exercise, each subject was depth interviewed

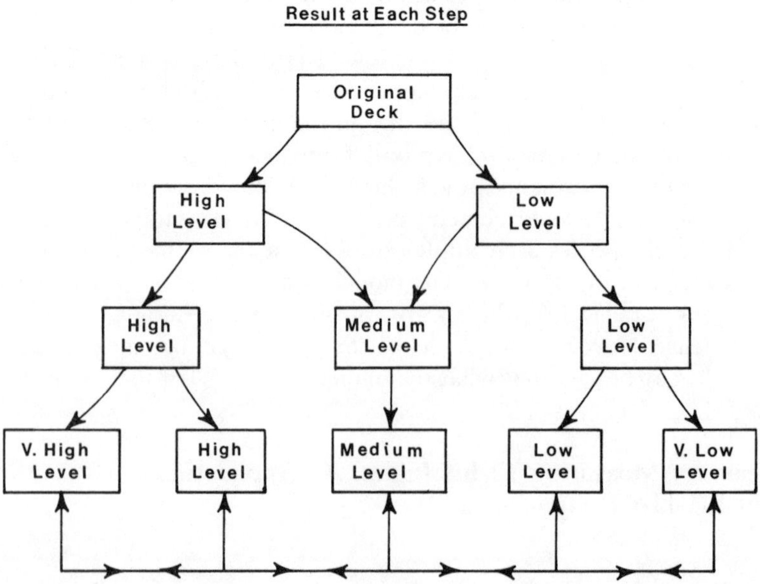

**Result at Each Step**

Figure 12–2. Result at Each Step of the Q-Sort Exercise

regarding the rationale for his Q-sort results. Each was asked to describe the criteria and dimensions he used to make his distinctions. A total of 53 criteria were obtained from these interviews. They included ease of use, newness of the field, complexity, and impacts on society.

### Factors and Measurement Dimensions

The descriptors from the Q-sort exercises were formalized in a 50-item questionnaire illustrated in table 12-1. This questionnaire was then administered to 48 engineers on three separate occasions. On the first occasion, the engineers were asked to complete the questionnaire for technology A in table 12-2. On the second and third occasions, they were asked to complete the questionnaire for technologies B and C respectively. Factor analyses were then used to reduce the questionnaire results to the four significant factors shown in table 12-3.

**Table 12–1**
**Sample Questionnaire Items**

Please indicate how strongly you agree with each of the following statements, relative to the above described new product. For each question, please draw a *circle* around:

SD if you *Strongly Disagree*

D if you *Disagree*

N if you are *Neutral*

A if you *Agree*

SA if you *Strongly Agree*

NA if you feel the statement does *Not Apply* to the above-described new product.

(1) The technology involved is *very new*. Most of the research in the field has been done only in the past few years.
SD _____ D _____ N _____ A _____ SA _____ NA _____

(2) The technology is highly dependent on a large amount of *basic research*.
SD _____ D _____ N _____ A _____ SA _____ NA _____

(3) The technology is extremely *complex*. It involves many interdependent and complicated relationships.
SD _____ D _____ N _____ A _____ SA _____ NA _____

(4) The technology is characterized by a high degree of *precision and accuracy*.
SD _____ D _____ N _____ A _____ SA _____ NA _____

**Table 12–2**
**Summary of Technology Descriptions**

---

*Technology A: "Personal" Portable Computer*

The ABC Company is attempting to develop a 100k-byte memory computer with an integral 150 character-per-second printer. The unit will have an integral video (CRT) display with full color capabilities. The entire unit will weigh no more than 35 pounds, and have a battery pack for portability that weighs no more than 25 pounds. The system will have the capability to use all the available computer languages (Fortran, Cobol, Basic, etc.), and it will have complete word processing and computer graphics capabilities. The user will have full dial-up capability to access other computer systems and data bases, through any commercial telephone. Many home and office applications are anticipated.

*Technology B: Anti-Gravity Device*

The XYZ Company is developing an anti-gravity device for material and human transport. This device is based on a new theory that all matter is held in place by its own unique electromagnetic force field. The theory itself is very complex and is not yet well understood. In lay terms, one implication of this theory is that people and objects can be moved or propelled at varying speeds depending on the degrees to which their force fields are modulated. Travel through time, both into the future and into the past, may also be possible through the application of this new theory. The XYZ Company has successfully demonstrated a small-scale model that illustrates the device they are now working on. This model, and the device they are working on now, is rumored to be powered by some type of high energy, solar-electronic phenomenon. However, the entire project has been shrouded in great secrecy, and little else is known about it.

*Technology C: Feather-Weight Claw Hammer*

The Home Corporation has been producing claw hammers for the building trades and for the home handyman for over 25 years. Home presently has a 70 percent share of the claw hammer market. One of their projects for the next year is to introduce a new light-weight claw hammer. This hammer is targeted for the home craftsman, especially for the growing market for female users. The problem is to make a durable, long-lasting, effective hammer that is light in weight, of the proper balance to be easily used, and has a comfortable feeling handle. Women often complain that most claw hammers are too heavy for them to use easily; not accurately balanced (which causes them to frequently miss hitting nails squarely on the head); uncomfortable to grip, either because of the shape of the handle or its composition; not well constructed (either the head detaches from the handle or the handle breaks off at the head soon after purchase); improperly shaped for them to gain enough leverage to easily pull out a nail with the claw part of the hammer.

Table 12–3
Technology Factors and Their Components

| Factor | Components |
|--------|-----------|
| 1. Impact | Affects other sciences |
| | Affects consumers (cost and utility) and non-commercial users |
| | Affects organizations and industries that deal with it |
| | Global impact on quality of life |
| | Radicalness of impact |
| 2. Accessibility | Ease in understanding the technology |
| | Ease in using the technology |
| | Can be explained and communicated in readily comprehensible terms |
| | Principles of the technology are codified in textbooks |
| 3. Connectedness | Requires diverse types of skills for development |
| | Requires interdependence among workers |
| | Draws upon diverse scientific disciplines |
| 4. State of the Art | Extent of development |
| | Knowledge of potential applications |
| | Extent of reduction to practice |
| | Robustness of the technology |

The first factor listed in table 12-3, impact, refers to the impacts of the technology on consumers, producers, other sciences, and the quality of life in general. The second factor, accessibility, reflects the availability of the technology to various stakeholders like researchers, users, and manufacturers. Some technologies are inaccessible to some users due to geographic limitations, the prospective user's limited skills and knowledge, the user's inability to comprehend them or inability to communicate the technology. The third factor, connectedness, reflects the extent to which the technology is integrated with other theories, principles, practices, and technologies. In general, a technology that is highly connected may be more useful than one that is not. An unconnected technology would seem to be less widely distributed, the variety of users would be more restricted and fewer users would know about it. The fourth factor, state of the art, reflects the extent to which the technology has been developed, elaborated, tested, and integrated with current practices.

*Technology Measurement Instrument*

A panel of experienced engineers and scientists was assembled in a brainstorming session to synthesize these results into a technology measurement device. Several instruments were suggested and developed. Table 12-4 shows one of these instruments.[4]

The panel chose a particular laser technology to illustrate the application of the instrument in table 12-4. According to the panel, the theory (CT) behind this laser technology has many impacts, is highly accessible, and is well connected to other related theories and concepts. However, the panelists did not feel that the state of the art was well advanced; basic research was needed to develop this theory fully. Therefore, the panel scored this technology 5, 5, 5, and 3 on the respective four CT dimensions in table 12-4. The panel thought that worldwide impacts of this laser technology were relatively meager because many potential users had only very limited know-how. They thought the theory was well-known and available but difficult to implement. Thus, they gave the technology a score of 2 on IT impacts and a score of 2 on IT accessibility. They did not think many users saw connections between this technology and others, thus leading them to give it a score of 3 on IT connectedness. Because they felt the state of the art in applications of the theory was thus poorly advanced, they gave it a score of 2 on IT state of the

**Table 12–4**
**Technology Instrument**

Technology Name _____

Instructions: Rate the above technology by placing an "X" along each of the three scales for each *dimension*.

| | *Scales* | | | | | |
| | *CT Scale* | | *IT Scale* | | *PT Scale* | |
| *Technology Dimension* | *Very Low* | *Very High* | *Very Low* | *Very High* | *Very Low* | *Very High* |
|---|---|---|---|---|---|---|
| Impact | 1 2 3 4 5 | | 1 2 3 4 5 | | 1 2 3 4 5 | |
| Accessibility | 1 2 3 4 5 | | 1 2 3 4 5 | | 1 2 3 4 5 | |
| Connectedness | 1 2 3 4 5 | | 1 2 3 4 5 | | 1 2 3 4 5 | |
| State of the Art | 1 2 3 4 5 | | 1 2 3 4 5 | | 1 2 3 4 5 | |

art. This adds up to a picture of this laser as relatively well-developed theoretically but poorly developed in its applications. Since the panel interpreted the PT scale as measuring the levels of know-how within a particular organization, and their charter was to develop and apply the instrument more generally, they did not attempt to use the PT scale.

In a separate application, six subjects individually scored technology A and technology B with the instrument in table 12-4. They then arrived at the consensus data shown in table 12-5. The subjects were engineering managers from various organizations who were all intimately familiar with both technologies. As the data in table 12-5 show, technology B was not well understood (accessibility equals 2, 2, 2) and was relatively unrelated to other established industry practices (connectedness equals 2, 2, 1). By contrast, technology A was older and better understood (accessibility equals 5, 5, 4) and its state of the art was more advanced (state of the art equals 5, 5, 5). Overall, the subjects felt that their results paralleled other independent assessments of these technologies.[4] It should be noted that all six subjects indicated they derived considerable benefit from the exercise of completing the instrument. The heuristic value of the experience, the intellectually enlightening discussions, and the sharing of expert opinions were repeatedly cited as significant benefits. These are the types of benefits typically cited for management decision aids. Like any decision aid, this instrument may be more valuable when used to help clarify judgments and focus discussions, rather than to divine correct answers.[3,4]

## Table 12–5
### Illustration of an Application of the Technology Instrument[a]

| | *Technology Scores* | | | | | |
| | *Technology A* | | | *Technology B* | | |
| | *CT* | *IT* | *PT* | *CT* | *IT* | *PT* |
|---|---|---|---|---|---|---|
| Impact | 3 | 3 | 3 | 3 | 4 | 4 |
| Accessibility | 5 | 5 | 4 | 2 | 2 | 2 |
| Connectedness | 5 | 5 | 5 | 2 | 2 | 1 |
| State of the Art | 5 | 5 | 5 | 1 | 1 | 2 |
| Total Scores | 18 | 18 | 17 | 8 | 9 | 9 |

[a]In this application, the dimensions are equally weighted. It should be noted that in another application the dimensions were respectively weighted 4, 3, 2, and 1. Then, the technology scores were multiplied by these respective weights to obtain weighted scores, which were then used to compare the technologies. For more on this, the reader is referred to note 4 at the end of this chapter.

## Technology versus Success

The technology instrument (table 12-4) was used to collect CT, IT, and PT data on projects in the data base. Means, ranges, and standard deviations were computed on the collected CT, IT, and PT values. The individual values ranged from 1 to 5, the means ranged from 2.74 to 4.21, and the standard deviations ranged from 0.99 to 1.25. Thus, the technologies studied here scored about 3 or 4 on the five-point scales of measurement. This is precisely the population hoped for: the "average" or typical technologies of American industry.

Correlation coefficients were computed between the CT, IT, and PT ratings from the instrument (table 12-4) and the outcomes of the projects (table 2-1). Surprisingly, there were only three statistically significant correlations. One of these was between the CT accessibility score and the project outcome. Another was between the IT accessibility score and the project outcome. The other was between the PT state of the art score and the project outcome.

At first, these results seemed odd. Why would only three of the 12 technology dimensions (table 12-4) be statistically significant? After reflecting on this, however, it became apparent that these results are not out of line. Most firms are usually involved in a range of technologies: some high impact and some low impact, some high connectedness, and some low connectedness. They can fail or succeed with any of these technologies for a variety of reasons. But one of the reasons for success or failure would surely relate to the availability of the concepts (CT accessibility). Success and failure should also relate to the availability of working embodiments of these concepts and theories (IT accessibility). Finally, success should relate to the firm's own internal ability to do something useful with these concepts and embodiments (PT state of the art) once they are successfully acquired. Thus, these results seem to be consistent with rational explanations.

### *Accessibility and Project Success*

Correlation coefficients were run between the CT accessibility and IT accessibility scores and the project technical degree of success (table 2-1). The correlations were statistically significant at the 95 percent confidence level.

What does this mean? The explanation is surprisingly simple: when one's ability to acquire a technology is low, one's success potentials are also low. Of course, this seems almost tautological. But consider the implications. These results run across all the organization climates and management techniques discussed in chapters 5 through 11. These results say that, all other things equal, irrespective of the climate or management techniques used, an inaccessible technology is likely to yield low degrees of success. This is a rather pessimistic result.

But why would anyone start a project on an inaccessible technology? There are two very good reasons. One reason is that the organization did not realize the technology was inaccessible until they were well into the project. This frequently occurred. Remember, the CT, IT, and PT ratings collected here are after-the-fact measures. They were taken after the outcomes of the projects in the data base were known. Second, the spirit of innovation is founded on optimism. Innovators generally believe they can overcome most barriers, including inaccessibility. This belief was widely held within the data base. As demonstrated in the next chapter, it is indeed possible to overcome inaccessibility. However, special circumstances are required and these circumstances are not often available.

## The State of the Art and Project Success

A correlation coefficient was computed between the scores for PT state of the art and the commercial outcomes for projects (table 2-1). This correlation was statistically significant at the 95 percent confidence level.

What does this mean? The interpretation is straightforward: firms that do not have high degrees of familiarity or experiences with technologies of this nature cannot expect to record high rates of commercial success. This is another rather pessimistic result for innovators.

## Implications of the CT-IT-PT Model

Three observations may now be made. First, low CT accessibility means that the theory to explain the technology is simply not available. The technology exists only as a disembodied idea. Innovators will nevertheless be challenged by this and by the potential to reap the profits of being the first to innovate with it. But the risks are high, as the results have shown. The likelihood of succeeding in developing a new product when the idea is only a glimmer in someone's eye is rather low. Of course, this is an obvious fact of life that new product developers have always coped with. What is interesting is *how* they have coped with it. Intermediary organizations are a common coping mechanism. They are often used to transform and incubate new technologies that are not readily accessible. More is said about this in a later section of this chapter.

Second, the data indicated that a high CT accessibility is a necessary but not sufficient quality for a high IT accessibility. The IT was seldom high when the CT was low, and the CT and IT scores were statistically significantly correlated. Thus, the ability to use a theory is not necessarily enhanced by its completeness. On the other hand, there cannot be many sound applications of undeveloped theories. Again, this is not a very heroic result. But the implications are rather important.

Third, the data indicated that high CT and IT are not sufficient for project success. High PT is also required. Having well-developed theories (CT) and having well-known applications (IT) are not sufficient for project success. The firm must have its own internal know-how (PT), and it must feel comfortable with that know-how. Note, however, that several cases were found where PT was high in the face of disproportionately low CT and IT values. In these cases, the firm had developed their own internal know-how or art, irrespective of the situation in the outside world. These high internal PTs seemed to work fine except for occasional cases where unexpected or anomalous research results occurred. Then the firm had no theory to fall back on to explain their results. Thus, high PT can occur with low CT and IT. But this is a rather insecure situation in which things work most of the time, but no one knows what to do in those occasions when things do not work.

All this is nothing new to an experienced manager of new product development efforts. But it is significant: what managers have always known intuitively can now be measured with the instrument in table 12-4. Moreover, all this adds up to a coherent theory of innovation that has long been lacking.

## Theory of Technology and Innovation

The above results lead to the following theory of the influence of technology on project success in new product innovations. First, a well-developed concept of the technology should be available to the innovating firm if it is to expect high degrees of success with that technology. This concept may be unavailable because it simply has not yet been developed, or because the prospective user can not acquire this knowledge. The user may not have the know-how to acquire the concept, may be unaware of it, or may be otherwise blocked from it.

Second, information about how to use this concept or body of theory must be available. Of course, the innovator can develop this information or the original theory. But this requires a set of basic research skills that are normally outside the realm of the typical new product developer. And time spent on these activities has potentially high opportunity costs. Time might better be spent on other new product development outputs. Thus, intermediary organizations, incubators, and technology developer organizations may be needed.

Third, organizations that do not have a high level of their own resident know-how in a technology are not very likely to have high degrees of commercial success with that technology. The optimum state is the one where there are established concepts or theories that provide a high level of public knowledge and predictability about the technology, there is an existing knowledge base about how to apply the technology, and the innovating firm has a depth of expertise in the area of the technology.

These are long-standing wisdoms, well-known to the experienced new product developer. But it is important that these long-standing wisdoms have been supported by the extensive empirical data base here. Furthermore, it is especially salient that these empirical findings generally transcend the conventional techniques used to manage technology. Even the "best" management methods could not consistently overcome the disadvantages of poor theory, poor know-how about applications, and poor internal expertise with a technology.

Though these are the general results, the correlations here are far from perfect. There were some cases of low CT, IT, and PT that were overcome by the firms, who then went on to create successful new product innovations. Let us now look at these cases.

## Marshaling Resources to Combat Difficult Technologies

The preceding discussions appear to indicate that staying close to home and remaining in familiar areas of technology is required for success with new product innovations. The corollary to this would be that radical innovation is not possible.

Not only do these tenets lead to ridiculous conclusions, but the data base confirms that these tenets are not correct. It is correct that moving into unfamiliar technologies (low PT state of the art) and difficult-to-acquire know-how (low IT accessibility) leads to lower degrees of success. But failures are not foreordained. Some firms effectively marshaled their resources to combat low degrees of IT and PT.

### Selection and Allocation Techniques

One way of combating difficult technologies (low CT, IT, or PT scores) is to select only those that are a good strategic fit to the firm. Another way is to provide these technologies with the highest quality and greatest amounts of resources possible. As table 12-6 shows, this is precisely how several firms were able to succeed with difficult technologies.

A strategic fit was a relationship between the technology and some familiar raw material, other product, other technology or long-range plan. In some cases, because the firm had some advantage elsewhere and the new technology was somehow related to that other advantage, a fit could be developed. For example, one respondent noted: We didn't have the foggiest

**Table 12–6**
**Analysis of Factors**

| Factors | Percentage of Successful Low IT Accessibility and Low PT State-of-the-Art Projects That Did Not Have This Factor[a] |
|---|---|
| Strategic Fit between Company and Technology | 9 |
| High Amounts of Resources | 12 |
| High Quality of Resources | 18 |

[a] Low IT Accessibility and low PT State-of-the-Art = scores less than 3 on the technology instrument (table 12–4).

notion how to do this. But we found out that our knowledge of synthetics gave us an understanding of these crystals. You wouldn't think so. But when you analyze it you can see it. So that's why our management went ahead with it. And we succeeded. But we couldn't have succeeded without our knowledge of synthetics.

In another example a respondent noted: Our long range plan specified a move into polymerics. As long as we were going in that direction, we might as well get into this area too. We saw the synergy, and it worked out. But, if we hadn't had the commitment and resources to go into polymerics we wouldn't have done this.

A quote from another respondent illustrates the extent of a strategic fit: We had the distribution channel for it. It seems like a big leap to get into something this different from your usual business. But one of the keys here is being able to get it to the customer, reliably and swiftly. Well, that's what we are good at. So, that is why we went into it. It turned out to be one of our best successes.

But operations like this have a cost. The firms paid heavily in terms of the amount and quality of resources absorbed from other programs. Comments like the following were collected at several firms. "It almost bankrupted us"; "It took away all the good people I had and caused me to fail"; "I think we lost a lot on all the other things we couldn't do because of it"; "One of these days our management is going to say that we don't have enough different products, and it will be because we put all our resources into this."

Thus, several of the organizations studied here appropriately recognized the difficulty of the low PT, IT, and CT technologies that they encountered. Some of these technologies were passed over in favor of less difficult alternatives. Others were selected and resources were marshaled on them in a determined effort to make them succeed. Nearly all the difficult technologies that were intentionally selected had some strategic relationship with current products and processes, marketing techniques, or other technologies.

## Incubating Strategies

Today's undeveloped technologies (low CT or IT) can be "incubated", with the prospect that they will either grow into or give birth to useful technologies tomorrow. Some incubating techniques found in this study included coventuring with other firms on the technology, funding research on the technology at universities or independent laboratories, and the use of internal think-tanks.

Funding basic research in an undeveloped technology is a time honored strategy that may or may not be feasible in some cases. Finding an independent laboratory or a faculty member who is both interested and competent in the area may not be easy. Moreover, negotiating patent rights and proprietary provisions can sometimes present serious obstacles.

Many forms of coventuring with other firms were found in the data base. Research through industry-wide consortia and trade associations are familiar ways to advance the state of the art. But such programs may be too general to aid any one firm, and proprietary rights are virtually impossible to protect. Subcontracting various portions of the work with other laboratories was a frequently found method. A variety of limited R&D partnerships (RDLPs) were also found.[5]

Internal think tanks or other arrangements for funding basic research and technology enhancements entirely within the firm were not often found in the data base. Though several of the firms studied here had central R&D facilities, management preferred that they devote their efforts to less risky, more mission-oriented and better defined work.

## Summary

In this chapter, a rudimentary theory was set forth to explain how the nature of technologies influences the success or failure outcome of new product developments. A scale was developed for empirically measuring technologies. This scale was used to test the theory and determine its implications. When used within the context of the theory, the measurement scale was demonstrated to be a useful tool for characterizing new technologies. The resulting information can be used to determine whether or not to undertake a new product development effort with this technology at this time, to further incubate the technology, to marshal resources for it, or to reject it in favor of other alternatives.

Thus, the technology measurement scale developed here has been shown to be useful for project selection decisions (see chapter 8), for resource allocation decisions (see chapter 4) and for deciding whether or not a technology is ready for development. The appropriate use of the scale can also indicate areas where the firm is weak, or areas where their know-how and capabilities for acquiring or using new technologies are too low to permit a high rate of new product success.

This chapter must be viewed as a starting point. Models for managing technologies are needed, but they are difficult to develop. Several results in this chapter are familiar to experienced managers, who have developed wisdom and heuristics, as well as intuition to help them cope with their difficult challenges. But without a comprehensive model that systematizes this knowledge, managers must fall back on hunch and intuition. New product innovations are far too important to be left to hunch and intuition.

## Notes

1. The author is indebted to Jay Bourgeois for suggesting some of these concepts.

2. Portions of this section are based on William E. Souder, *Management Decision Methods* (New York: Van Nostrand Reinhold, 1980), pp. 4-7 and 81-115.

3. For more details see William E. Souder, "Field Studies with a Q-Sort/Nominal Group Process for Selecting R&D Projects," *Research Policy 5*, no. 4 (April 1975), 172-88; and William E. Souder, *Project Selection and Economic Appraisal* (New York: Van Nostrand Reinhold, 1984), pp. 78-85.

4. This is only one of many different types of scoring models that could be used. The choice of weighting factors and model types will depend on the user's needs and the application at hand. For more on this, see William E. Souder, *Project Selection and Economic Appraisal* (New York: Van Nostrand Reinhold, 1984), pp. 78-89.

5. For more on this topic, see William E. Souder, "Research and Development Limited Partnerships: A New Form of Research Collaboration," in *Strategies and Practices for Technological Innovation*, D. Gray, T. Solomon, and W. Hetzner, eds. (Amsterdam: Elsevier Science Publishers, 1986), pp. 69-77.

# 13
# Technology Transfer: From the Lab to the Customer

Technology transfer refers to the process of moving or transferring technologies from one organizational entity or location to another. Technologies may be transferred in a wide variety of ways, from a variety of sources to a variety of users. The technologies being transferred may exist in many different levels of embodiment, from embryonic ideas to finished products.

This chapter examines the effectiveness of the technology transfer processes found in the data base. Based on the analyses, rules are devised for selecting the most effective process under various circumstances.

## Technology Transfer Processes

Figure 13-1 illustrates the technology transfer processes observed at one firm in the data base. Organizations often purchase and license technologies from others, obtain technologies through the acquisition of other firms and organizations, or acquire technologies from outside laboratories, universities, suppliers, and customers. Organizations often sell or license technologies to these same parties. Some of these transfers may involve only R&D personnel, while some may involve personnel from other departments. Thus, a myriad of pathways and processes may exist for moving technologies between an organization and its environment.

As figure 13-1 shows, many active pathways of technology transfer can exist within most organizations. The continuous transfer of ideas, products, and processes from one department to another are essential for the success of most organizations.

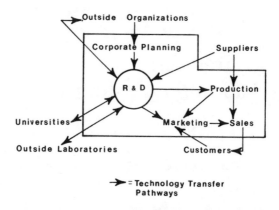

Figure 13–1. Some Typical Technology Transfer Processes

## Phase Transfer: Internal Technology Transfer

A phase transfer is a managerial process for passing a technology from one phase of its life cycle to another.[1] Phase transfer is internal or intra-organization technology transfer.

As an example of a phase transfer process, figure 13-2 depicts the life cycle phase transfers for one of the products in the data base. The idea for this device originated in the firm's central research laboratory. It remained there until it was further refined by the inventor, at which time management decided to transfer it to one of the firm's divisional research facilities. The divisional facility converted the idea into a product concept, which was then transferred to one of the firm's divisional engineering departments. The engineers further developed the concept, then transferred it to the manufacturing department. After proving pilot feasibility, it was then transferred to the firm's marketing division. They contracted for its routine manufacturing outside the firm and handled its routine sales. Thus, the technology evolved through several phases of maturity and was accordingly transferred across the interface between each phase.

## Core Models of Phase Transfer

Figure 13-3 depicts a core model of phase transfer over the life cycle of a typical new product development project. The model shows the core technology phases, the corresponding core personnel and personnel skill types within each phase, the major decision roles played by these core personnel,

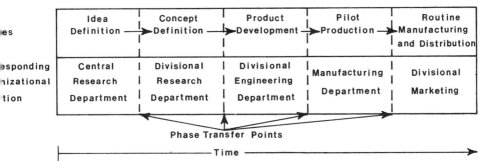

Figure 13–2. A Typical Phase Transfer Process

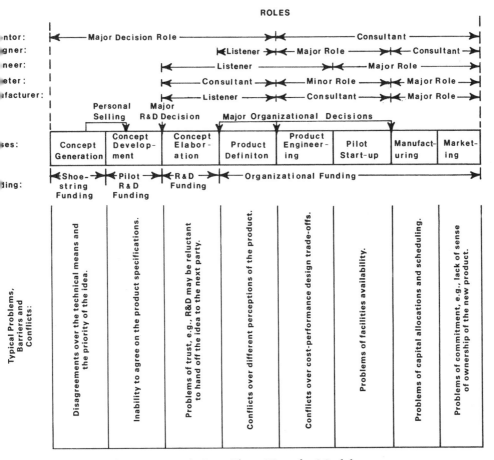

Figure 13–3. A Core Phase Transfer Model

and the typical problems and barriers encountered within each core phase. A core model details the essential or core phases, functions, and roles that must be carried out in most phase transfers.[2]

This model depicts eight core phases. Some phase transfer processes may have more or fewer core stages. For example, the concept generation, development, and elaboration phases may be combined in some cases. For some technologies, the pilot manufacturing phase may be eliminated and the product may go directly from engineering to routine manufacturing. There are many other possibilities: the manufacturing phase was contracted out in the example given earlier. These are simply variations in the application of the general core model in figure 13-3.

Note how the core personnel and their roles may change over the life cycle of a technology, as illustrated in figure 13-3. In the very beginning, there may only be the lone inventor with an idea. Though he may play the major decision-making role for some time, a point will be reached when extensive R&D resources must be obtained if the work is to proceed. If a decision is made to proceed, then designers, engineers, and other personnel will usually be brought in. These others may play the roles of consultants, listeners, decision makers, or performers. If the technology grows and evolves, there will be many changes of roles over the life cycle of the technology. Major players in one period may become consultants in subsequent periods, or have no association with the project in still later periods. Consultants in some periods may play major decision roles in subsequent periods. Many dynamic changes and evolutions of roles are thus possible over the life of the technology.

Several problems or barriers will likely appear during the life cycle of the technology. Problems in cooperation and collaboration may arise among the various personnel and departments. Differences in the perceptions of the various parties may create problems in setting priorities. Difficulties may arise in obtaining funds, and problems of emotional commitments may arise within the various stages, between the various parties. Some of these problems are noted in figure 13-3.

## Three Core Phase Transfer Models

The data base revealed the presence of three distinct types of core phase transfer models. These models differed in terms of the nature of the transfer points, the events at the transfer points, the types of responsibilities transferred, the nature of the transfer and the duration of the transfers. The author labeled these three models: the stage-dominant (SD) model, the phase-dominant (PD) model, and the task-dominant (TD) model.

## The Stage-Dominant (SD) Model

The SD model is characterized by formal groups or functions that are organizationally specialized and separated from each other. The functions are rigidly and narrowly defined to include only very specific activities.

Participants in the SD model describe their activities in terms of finite responsibilities and limited authorities. They talk about their work in terms of which portions are their perceived responsibilities and which other portions are someone else's. They have little awareness or feeling of responsibility for the entire new product development effort. They are concerned only with their assigned portions of the effort. Institutionalized transfer points exist at several predetermined places throughout the new product development process.

At each transfer point, the technology may be physically handed off by one party to another or formally transferred by one party signing off and the other signing on for its responsibility. The transmitting party formally relieves itself of all further responsibility for the technology and the accepting party assumes all further responsibility for it. A major consequence of the SD model is the termination of the emotional commitment and the sense of responsibility for the future of the technology by the transferring party. The SD model does not provide any mechanism for involving personnel from any prior phase in a future phase. Moreover, emotional commitments and future visions are confined within each phase. No one party has the responsibility for the entire multiphase effort.

Examples of SD models from the data base are depicted in figure 13-4. The key elements of the SD model are the presence of formal transfers of responsibility, the linearity of the process, and the complete transfer of commitments at the transfer point. Once transferred, a technology is not expected to ever return to a prior phase or to a prior organizational entity.

## The Process-Dominant (PD) Model

The PD model is also characterized by specialized functions. Unlike the SD model, however, there are no apparent discrete transfer points where one party hands off their finished portion of the project and another party signs on for it. Rather, the transfer points involve the gradual transition of technologies and personnel. There is no abrupt reassignment of personnel to new jobs or technologies. The personnel that are giving up a technology gradually ease out of some assignments and go on to others. Personnel accepting a technology gradually pick up a greater share of the responsibility and workload.

The participants talk about their work in terms of finite periods of inter-

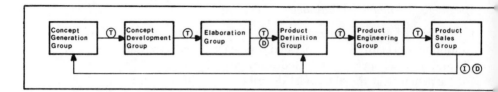

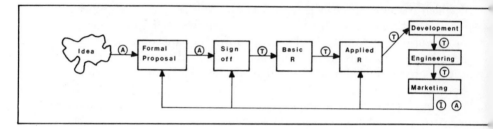

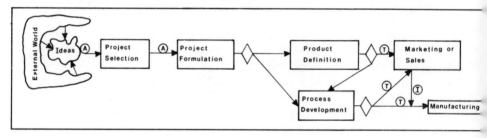

Key: Ⓐ = approval process
Ⓣ = transfer point
Ⓘ = inputs
Ⓓ = direction
R = research

**Figure 13–4. Examples of Stage-Dominant (SD) Models**

action with the other parties, instead of continual interactions or distinct hand-off points. They identify with their functional specialties, but they also have considerable awareness of the adjacent functions. However, this awareness diminishes beyond the immediately adjacent functions. The viewpoints expressed are focused on the functions: the personnel talk in terms of individual functions (research, marketing, etc.) when asked about their work. But, unlike the SD model, there are few paperwork systems and there are few actual sign-offs. Rather, the parties agree to work together for a finite period, until both are satisfied that the incoming party has the know-how and where-withal to continue the work. This is in contrast to the SD model, where the transfer can be pinpointed as occurring at a particular point in time, at the

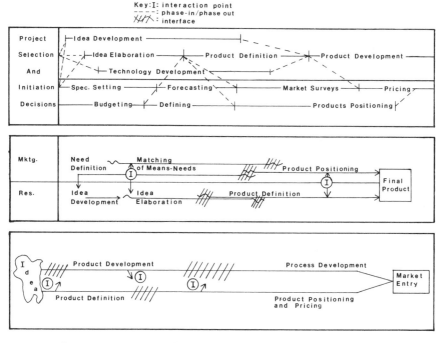

**Figure 13–5. Examples of Process-Dominant (PD) Models**

moment of physical hand-off or the signing of a specific document. In the PD model, the transfer is more aptly pictured as a kind of short-term miniature task force, involving two or more persons, between two adjacent linear phases. Examples of PD models from the data base are presented in figure 13-5.

## The Task-Dominant (TD) Model

In the TD model, there are no identifiable hand-off points. There are no formal transfer points and no formal transfers of personnel.

Personnel are functional specialists but they are not rigidly designated as such. And they do not exclusively identify with only one area of expertise. They talk in terms of the end product and the time schedule for that product. Personnel identify with their technical and organizational specialties, but not to the exclusion of their identification with the total process. They describe their individual responsibilities in terms of total project contributions rather than their individual functions. They view their individual responsibilities as extending over the entire task, rather than being limited to their own particular specialties. The personnel feel free to cross organizational boundaries,

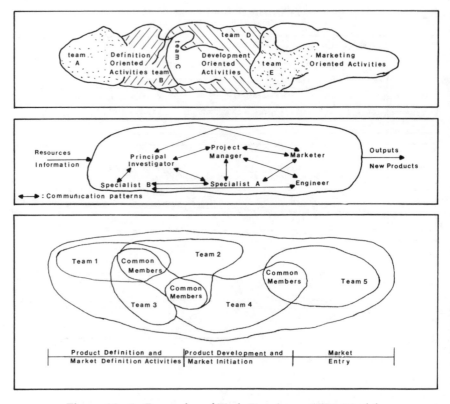

**Figure 13–6. Examples of Task-Dominant (TD) Models**

and they have frequent informal contacts and conversations with parties in other areas of the organization. Communication channels are frequently crisscrossing and overlapping.

Examples of TD models from the data base are presented in figure 13-6. The TD model is distinguished from the SD and PD models by its total team focus. Instead of a linear flow process, the TD model is characterized by an organic process: each function is systematically related and interdependent with every other. There is yet another important facet that distinguishes the TD model from the SD and PD types. The TD model has a dynamic quality of people and roles and a true team spirit. Roles overlap and individuals do whatever is needed to get things done. Unlike the more linear SD and PD models, the TD model has a kind of flexible responsiveness that enables it to cope with many emerging threats and changing environments.

## Differences among the Three Models

The data base was examined for specific differences among the three models. Using correlation analyses, six characteristics of the models were found that distinguished them. These differences are summarized in table 13-1.

The SD model was characterized by infrequent, brief personnel interactions. The tasks or work packages in the SD model were well defined. Information was primarily written and limited to the need to know. The coordi-

**Table 13–1**
**Six Characteristics That Distinguished the SD, PD, and TD Models**

X = This item characterizes this model

| Significant Characteristics | Phase Transfer Models | | |
|---|---|---|---|
| | *SD* | *PD* | *TD* |
| 1. Personal Interactions | | | |
|     Infrequent, Short Duration | X | | |
|     Periodic, Short Duration | | X | |
|     Frequent, Continuous | | | X |
| 2. Division of Tasks | | | |
|     Well-Defined | X | | |
|     Flexible Boundaries | | X | |
|     Overlapping | | | X |
| 3. Information Flows | | | |
|     Limited to Need-to-Know | X | | |
|     Exchanged Only at the Technology Transfer Points | | X | |
|     Free Flow, All and Anything | | | X |
| 4. Communication Media | | | |
|     Written Only | X | | |
|     Primarily Verbal | | X | |
|     All-Channel, All-Media | | | X |
| 5. Coordination Mechanisms | | | |
|     Clearly Defined, One Person | X | | |
|     Spread among Several Persons | | X | |
|     Diffused among Team Members | | | X |
| 6. Cost Control Center | | | |
|     Department Cost Center | X | | |
|     Two-Department Center | | X | |
|     Project Cost Center | | | X |

nation mechanisms were well defined and one person was formally in charge at all times. The cost center resided in the department that was primarily responsible for the technology at that point in time.

The PD model was characterized by periodic, brief personnel interactions. The tasks were well defined but highly flexible. In effect, the PD model was characterized by the use of temporary teams with limited memberships and very finite durations. Information flows were not unlimited, but they were free-flowing during the periods when technology was being transferred. Unlike the SD model, information exchange was primarily verbal and written formalities were minimized. Coordination was spread among several persons instead of being vested in a single person. Involved departments were jointly responsible during the transfer, and both served as cost centers for the transfer effort.

In the TD model, personnel interaction was continuous and frequent. Personnel often sought new contacts and they interacted continuously with their counterparts throughout the duration of the entire project. There was seldom any formal separation of tasks and work flows, which overlapped considerably. Information flows were free: nothing was confidential and everything that anyone thought important was brought up for discussion. Both written and verbal communication were used, sometimes redundantly. The cost center for the work was the entire task, which was designated a formal project.

Table 13-2 summarizes the behaviors and technology transfer techniques found within each model. Note how the SD model uses rather bureaucratic methods, while the TD model depends greatly on the interpersonal initiatives of the individuals. The PD model uses some of the behaviors and transfer techniques of both the SD and TD models.[3]

## Relative Effectiveness of the Three Models

Is one of the three models the most effective? Is one of the models superior under some circumstances? To answer these important questions, the effectiveness of each model was analyzed under easy and difficult technologies, and easy and difficult market environments.

### Difficult Technologies

In one of the instruments,[4] the degree of technical difficulty of each project in the data base was scored by consensus of all the technical principals assigned to it. Technical difficulty refers to the perceived difficulty of meeting the established technical or laboratory targets on the project. Projects with

## Table 13–2
## Characteristic Behaviors and Transfer Methods Used within Each of the Three Models

The following methods were commonly used by R&D and engineering departments to attract interested parties from marketing, sales, or other user department and to transfer their outputs to them.

### SD Model

| | |
|---|---|
| Status Report. | A technical report is distributed describing work done and technologies available. |
| Management Edict. | Top management issues a letter stating that a particular technology is ready for transfer and a certain party is expected to accept it. |
| Executive Communication. | A high level R&D or engineering executive distributes a letter stating that his portion of the work is complete and someone else should now accept it. |
| Termination Report. | R&D or engineering issues a report stating that their agreed-upon work is complete and no further work will be done. |

### PD Model

| | |
|---|---|
| Bi-joint Planning. | Two adjacent parties assemble to plan the transfer across their interface at the time a transfer point is reached. |
| Advanced Transfer Plan. | Two adjacent parties meet to work out the details of the transfer before the transfer point is reached. |
| Renegotiation Involvement. | Two adjacent parties work together in an ad hoc fashion, doing whatever is needed and renegotiating their preconceived notions of their proper roles, in order to arrive at a complete transfer of a technology. |

### TD Model

| | |
|---|---|
| Active Outreach. | R&D or engineering personnel actively seek out potential users in marketing or other departments and cultivate mutual understanding of each other's operations and needs. |
| Partnership Involvement. | The R&D, engineering, marketing, and other parties that may be involved come together in planning meetings early in the life of the effort and throughout the effort to collaborate and coordinate their activities. |
| Multidirectional Flow. | Technology moves back and forth among several parties to adjust, modify, fit and bend it to make it a more effective product in the eyes of all the involved parties. |

degree of difficulty scores above the mean for all the projects were labeled "difficult technologies." The others were labeled "easy technologies."

In the interviews, the same persons were asked to describe the difficulties they perceived in achieving phase transfer success and to score the project's degree of phase transfer success on a scale from 1 to 5. Projects with degree of phase transfer success scores above the mean for all the projects were labeled "transfer success projects." The others were labeled "transfer failure projects." These two statistics, difficult versus easy and transfer success versus failure, were then compared.

The results of this comparison are shown in table 13-3. When the technology was easy, the SD, PD, and TD models all gave about the same percentage of transfer success projects. But, when the technology was difficult, differences occurred. As shown in table 13-3, the SD model was relatively ineffective when the technology was difficult. Only 33 percent of the difficult technologies became transfer successes when the SD model was used on them. By comparison, 77 percent of the easy technologies became transfer successes under the SD model. The PD model was also not very effective on difficult technologies: only 56 percent of them became transfer successes. By comparison, 84 percent of the easy technologies became transfer successes under the PD model. In contrast to these results for the SD and PD models, the TD model remained effective under both easy and difficult technologies. High percentage transfer successes were recorded under both easy and difficult technologies with the TD model.

Thus, for phase transfer success, it may not matter greatly whether the SD, PD, or TD models are used on easy technologies. However, it does matter which of these three is used on difficult technologies. The TD model is the only effective choice for difficult technologies.

Table 13–3
Relative Effectiveness of SD, PD, and TD Models for Technology Transfer under Various Technical Environments

| Technical Environment and Model | Relative Effectiveness: Percentage of Transfer Succcess Projects |
|---|---|
| Easy | |
| SD | 77 |
| PD | 84 |
| TD | 81 |
| Difficult | |
| SD | 33 |
| PD | 56 |
| 'TD | 78 |

## Difficult Market Environments

Data collections and analyses analogous to the above were carried out for the degree of market difficulty of each project.[4] The degree of market difficulty refers to the perceived difficulty of meeting the commercial objectives set for the project, that is, meeting the users' requirements and achieving the financial and market share goals. The principal marketing (or other commercial) personnel on the projects were the respondents here.

The results of these analyses are summarized in table 13-4. The results are analogous to those above for technical difficulty. The TD model was the most effective when the market environment was difficult. Under easy market environments, however, no major differences were found in the effectiveness of the three models. Thus, the TD model is again the most effective.

## Selecting the Best Model

Thus, the results here indicate that it may not matter which of the three models is used when the project is not difficult from either a technical or market standpoint. All three models appear to be about equally effective in achieving phase transfer success.

However, when the project is difficult from either the technical or market standpoint, the TD model is the best choice. It is the most effective for achieving successful phase transfers. When the TD model is used on difficult projects they experience relatively few interdepartmental conflicts, personnel collaborate better, the technologies generally move along more swiftly, and transfers generally occur with fewer difficulties. Technologies move more smoothly from phase to phase in a timely fashion, and the involved personnel

**Table 13–4**
**Relative Effectiveness of SD, PD, and TD Models for Technology Transfer under Various Market Environments**

| Market Environment and Model | Relative Effectiveness: Percentage of Transfer Succcess Projects |
|---|---|
| Easy | |
| SD | 60 |
| PD | 65 |
| TD | 79 |
| Difficult | |
| SD | 32 |
| PD | 39 |
| TD | 68 |

and departments are more willing to accept new technologies from those who want to pass them on. In general, the typical problems and barriers listed in figure 13-3 were perceived to be greatly diminished when the TD model was used.

It must be noted that even the highly effective TD model is not perfect. As can be seen from the results in tables 13-3 and 13-4, some phase transfer problems and barriers arose when the TD model was used. However, the TD model is clearly the most effective of the three models.

## Technology, Phase Transfer Models, and Project Success

The analyses and discussions considered only phase transfer success: the evolution of the technology through appropriate and timely transfers between various performers during its life cycle. Though an effective phase transfer process is important to the success of the entire project, it is not synonymous with project success. A project can be effectively phase transferred throughout its life cycle and still fail for other reasons.

Nevertheless, core phase transfer models (figure 13-3) would seem to be powerful mechanisms for handling many obstacles to project success. In particular, they might be effective management tools in those cases where the technology is not well understood and the project is ill defined. We will now turn to these aspects.

### Accessibility and Phase Transfer Model Effectiveness

Chapter 12 demonstrated how the accessibility of the technology underlying a project can significantly affect that project's outcome. Highly accessible technologies promoted project success. Inaccessibility hindered success. It is reasonable to suspect that some core phase transfer models may be more effective than others for handling inaccessible technologies. If so, then couldn't these same models be potent devices for fostering project success?

To investigate these suspicions, the data examined in chapter 12 were reexamined here. Recall that subjects at each firm provided IT accessibility scores for each project, on a scale of 1 to 5. These scores measured the subject's perceptions of the ease with which the know-how to create useful devices from the technology could be obtained and integrated into the organization.

Using a score of 3 or greater as an accessible technology (and less than 3 as an inaccessible technology), the percentage of successful projects was computed for each of the core phase transfer models under inaccessible and accessible conditions. The percentage successful statistic was defined as the percentage of projects that met or exceeded their commercial expectations (see table 2-1). The results of this analysis are shown in table 13-5. The data in table 13-5 show that the effectiveness of both the SD and PD models falls off significantly when the technology becomes inaccessible. The superior power of the TD model is aptly demonstrated by these results. The TD model gives about the same percentage of successful projects, whether the technology is accessible or inaccessible.

What characteristics of the TD model account for its superior effectiveness? How does it cope with an inaccessible technology? Recall from table 13-1 that overlapping tasks, coordination diffused among the team members, and all-channel/all-media communication were features of TD models. With this in mind, consider cases A, B, and C from the data base presented in table 13-6. These three cases typify the situations with inaccessible technologies where the TD model was applied. Note the emphasis on the use of interdisciplinary teams, open communication flows, overlapping roles and authorities, and the free flow of information (sometimes without regard for competitive secrecy). Elements of risk-taking and sociotechnical responsibility are also prominently revealed. The desire to create a technological "brave new world" appears as a prominent motive in all three cases.

*Organizational Competence and Phase Transfer Model Success*

Though a technology may be accessible, the organization may not know how to use it. The organization may not have the requisite skills, facilities, personnel, or know-how to enable them to use it. Recall from chapter 12 that this was termed the PT state-of-the-art factor. It was measured on a scale of 1 to 5 by the respondents at each firm. When a score of 3 or greater is re-

Table 13–5
**Relative Effectiveness of SD, PD, and TD Models under Accessible and Inaccessible Technologies**

| Technology and Model | Relative Effectiveness: Percentage of Succcessful Projects |
|---|---|
| Accessible | |
| SD | 59 |
| PD | 68 |
| TD | 73 |
| Inaccessible | |
| SD | 23 |
| PD | 31 |
| TD | 66 |

**Table 13–6**
**Three Cases of Inaccessible Technologies That Were Handled through the Use of TD Models**

*Case A*

At first, we said, hell, we don't know how to do this and neither does anyone else. That know-how just doesn't exist. But, then, we started a literature survey and we went out and talked to a lot of people. And we began to see how you could maybe put it together. It was a gamble. We didn't have the expertise, and neither did anyone else. But you could maybe put together the right teams of contractors. Well, our management bought it, and we started subcontracting the assembly of this whole new know-how. Man that was a kick! Imagine that: you're going out and actually creating a whole new technology by picking a team of subcontractors to do some phase, then passing that work on to other teams until you get the whole thing. Each time a new subcontractor came on we had to teach him the technology, or at least what we had learned about it up to that point. We used overlapping teams. The previous contractor stayed around as a consultant until the new one got completely up to speed. Sometimes we called on some of the older contractors we used in the early stages and made them part of the new teams. It got pretty confusing sometimes with all these people running around. And most of them weren't your own employees. Sometimes you couldn't tell who worked for who. But that's what made it so much fun. Everybody worked together and did whatever they saw that needed to be done. We really had some motivated people. And we had a good time, too. And that's what made it work.

*Case B*

We actually had to create a new field here before we could develop it. The way you do that is to bring together all the current states of arts in closely related fields and all the top people in those related fields. You supply them with whatever they need, within reason, give them the broad goals, and let them proceed to develop the new field. We had our suppliers, our competitors, our own people, and our users all on the taskforces. It's the only way to do it. We developed a technology that everyone can use. We made it more available for the whole world. Of course, we incidentally helped our competition. But most of all, we helped the industry. And that helps us. We're the leaders, and if we hadn't done it the whole industry would have suffered.

*Case C*

You have to get over two hurdles to succeed. First, the knowledge has to exist in the world around you. Second, you have to know how to use it. Now, in this case, it didn't exist, so we didn't have it. But, through the trade association we got the government to fund a lot of studies. This wasn't basic research—it just put together a lot of knowledge. But that opened up the field, and with our background we quickly learned how to use it. Sure, we often got the trade association to run the tests we wanted and we learned more from these tests than the other members. But that's how you stay ahead of your competition.

corded on the PT state-of-the-art factor, consider the organization to be competent in that technology. Otherwise, it is incompetent.

Following the methodology used before for accessibility/inaccessibility, table 13-7 was developed. As the results in the table show, the effectiveness of the SD and PD models falls off significantly in going from competent to incompetent conditions. The TD model does not. The TD model is superior to the other two models under incompetent conditions.

Why is the TD model so superior for handling organizational incompetency with respect to a technology? To answer this question, several project interviews were examined. Three cases from the interviews are reproduced here in table 13-8. It is apparent from reading these cases that the superior capabilities of the TD model are its integrating and knowledge synthesizing capabilities. The TD model provides an atmosphere that catalyzes personnel interactions and the exchange of know-how. This atmosphere also fosters the synthesis of know-how into creative new forms, shapes, and developments.

## Conditions for Using the Three Phase Transfer Models

The results and their associated discussions might be interpreted to imply that the TD model should universally be used for all phase transfers. This does not appear to be a correct interpretation. The SD and PD models each have their place. In fact, there may be some circumstances when the TD model

Table 13–7
**Relative Effectiveness of SD, PD, and TD Models under Competent and Incompetent Conditions**

| Organizational Competency and Models | Relative Effectiveness: Percentage of Succcessful Projects[a] |
|---|---|
| Competent | |
| SD | 69 |
| PD | 62 |
| TD | 72 |
| Incompetent | |
| SD | 20 |
| PD | 31 |
| TD | 69 |

[a]Percentage of projects that met or exceeded their commercial expectations (see table 2-1).

Table 13–8

**Three Cases of Organizational Incompetency That Were Handled through the Use of TD Models**

*Case 1*

We didn't have the competency to do the job within our organization. It wasn't a matter of the technology not existing. We just had to go out and learn it. So we put together a "think tank SWAT team." We got some people from marketing, engineering, research, and operations and we set them up as a taskforce. And we spent day and night reading, running experiments, buying consultants' time, whatever it took. We had a carte blanche on equipment, contractors, travel, literature. We could have anything we wanted, within reason. We could talk to anyone and we sought advice from just about everybody. We weren't limited by any organizational boundaries and we each played a variety of roles. One day I'd putter in the lab, one day I'd travel to one of our plants, and the next day I'd spend reading some reports. I'm a pure research person, but I learned a lot about marketing on this assignment. One time I even argued against our marketing people, using their own data. And I won the argument!

*Case 2*

We usually take a pretty rigid approach in managing our projects. But you can't do that if you don't know the technology. Then you have to use a more open kind of team approach. Then there is a lot of free and open communication. It's a learning situation. People have to be interested in learning from each other. They are in a search for knowledge, and that has to be their whole motivating force. They can't be burdened with budgets and the need to show some output every week. If you know what you're doing, you plan it and then manage it carefully. If you don't know what you're doing, that doesn't mean you should shy away from it. If the technology exists, maybe you should acquire it. To do that, you have to use a whole different management approach.

*Case 3*

A team can actually create know-hows. They actually create technologies by sharing their thoughts. One person says something, another picks up on it, and then some others add their thoughts. The human mind does the rest: puts it together in a new form, a new technology. Teams are incredibly powerful when they're used like that. You can actually build whole new technologies if you put together the right teams and manage them properly.

should not be used because it does not fit all of the conditions within those circumstances.

Let us define the best phase transfer model as the one that fosters the most timely, smooth, barrier-free transfer of technologies across phase boundaries throughout the life cycle of those technologies. Using this definition, a case-by-case analysis of the data base revealed that there are many complex factors that may determine the best phase transfer model to use in any particular circumstance. Table 13-9 was developed as a result of this case-by-case analysis. It is clear from the table that there are indeed many contingent conditions that can influence the choice of the best model.

Proving all the relationships and contingencies in table 13-9 would constitute a major research undertaking. However, sufficient evidence has been compiled in the cases here to warrant using table 13-9 as a general guide in selecting the best models to use under various circumstances. All the analyses

**Table 13–9**
**Contingent Conditions for Using the Three Phase Transfer Models**

| | Use the Following Model | | |
|---|---|---|---|
| *Under the Following Condition* | *SD Model* | *PD Model* | *TD Model* |
| Environmental Uncertainty Is | Low | Medium | High |
| Market Dynamics Are | Stable | Variable | Constantly Changing |
| Technology Is | Routine | Specialized | Poorly Understood |
| Innovation Is | Incremental | Continuous | Radical |
| Task Objectives Are | Rigid | Flexible | Fluid |
| Jobs Are | Well-Defined | Ill-Defined | Undefined |
| Responsibilities Are | Rigid | Open | Undefined |
| Communication Is | Vertical | Horizontal | Multi-Directional |
| Organization Structure Is | Centralized | Decentralized | Matrix |
| Major Goal Is | Minimum Costs | Implementation | Idea Generation |
| Emphasis Is On | Cost Control | Activity Control | Creativity |
| Source of Funds Is | Corporate | Division | Project |
| Source of Decisions Is | Top Management | Project | Group |
| Familiarity with Technology Is | High | Moderate | Low |
| Familiarity with Customer Is | High | Moderate | Low |
| Accessibility of Technology Is | High | Moderate | Low |
| New Product Management Method Is (see chapter 9) | Top Down Structures | Project Manager Methods and New Product Structures | Teams and Taskforces |

in this chapter and throughout this book generally support the central hypothesis underlying table 13-9. This hypothesis is: There are some circumstances under which some phase-transfer models are more effective than others. The models vary in their appropriateness for various circumstances, or the extent to which their characteristics fit the needs of the situation. It appears that the SD, PD, and TD models examined here are in fact very complex, and they demand a consistent set of circumstances if their effectiveness is to be maximized.[3]

## Choosing the Best Model for the Situation

When used outside of the contingent conditions shown in table 13-9, the effectiveness of the various models may be compromised. For example, the effectiveness of the TD model was found to be impaired whenever it was used under the following set of conditions within the data base: low environmental uncertainty, stable market dynamics, routine technologies, rigidly defined task objectives, hierarchical R&D organization structures, and heavy emphasis on paperwork flows. Under these circumstances, the personnel became bored with the simplicity of the technologies and they freely interacted with each other to build more elaborate products than the customer wanted. When management attempted to constrain and control the personnel to more rigid roles and behavior patterns, considerable conflicts erupted that delayed the progress of the transfers. The heavy emphasis on paperwork and frequent reporting was emotionally debilitating to the personnel and the transfers did not proceed smoothly. On the other hand, few such problems resulted when the SD model was used under the same types of conditions.

Cases of this kind of mismatch between the circumstances and the models were not often found in the data base. Apparently, many managers are able to select the best models for most circumstances. However, the preceding example is sufficient evidence to show that the TD model can indeed be far too powerful to be universally used, under all conditions. Even if the TD model were effective under all conditions, there is no reason to use it when a simpler model will suffice. The TD model is a relatively complex model to use, requiring a diversity of personnel skills, mature behavior patterns, and experienced management. Some managers are not fully attuned to the open, decentralized style required to make the TD model work well. The SD and PD models may be more consistent with many prevailing management philosophies and organization structures.

The choice of the best model is therefore a complex decision. It requires a consideration of many factors and finely tuned judgements about their impacts in particular cases. There will not be many real life situations that are as precise as those defined in table 13-9. In practice, a mixture of the contingent conditions for the SD, PD, and TD models is more likely to exist. For example, suppose the market dynamics are stable and a radical innovation is desired from a specialized technology. A brief look at table 13-9 shows that these specifications cut across the conditions for all three models. It is impossible to tell, from this information alone, which model would be best.

Nevertheless, table 13-9 serves as a general guide and a reference for thinking about the choice of the best model. Until deeper study can clarify some of the underlying complex contingencies, table 13-9 will serve as a useful guideline.

## Summary

Important relationships between various models of technology transfer, the nature of the underlying technologies and the environments of these models have been defined in this chapter. These models have been termed "core phase transfer" models because they are concerned with core aspects of the internal transfer of technologies between departments and functions within the organization.

Three types of core phase transfer models were elaborated: the stage-dominant (SD) model, the phase-dominant (PD) model, and the task-dominant (TD) model. Each model was found to differ with respect to several characteristics. The effectiveness of each model was found to vary with the circumstances.

In general, the TD model was found to be the most powerful. It was the only model capable of handling difficult technologies and markets, technologies that were not readily accessible, or technologies where the organization was not competent. However, the TD model was not universally effective for phase transfers. There were some circumstances where the TD model appeared to be too powerful because it went beyond the demands of the situation. In those cases, its use created more problems than it solved. Thus, a series of contingent conditions or guidelines was devised to help managers select the best models for transferring technologies within their particular new product development processes.

## Notes

1. The author originally invented this term in 1973 to describe processes observed in a research study on relationships between R&D and marketing groups. However, it appears to be quite suitable for describing many different intergroup processes.

2. The author originally conceptualized the core model idea in 1977 for visual-

izing alternative ways to manage R&D projects for a client firm. However, the core concept appears applicable to many situations.

3. The author and his students and colleagues have extended these models elsewhere. For more details see William E. Souder and A. K. Chakrabarti, "Managing the Coordination of Marketing and R&D in the Innovation Process," *TIMS Studies in the Management Sciences,* 15 (Amsterdam: Elsevier, 1980), pp. 135-50; and William E. Souder and Paul Shrivastava, "Phase Transfer Models of Technological Innovation," in *Advances In Strategic Management,* vol. 3, R. Lamb and P. Shrivastava, eds. (Greenwich, Connecticut: JAI Press, 1984), pp. 135-47.

4. See the instrument package, especially instruments 10 and 12-2, available from the author.

# 14
# Principles of Managing
# New Product Innovations

You can't steal second base while keeping one foot on first.
—Anonymous

S omeone once said that research only proves the obvious and confirms the best practices. Perhaps there is more truth in this statement than most of us want to admit. But these are valuable contributions. It is always worthwhile to verify the prevailing wisdoms, standardize on the best practices, and make this knowledge generally available to everyone. This is the spirit in which this book has been written.

This chapter attempts to further this spirit by summarizing the findings in this book in a conveniently useful form for innovators, managers, and students of innovation processes. The following ten "principles" are meant to be guidelines to the best state of the art. Rigid adherence to them will certainly not guarantee success with new product innovations. However, the empirical evidence in this book indicates that practicing them well will significantly increase the chances of success.

## Ten Principles

*Principle 1. Because Innovations Are Special, They Require Special Management Qualities*

Innovation projects fail and succeed as a result of numerous, complex conditions. The art of management is orchestrating the proper confluence of conditions that will foster success. Though precise rules cannot be stated, success with new product innovations usually requires the following seven conditions: (1) a high degree of understanding of emerging worldwide technologies, (2) a climate in which creative ideas can flourish, (3) the spontaneous teamwork and collaboration of many specialists, (4) systematic decision making and risk taking, (5) an in-depth knowledge of technologies, (6) an understanding of how to transform technologies into want-satisfying products, and (7) an intimate understanding of changing customer needs.

A precise recipe cannot be given for management qualities that will always lead to these bountiful conditions. However, there are five things that foster the above conditions. First, successful managers of innovations demonstrate a willingness to accept calculated risks. Second, they use participative decision-making techniques and they are always open to oblique ideas. Third, they develop flexible organizations that emphasize open communication, free movements of personnel across departmental boundaries, and individual initiatives within team settings. Fourth, they maintain close contact and trusting relationships with potential customers. This results in customers that are willing to try out new products recommended by the developers, and developers who only work on the most relevant innovations for their customers. Fifth, they are continuously involved with customers, new technologies, trade societies, and professional activities. This places the firm in the mainstream of information flows, interpersonal influence, and new ideas. It puts the firm in a position to intercept new trends, build power, and influence its environment.

### Principle 2. Because Success Is Not a Smooth Process for Any Innovation, Great Patience Is Needed

Even the best ideas under the best conditions cannot sweep themselves into success. Numerous individuals who can provide various kinds of moral and financial support for the idea must be on the bandwagon. Specialists with various intellectual and physical resources are needed to process the idea and develop it into a commercially viable product. Many persons must cooperate to play several roles that will help the idea navigate its environment. A variety of users must exist who are willing to try out and adopt the new innovation. A cadre of persons is needed who can persuade and inform the users, reducing their apathy and hostility to the new innovation.

But even all this will not guarantee success. The road to success is a roller coaster of fits and starts. Most successful innovations evolve through painful cycles of growth and decline until they become strong enough to break through the barriers that accord them a place in the realms of success.

### Principle 3. Do Not Try to Control Innovation Projects with Traditional Budget Techniques

In some industries, innovation projects are time-intensive: they take relatively more time than money. Other industries are characteristically cost-intensive: their innovation projects require a lot of money to be spent in a brief time period. In some industries, innovation projects have a relatively constant cost/ time ratio during their life cycles. In other industries, the projects exhibit wide swings in their cost/time ratios. Some industries are characterized by fore-load patterns, in which the bulk of the project costs are in the R&D and product engineering stages. Other industries are characteristically aft-load: their project costs are concentrated in production and marketing activities.

Thus, the effective financial control of innovation projects is a complex matter. Different procedures must be used for fore-load, aft-load, cost-intensive, time-intensive, constant cost/time ratio and variable cost/time ratio types of projects. The methods that are traditionally used to control the costs of engineering and development projects will not work for innovation projects.

## Principle 4. Do Not Try to Use Classical Organizing Approaches with Innovations

Classical approaches emphasize bureaucracies, hierarchies, narrowly defined jobs, behaviors that conform to established rules, centralized decision making, communications that flow from the top of the organization down, and economic efficiency as the singular goal. To the extent that any of these climates are present within an organization, innovation will be severely constrained.

Innovation requires an organization that can adjust to fit the needs of its members and the needs of its customers. Responsibility must replace authority, so that things get done through a mutuality of agreement and a community of interest. Communication must be multidirectional, resembling consultation rather than command. Personnel are more naturally motivated by the achievement of the task and the thrill of success than by orders and policies. Newness, creativity, acquiring new markets, and fulfilling customer needs are internalized organizational goals in innovative firms. Teams, task forces, and project management methods are frequently used. Organization structures that incorporate new enterprise activities and project management methods provide the best climate for innovations to emerge, grow and mature. Managers are responsible for these aspects. They design the organization and set its tone, posture, and prevailing attitudes.

## Principle 5. Take a Systematic Approach to the Selection of the Best Projects

Getting the best new product innovations begins with selecting the best project proposals. Because this is a subjective process of information sharing and participative decision making, a systematic process is required. Every idea must be viewed as a precious commodity. Idea generation and flow processes must be highly developed and well maintained. Collected ideas should be carefully housed and processed, with the idea submitter involved throughout this warehousing process. Every involved person within the organization should participate in the analyses of the ideas and the decision processes used to sort out the best ones. These decision processes must use established criteria that relate to the organization's goals and purposes.

Whether or not sophisticated mathematical models and decision aids are used to assist in this process is not important. The important point is that the process be systematic and open, rather than haphazard and autocratic.

### Principle 6. Carefully Select the Most Cost-Effective Method for Managing Each Innovation Project

Different methods are required for managing innovation projects, depending on whether they are operating under well understood or poorly understood technical and market environments. The least demanding condition exists when both the technology and the market environments are well understood. Under these circumstances, the relatively inexpensive commercial line management method can be used effectively. When the market environment is well understood but the technical environment is not, then more expensive methods are required. Here, the technical line management method is the most cost-effective. When the technology is well understood but the market is not, then commercial line management methods are the most cost-effective.

The most demanding condition exists when both the technical and market environments are poorly understood. Then the most powerful and costly methods are required: commercial project manager, new product committee, or dyads and counterparts methods. The choice of one of these three over the others will depend on the availability of appropriate personnel to staff the method.

### Principle 7. Eliminate Disharmony between R&D and Marketing Groups

Lack of understanding, lack of appreciation, lack of communication, and distrust between R&D and marketing parties must not be permitted. They severely constrain the success of innovations.

Managers can take several steps to eliminate and avoid these problems. These steps include breaking large projects into smaller ones, eliminating mild problems before they grow into severe ones, making open communications an explicit responsibility of every employee and using more joint R&D/marketing task forces. It is management's job to see that the R&D and marketing parties are jointly involved with each other early in the life of the project. They must come to feel a deep appreciation and respect for each other's work.

## Principle 8. Carefully Analyze the Customer's Level of Product Sophistication and the Product Developer's Level of Technical Sophistication

There is only one situation where a weak R&D/marketing interface can succeed. It is: when the customer knows his needs and can translate them into product specifications, *and* when the new product developer understands these specifications and has the means at hand to develop the product. This situation is relatively rare. Few customers fully understand their own needs, let alone possess the technical knowledge to translate them into detailed product specifications. Few developers are sophisticated enough to completely understand every specification and proceed directly to develop a product from it. For most situations, strong collaborative roles are required between R&D and marketing to create an innovation that fulfills a customer's needs.

The types of collaborative roles and the postures that the R&D and marketing parties must take will depend on whether the idea for the innovation originates from R&D, from marketing or from outside the firm. Ideas that originate from R&D require marketing to play a strong leadership role in searching out potential creative uses for the idea, and to play the role of change agent in moving the idea into a more useful form. Ideas that originate from marketing require R&D to make an open-minded and honest assessment of their capabilities before undertaking the development of that idea. If the idea comes from outside the firm, then both parties must take great care that their pride and sense of self-esteem do not get in the way of an honest assessment of the idea and its potentials.

## Principle 9. Marshal Resources According to the Nature of the Technology

Always carefully measure and understand two dimensions of any technology: accessibility and state of the art. An inaccessible technology is disembodied know-how that must be synthesized and fully elaborated before the organization can develop useful new product innovations from it. In a low state-of-the-art technology, the organization must upgrade its know-how before it can make use of the technology.

Management can use two techniques to overcome these barriers. First, if the technology has some strategic fit to the firm, then the firm's ability to handle it is enhanced. However, large amounts of high quality resources will be required. Managers should stop to consider whether or not they can afford these costs before they commit to such technologies. Second, managers can use various incubating strategies to nurture and grow the technologies until they are ready for the firm. Some typical incubating strategies include co-venturing with other firms, sponsoring the refinement of the technology at universities and engaging in various forms of research consortia.

*Principle 10. Pay Close Attention to Internal Technology Transfers*

The timely transfer of ideas and the flow of technologies between various departments within a firm are essential to the success of an innovation project. When the technology and markets are well understood and familiar to all the parties, a linear sequence of activities can be prescribed to guide this flow. In all other cases, the only effective way to transfer technologies is to use a core phase transfer model. This is a dynamic, interacting team concept in which the team memberships and member roles change during the life cycle of the technology.

The core phase transfer concept is based on the idea that as a technology grows and evolves from one phase to another, the skills and know-how required to handle that technology must also evolve. To respond to this, the core membership of the technology transfer team and the roles of its members must change. For example, basic scientists, who are the primary decision makers in the early phase of the work, are gradually replaced by applied scientists in a later phase. The applied scientists are, in turn, replaced by engineers. The engineers are subsequently replaced by marketers in later phases. Key decision makers in one phase become consultants in later phases. Thus, the technology is gradually passed from one party of specialists to another as it matures.

## Applying the Principles

These ten principles repeatedly telegraph the same rather tautological message: To innovate requires innovative managers. Managers must be innovative in harmonizing people and things with the emerging opportunities around them.

This is a disappointing message for those who are expecting a recipe for managing innovations. No such recipe exists. Perhaps someday, when the state of the art in innovation management has advanced, more precise prescriptions and "how to do it" rules can be offered. This is a very young field, with a myriad of exciting research opportunities and a wealth of rich findings waiting to be uncovered.

Until then, these principles remain the best state of the art. And success in innovating remains a matter of how well managers are capable of practicing them.

# Index

# About the Author

William E. Souder is an authority in the fields of innovation management, systems analysis, and organization behavior. He teaches at the University of Pittsburgh, where he is Professor of Industrial Engineering and Engineering Management, and Director of the Technology Management Studies Institute. Dr. Souder has a B.S. with Distinction in Chemistry, an MBA, and a Ph.D. in Management Science. He has been conducting field studies on the management of research and development and innovation for over 20 years. He is the author of over 70 research papers and four books on research and engineering management, and he serves on the editorial boards of three prominent journals. Dr. Souder is the recipient of numerous awards, including an award from the White House for service on the President's advisory council on federal policies for innovation. He has over 12 years of industrial experience with the Monsanto Company, where he served as Lubricants Engineering Chemist, Project Manager, Assistant to the Director of Research, Operations Research Specialist, and Senior Mathematician. Dr. Souder is the president of Scientific Management Associates, Inc., a consulting firm with extensive experience in the design of new product management systems. He also serves as a director of Information Research Analysts and as a faculty research associate in the human factors laboratory of the U.S. Bureau of Mines, where he conducts research on behavior modification and the adoption of innovations.